Education and Capitalism

W8-BYT-135

Education and Capitalism
Struggles for Learning and Liberation

Edited by Jeff Bale and Sarah Knopp

HaymarketBooks
Chicago, Illinois

Copyright © 2012 by Jeff Bale and Sarah Knopp
Published in 2012 by Haymarket Books
PO Box 180165
Chicago, IL 60618
www.haymarketbooks.org
773-583-7884

ISBN: 978-1-60846-147-9

Trade distribution:
In the US, Consortium Book Sales and Distribution, www.cbsd.com
In Canada, Publishers Group Canada, www.pgcbooks.ca
In the UK, Turnaround Publisher Services, www.turnaround-uk.com
In Australia, Palgrave Macmillan, www.palgravemacmillan.com.au
All other countries, Publishers Group Worldwide, www.pgw.com

Cover design by Josh On.
Cover image of children attending a Freedom School in an integrated public hous-
ing project in Cincinnati during a one-day boycott of city schools organized by the
Congress for Racial Equality in 1964. © Gene Smith, Associated Press Photo.

Published with the generous support of Lannan Foundation and
the Wallace Global Fund.

Printed in the United States by union labor.

Library of Congress cataloging-in-publication data is available.

10 9 8 7 6 5 4 3 2 1

 (28)

SUSTAINABLE FORESTRY INITIATIVE

Certified Sourcing
www.sfiprogram.org
SFI-01234

To Michal Myers, Kevin Chojczak,
and all other socialist educators who didn't live to participate
in a truly liberated educational system.

¡Presente!

Contents

Foreword
Adam Sanchez Interviews Bill Bigelow

Rethinking Schools magazine began in Milwaukee, Wisconsin, in *1986 as a local effort to address problems such as racial bias in schools and standardized testing. Since its founding, it has grown into a nationally renowned venue for critical perspectives on teaching and education, as well as an active publisher of educational materials such as curricular guides. While writing for a broad audience,* Rethinking Schools *emphasizes problems facing urban schools, particularly issues related to racism. Throughout its history,* Rethinking Schools *has tried to balance discussion of classroom practice and educational theory. It addresses key policy issues such as market-oriented reforms, funding equity, and autonomy and collective bargaining rights for teachers.* Rethinking Schools *defines its project as being "both visionary and practical: visionary because we need to be inspired by each other's vision of schooling; practical because for too long, teachers and parents have been preached at by theoreticians, far-removed from classrooms, who are long on jargon and short on specific examples."*

Rethinking Schools has been an inspiration to teachers, including the contributors to this book, to see themselves as visionaries and strategists instead of implementers of mandated curriculum. Because it's an activist publication, with articles written by and for teachers, parents, and students, it imagines a future where the "doers" are also the thinkers.

Bill Bigelow is curriculum editor of Rethinking Schools *magazine. Here, he talks to Adam Sanchez, a teacher in a Portland public school and his former student, about the relationship between curriculum and struggles for justice.*

Adam Sanchez: Many who have gone through the public school system in the United States leave feeling dissatisfied, bored, and/or alienated. Why do you think public schools are worth fighting for?

Bill Bigelow: You could make an even stronger case against public schools for many students. They push students out; they criminalize behaviors that don't conform to middle-class norms; schools are many students' introduction to institutional punishment. More times than not, they teach an inaccurate and flag-waving version of US history and how the world works. In essence, they often strengthen racial and class inequality as well as militarism.

But public schools can also be places where students learn to read and write and to ask deep questions about the world. They can be places where young people talk with their peers about their lives and the broader world. They can learn to sing, play an instrument, act, paint, hit a curveball. And public schools are places where students can come to think of themselves as activists for social justice. Of course, any school—public or otherwise—can be excellent academically, and can teach for social justice. But public schools are charged with serving *all* children. The *public* in public schools acknowledges that education is not a commodity that we buy as individuals in the marketplace. Public education reflects a social commitment to one another and to the future.

What do you think of Obama's education policies and his choice of Arne Duncan as secretary of education?

I agree with Diane Ravitch that, with respect to education, Obama's presidency has been like George Bush's third term. In fact, Race to the Top—Obama's initiative that takes a relatively small amount of money, dangles it in front of resource-starved states, and says, "You might get it if you allow more privatization and link teacher evaluations and pay to test scores"—it's Bush's No Child Left Behind on steroids. I can't think of any substantial difference between Barack Obama and George Bush when it comes to education; in fact, Arne Duncan has been cozy with New Jersey's Governor Chris Christie, a huge privatizer and a hater of teacher unions. I confess that Obama and Duncan's attacks on teachers and teacher unions are puzzling to me, as the unions have been some of the Democratic Party's most loyal supporters. For example, both Duncan and Obama cheered when teachers at Central Falls High School in Providence, Rhode Island, were removed en masse. But ideologically, Obama seems committed to a neoliberal model of development—look at his pursuit of free trade agreements all over the world—so I suppose that it shouldn't surprise us when he follows similar "let the market lead" policies when it comes to education. It's absurd that at a moment when the capitalist system cannot provide work for huge numbers of people, cannot provide decent health care for all, cannot provide housing for all who need it, and has brought the world to the brink of ecological collapse, that anyone should look to that same system—and the people who manage it—to address our educational woes.

Many social justice educators feel that their teaching is their activism, yet at the same time teachers increasingly have less control over curriculum. For those who believe in social justice education, is what we do inside the classroom enough?

I want to start by flipping that question on its head. I've known a lot of teachers who believe that their activism outside the classroom is sufficient. And it's not. It's not enough to be a good "social justice unionist," or to participate in teacher antiwar committees or worker-community alliances. I believe that teacher activism begins in the classroom, with our commitment to our students and to the communities that we serve as educators. Our first job is to be an outstanding teacher. That said, as you point out, how well we are able to serve our students and the society as a whole is being shaped—distorted, really—by forces that are outside of what is going on in the schools themselves. As we regularly editorialize in *Rethinking Schools*, protecting our classrooms, protecting our craft, requires that we challenge all kinds of social priorities. As the recent struggles in Wisconsin show, the wealthy and the politicians they've hired are attempting to defund and deform public schools. Yes, we need to teach about this and equip students to understand the roots and motives of these initiatives. But we have to be out in the streets opposing all these right-wing schemes. I do think that good teaching is a kind of activism, but the space for critical teaching will become increasingly narrow unless we get active beyond our classrooms.

The introduction to *Rethinking Our Classrooms*, one of the first books put out by *Rethinking Schools*, argues that curriculum should not only be critical, antiracist, and pro-justice, but also participatory, culturally sensitive, experiential, and grounded in the lives of students. In your opinion, what is the importance of pedagogy—how we teach—in relation to the content we are teaching?

They are intimately connected. How can students develop their capacity to work together—critically and collaboratively—if they are being lectured at or handed worksheets or, as is the case more and more, planted in front of a computer to do test-prep reading drills and the like? Our pedagogy—how we engage students—should reinforce the content of the curriculum. For example, when I teach about the abolition movement and the role that struggle played in ending slavery, I want to bring the movement into the classroom. I want to encourage students to think like organizers, to confront the dilemmas that actual antislavery campaigners confronted in the nineteenth century. I wrote a role-play in which all students take on the roles of members of the American Anti-Slavery Society and have to meet with one another to talk through some of the difficult choices that faced actual abolitionists. One question focuses on 1848, when women abolitionists announce that they are going to meet at Seneca Falls, New York, to draft a set of demands for women's rights. Do we, playing the role of abolitionists, support this movement, or do we see it as a distraction from fighting the main social evil: slavery? In 1857, after the Supreme Court declared in Dred Scott that Black people "had no rights which the white man was bound to respect," should abolitionists support armed efforts to confront slave owners? The point is that students need to learn about social movements from the inside, and they can only do this together, through problem-posing and participation. So in school, learning what matters most depends a lot on the pedagogy, on the how of teaching, not only the what.

That same introduction to _Rethinking Our Classrooms_ also proclaims, "classrooms can be places of hope, where students and teachers gain glimpses of the kind of society we could live in and where students learn the academic and critical skills needed to make it a reality." Can you give a few examples from your experience as a teacher of lessons where you have been able to glimpse this more hopeful society?

I've been in a number of social justice curriculum groups over the years, and this is the key conundrum that we always return to: how can we teach fully and honestly about the enormity of injustice in the world and yet not totally discourage students? I think that "hope" begins with students' experiences in the classroom. It seems to me that when students feel themselves changing and growing in positive directions, it becomes easier to imagine others changing and growing—which is fundamental to believing in the possibility of a different kind of society. One simple example is giving students a chance to write about their lives and share their stories with one another—encouraging them to offer each other positive feedback and to ask big questions about how our personal stories connect to broader social patterns.

We also need to give students the opportunity to feel themselves as "activists"—broadly understood. So, for example, when we study about we live our lives, and yet invisible. So much of the official school curriculum teaches students to not-think. And the curriculum especially teaches students to not-think about capitalism. Obviously, it's totally off-limits to question capitalism, but really the idea is to teach kids to ignore it.

Isn't it a "basic skill" to be able to think clearly about the nature of the economic system that shapes how we produce and distribute goods, how we organize work, how we allocate wealth, how we appropriate nature? As I mentioned earlier, it seems especially important for students to think critically about capitalism because capitalism privatizes the rewards but socializes its ecological impact. The curricular implications are that educators need to find as many ways as we can to help students interrogate the nature of capitalism.

The Thingamabob simulation that I just mentioned is one example of an activity that encourages students to recognize capitalism as a system, and to think critically about some of the dynamics of that system. Another is a simulation called "Organic Goodie" (included in *The Power in Our Hands: A Curriculum on the History of Work and Workers in the United States,* written with Norm Diamond and *Rethinking Our Classrooms: Teaching for Equity and Justice,* vol. 1). In Organic Goodie, I tell students to imagine that we're going to live the rest of our lives in the classroom, but we're in luck because we have a machine that produces "organic goodies" and we'll be able to survive in good shape. I correct myself to tell them that really, *we* don't have this machine, *I* do—I own it. I hire half the students as workers and the other half are unemployed and receive meager welfare payments. I proceed to drive down wages, by hiring the unemployed to work for less and then demanding concessions from my workers—until finally they begin to organize. Sometimes they go on strike, sometimes workers ally with unemployed, sometimes they seize the machine—but there is always some kind of organizing that goes on. After the game, we talk about how students responded, and we also talk about the attitudes that, as the owner, I wanted them to have: that it was my right to do as I pleased with the machine because it was mine, and questioning my ownership and control was off-limits; that they could not count on or trust one another to work together; that I deserved more wealth because I owned the machine. We also talk about what would have been the best way to run the machine had I not asserted my ownership rights. Universally, students say that the best route would have been for everyone to have a say in running the machine and sharing the goodies. I ask them, "So why didn't you do that?" I want students to see that how a society's resources are owned and controlled is not ordained by God, but is the product of human choice and the struggle between different social classes. Of course, all these simulations are partial and emphasize some aspects of capitalism while neglecting others, but the point is that it's essential for teachers to help students think critically about the nature of capitalism—to get the fish to think about the water.

A number of public school teachers from all over the country got together to write Education and Capitalism: Struggles for Learning and Liberation for several reasons. The authors share the idea that teachers should also be social critics, visionaries, strategists, and public intellectuals. Hopefully analyzing the world and changing it go hand in hand. How do you think this book contributes to that project?

This is such an important premise. More and more, teachers are regarded as simple implementers of curriculum that has been developed by big corporations—curriculum that supposedly aligns with content standards written by invisible experts. A word that has become more popular with school administrators these days is "fidelity"—in other words, "How faithfully are you teaching what we've ordered you to teach?" So a book like *Education and Capitalism* that imagines a fundamentally critical and creative role for teachers is such a welcome contribution. This is the kind of work that *Rethinking Schools* stands for—teachers as writers and researchers, critics and activists.

I think that what the book's editors are also trying to insist is that there is a relationship between social struggle and curricular imagination. Teachers don't develop insights about the world or about how to help students think more critically simply by sitting at a computer trying to come up with good lesson plans. For example, in the most recent issue of *Rethinking Schools* magazine we have three pieces from teachers about imaginative ways to engage students in thinking about how societies change, and how people can work together for more rights and to defend public schools. This curriculum did not occur to teachers from simple contemplation; it grew out of their involvement in struggles in Wisconsin and New York. This has been true in my own teaching and curriculum work, too. My involvement with the anti–Vietnam War movement, South Africa and Central America solidarity movements, democratic and antiracist education struggles, and most recently in environmental justice work, has helped me generate teaching ideas—both in terms of the content that is worth teaching, but also pedagogically. But it works the other way, too. My work with students, seeing what moves them and hearing their insights, and my own learning the content more deeply as I have to teach it, has influenced my outside-of-school activism. It was teaching about apartheid and the complicity of the US government and corporations in sustaining racial inequality in South Africa that made me want to take action beyond my own classroom. So I'm delighted that here is a book that urges teachers to see ourselves broadly, as you say, as social critics, visionaries, strategists, and public intellectuals. That's exactly what we need.

Preface

A Defense of Public Education
and an Action Plan for Change

In the opening decade of the twenty-first century, public education globally has come under attack. Since 2007, the Great Recession has been used as cover to gut living standards for most working Americans and to impose massive cuts in social spending. As the biggest and most wide-reaching public institution, schools—and the students and educators in them—have borne the brunt of these attacks. Class sizes have shot up, and business models of "accountability" have recklessly driven the education agenda like a car with a stuck accelerator, careering away from research-based best practices. Teachers and their unions have not only been blamed for the dire state of education, but, as the largest sector of unionized workers left in this country, have had the teetering economic crisis itself hung around their necks. Many school districts have significantly reduced their teaching force and cut or frozen teacher salaries.[1] In a world obsessed with the privatization of public resources, charter schools have become the weapon of choice, as much for organizations like the Walton Foundation and the Bill and Melinda Gates Foundation as for politicians, Republicans and Democrats alike, bent on imposing business models on education. This has only increased the criminal levels of segregation in our schools.[2]

People tend to be of two minds about public education. On the one hand, many of us who attended public school remember some positive

1

experiences: some teachers we liked, some classes that were interesting, a place where we developed lasting friendships, a dance club, robotics club, or sports team that sparked our passions. For some, school is a welcome respite from a very challenging home environment. A few others actually did use our schooling experience to get better jobs than our parents had—although that was much more common two generations ago than it is now. And some remember learning to love learning at school.

The explosion of protest in Wisconsin in the early months of 2011 reflects in part the deep connectedness that many people have to their schools and their teachers. Thousands of people—teachers, students, parents, other unionists, and allies—took over the state capitol building to protest Governor Scott Walker's attempt to strip collective bargaining rights from public employees and effectively cut salaries by 20 percent. One of the most common signs paraded through the capitol read: "Care about your teachers the way they care about your child." Students and teachers in Madison were at the forefront of these protests: they led spontaneous walkouts on February 16, 17, 18, and 21, 2011, helped to block legislators from getting into the assembly meeting to vote on Walker's bill, camped out in the capitol building, festooned the balconies with banners proclaiming such slogans as "Tax the Rich," and sang out chants like "This is what democracy looks like!"[3] Clearly, the widespread public support for mass action in Madison showed that the media onslaught against teachers and their unions, begun under the cover of the Great Recession, is not an accurate reflection of public opinion.

However, many people also believe that public education is failing and in crisis. That ideas like "Tax the Rich" were so popular at the Madison rallies reflects a general understanding that there is not just *one* public education system in America but rather two. There is widespread acknowledgement that schools vary greatly depending on the economic status of the neighborhood where they're located and the degree of racial segregation of their students. Many of the authors of this book are teachers in urban public schools. As such, we work daily in schools where young people in segregated classrooms are drilled with math and English "test prep," are taught to obey rules that seem designed just for the sake of having rules, and are punished sharply if they don't. Our classes are often packed with forty students or more. We administer soul-sucking tests, struggle to provide enough support for English language learners, and watch our graduates struggle to afford college and to keep up in college once there. In the case of our undocumented students, we watch as the door to higher education or the potential for a good job is slammed in their faces, based merely on their immigration status. We often act as counselors to students suffering from a range of social problems, and help to find resources to alleviate our students' health care problems, from needing glasses to see the board to dental care and psychological services. These are all resources that should be provided in schools in communities that are struggling.

One needn't defend the status of public education as it stands today to defend the right that we all should have to public education—and a much better one than that on offer now. After thirty years or more of neoliberalism, society has been stripped of almost all public services and communitarian cultural events and spaces. Basic programs to ensure universal health care and an actual social safety net, in the forms of elder care, subsidized child care, and public income assistance at the level of living wages, for example, would make a huge difference in the lives of millions. Having more public green space for recreation and socializing would be a huge step forward for all cities. But we have precious little of any of this.

The first reason, then, to defend what we have left of public education is because it is one of the last public spaces that remain in this country, and one of the only services that most people expect the government to provide with our tax dollars. In his book *City Schools and the American Dream: Reclaiming the Promise of Public Education*, Pedro Noguera underscores this point by highlighting the central role that schools often play in the most impoverished sections of major urban areas. He states:

> In economically depressed inner-city communities like Pico Union, public schools play a vital role in supporting low-income families. Even when other neighborhood services, including banks, retail stores, libraries, and other public services, do not exist, are shut down, or are abandoned, public schools remain. They are neighborhood constants, not because they succeed in carrying out their mission or because they satisfy the needs of those they serve, but because they have a relatively stable source of funding ensured by the legal mandate to educate children. Urban schools frequently serve as social welfare institutions.[4]

Second, we should defend public education because so much of what its enemies say about it is a lie. For example, education is supposed to be the cure for poverty. Logically, then, if poverty still plagues our society, our schools must be to blame. The education system becomes a convenient scapegoat for our social problems when, in reality, the blame should be placed on an economic system that rests on low-wage jobs. Education can't cure poverty if there aren't decent careers for graduates. A 2010 study from the Georgetown University Center on Education documented that one in four workers in America has a job that pays poverty-level wages.[5] Seven of the ten jobs that have the most openings right now pay less than 150 percent of the official poverty threshold.[6] Worse still, according to this same study, more than half the jobs being created today (think service sector) require less than a bachelor's degree.[7] If education is expected to solve the problem of poverty in the United States, then it can always be said to be "failing." In other words, education alone is incapable of solving the problem of poverty without a major jobs program that changes the economic prospects for students upon graduation, and without a union movement that fights for all jobs to provide living wages. Yet the enemies of public education twist this reality around and blame schools—and above all, the teachers in them—for not lifting their students out of poverty. Blaming teachers and their unions for this "failure" is an obvious attempt by political conservatives to break the power of the largest section of the American labor movement, as well as to undermine the academic freedom that has allowed some space for teaching critical thinking.

A third reason to defend public education relates to the contradictions between the ideology about the purpose of schools and the reality of schools as they exist. The gap between what we are told to expect from school and what school usually delivers is often the fuel powering many struggles for educational justice and equality. As several of the contributions to this book explain, demands for access to relevant, quality education have been an integral part of almost all the social movements of the twentieth and twenty-first centuries.

Finally, defending public education can also draw attention to the contradictions that exist in society overall, not just in terms of school. Indeed, after a decade of war and occupation in Afghanistan and Iraq, this point is increasingly self-evident. In the wake of the Great Recession, politicians and policy makers repeatedly cry poverty as they try to solve school budget crises on the backs of teachers and students. Yet those same politicians and policy makers always manage to find endless pots of money to wage war. A recent report from Brown University's Watson Institute for International Studies estimated the true cost of the wars in Iraq and Afghanistan to be between

$3.2 trillion and $4 trillion.[8] In this context, a campaign around "Money for Schools, Not for War" can be central to defending public education and funding for it, but also for raising more fundamental questions about the very society that prioritizes war over education to begin with.

The purpose of this book is to use critical analysis informed by Marxism both to understand the social context in which our schools are situated and to contribute to a plan of action for change, inside and outside schools. To do this, the book is structured around three major themes. The first is historical analysis of past struggles over schooling, in particular civil rights and union-led movements. Civil rights and union-led struggles for racial and social justice have had a more profound impact than any other factor on what schools look and sound like in the United States. Indeed, what the histories of these movements have taught us is that education, if it is to be genuinely liberatory, has to be connected to struggle. Thus, the historical analysis that runs throughout the book functions both to set the record straight and to inspire hope about the possibilities for change when educational demands are tied to social movements.

Second, we argue that our schools are designed to serve the needs of capitalism, a system that is organized mainly for the purpose of generating profit. Consequently—and absent mass social struggles—there is always enough money for war, and there is always enough money to bail out big banks and corporations, but never enough money for public schools. Moreover, in our society, and specifically at work, there is no economic democracy. This basic fact profoundly impacts how schools are structured and how they function to socialize students. Obviously, this needs to change in order for people in general to be liberated. However, for schools to become sites where freedom of expression, community-based empowerment, and true enlightenment are practiced, society itself must change fundamentally. We implore teachers to join the struggle for such a transformation.

Third, we focus on the role that teachers can play both inside and outside the classroom. On the one hand, we argue that teachers' unions can and should be a key tool in defending public education and leading broader social struggles for economic, social, and racial justice. Our argument is rooted in a Marxist analysis of trade unions in general, as well as the idea that teachers are workers—not merely "professionals"—who need unions as much as any other section of workers in society. On the other hand, we argue that union activists need to engage in social justice and liberatory pedagogy, too. "Liberation," as a Marxist concept, means having control over the conditions of one's own life, both individually and as a community. It means that vital decisions—like whether resources are used for war or for developing renewable energy resources, how many hours people should work, how our workplaces and schools should run, and how to make and distribute healthy food—should be made by the people affected, not by a tiny minority of elites. Knowledge is power only if it helps us to have more control over the resources in our communities.

The social movements that can lead to this sort of liberation certainly require ideas and informed debate. It is in this spirit that we have compiled this collection of essays about education, capitalism, and the struggles for an education that empowers students and teachers to change society. The authors' own experiences—as teachers and teacher educators in urban public school systems across the United States, as political organizers, as unionists, and in many cases as socialist activists—have directly shaped our understanding of schooling in terms of what is *needed* and what is *possible*. It is our hope that these essays will contribute to the important debates within current and future struggles over public education.

We should state at the outset, as well, what this book is *not* meant to do. On the one hand, it is not meant to review or respond to every strand of progressive, radical, or Marxist writing on public education, whether from popular, political, or academic sources. While many of the best and most controversial perspectives are cited and engaged throughout the chapters, these essays are not meant to be comprehensive overviews of left thought on public education. In addition, this book does not attempt to speak to every oppressive or exploitative aspect of public education, or to explore each and every reform that we could or should fight for. Nor is the book meant to be a practical "how to" guide for creating social justice curriculum, although those hoping for such will find some examples and ideas interspersed throughout the book. Instead, we have tried to frame each chapter around key questions facing public education or key debates in struggles to improve our schools and the educational experiences of students.

In no way is this collection of essays meant to be a definitive outline of Marxist theory about schooling under capitalism or what liberatory education could look like. But given the scale of attacks on our public schools, in particular on the students and teachers in them, the need to revitalize socialist strategies about education is as urgent as ever. The guiding philosophy of the contributors to this book is, in the words of Karl Marx, "The weapon of criticism cannot, of course, replace criticism of the weapon, material force must be overthrown by material force; but theory also becomes a material force as soon as it has gripped the masses." We have to join struggles for equality and justice in the streets, in workplaces, communities, and society at large, and we have to build organizations that aim to engage in these struggles as well. We hope that these essays make a useful contribution to that project, and above all, to building stronger and broader social movements for genuine learning at school and liberation in society.

1

Schools, Marxism, and Liberation
Sarah Knopp

*Schooling has been at once something done to the poor and for the poor. . . .
The unequal contest between social control and social justice is evident in the
total functioning of US education.*
   —Samuel Bowles and Herbert Gintis, *Schooling in Capitalist America*[1]

*The weapon of criticism cannot, of course, replace criticism of the weapon,
material force must be overthrown by material force; but theory also becomes a
material force as soon as it has gripped the masses.*
   —Karl Marx, *Contribution to Hegel's Philosophy of Right*

Education, Poverty, and Inequality
Most people hope that public education will fulfill its promised role as "the
Great Equalizer," as described by Horace Mann, one of the most influential
early voices in public education. People all over the world hang such high
hopes and aspirations on the rewards of education in the advanced capitalist
countries that they are willing to make huge and sometimes dangerous sac-
rifices—parents risk their lives in the deserts of the US-Mexico border, for
example—to gain access for their children to a "better life." While many
want education to help children to achieve the "completion of themselves
as human beings," to paraphrase Paulo Freire, mainly it's expected that
schools will help the next generation to have access to better jobs and careers.

   In October 2011, during a meeting of public school teachers to discuss
how to bring the Occupy Wall Street movement to our own district in Los
Angeles, we were formulating demands. We wanted the twelve hundred
teachers laid off by our district to be rehired, we wanted schools run by families and teachers, not billionaires (our school "reform," not theirs), and we

9

wanted to tax the 1 percent to pay for it. Someone laid out some of the grievances of the Occupy Wall Street protest, as posted on its website, which include a living wage for all, employed or unemployed, universal health care, and access to free quality education through college. One teacher said, "We need to put education at the forefront of the demands. People need to see that we (educators) are the solution to the demands that are raised by the occupiers." The sincerity with which she said this and the earnestness with which some teachers approach their jobs as a weapon for equality are inspiring. And yet it remains true that even quality education cannot be the antidote for the social ills of the majority without a dramatic restructuring of the economic power structure.

This chapter will first look at the commonsense logic (on both the left and the right) that education can act as a social leveler. Then, I draw on Marxism as a useful tool for understanding the world in which we are teaching. Specifically, a Marxist set of theories helps us to understand how knowledge is structured under capitalism, to sketch out an alternative way of thinking about knowledge and learning, and to describe the way that the economic system we live in shapes the schools in which we work and learn.

Marxism also helps us to craft a plan of action and an alternative vision of education. Social justice educators can be "transformative intellectuals" who wield a working-class, liberatory pedagogy. We can lead critical inquiry in our classrooms, even as we recognize the limitations of what we can achieve as individuals. To achieve more, though, we also need to fight against racism, segregation, and poverty, and fight for equal access to—and far more resources for—quality public education. Lastly, the logical conclusion of the arguments presented here is that schools will not be able to satisfy our extremely lofty expectations of them without a revolutionary transformation of the economic and social system in which schools operate.

Fighting for better schools and more equal access has been, will be, and must be a part of the social movements that will ultimately be the key to a more profound transformation of the economy, and in turn, the broader society. Marxism is the politics of hope; it argues that learning is a social phenomenon and that the thirst for it is deepest when it serves the cause of liberation, as it does when it is connected to movements for social equality, justice, and power. Knowledge must be combined with struggle against those who have a monopoly on power for it to be a force for empowerment. We have to envision the concept of "education" more broadly than it is defined today.

The World Into Which Students Are Graduating

There is a basic problem with viewing the public school system as the route to economic stability for the majority of young people in the United States. The economy these students are graduating into will only grant a minority of workers comfortable, middle-class status. From 2007–09, the real rate of unemployment in the United States (which adds to the government's official statistics people who have given up looking for work) was 17 percent, and among Blacks and Latinos, it was above 25 percent.[2] In 2011, according to the Economic Policy Institute, there were 4.4 job seekers for every open job.[3] Education only leads to financial stability if the economy has jobs to offer.

The following three books, written over the past thirty-five years, look at education in an economic context and draw similar conclusions. In 1976, Herbert Bowles and Samuel Gintis wrote the paradigm-shifting *Schooling in Capitalist America: Educational Reform and the Contradictions of Economic Life*. In 2005, Jean Anyon published *Radical Possibilities: Public Policy, Urban Education, and a New Social Movement*. And most recently, John Marsh's 2011 *Class Dismissed: Why We Cannot Teach or Learn Our Way Out of Inequality* reviews the best and most recent statistical research about education, poverty, and inequality. All these books survey the research available at the time they were written, and all argue that education cannot solve the problem of poverty. Further, educational attainment, or lack of it, is not the largest factor in predicting one's social status, income, or wealth.

For example, according to the Organization for Economic Cooperation and Development (OECD), in the United States, about half of one's income as an adult can be predicted by one's parents' income.[4] Half may not seem like a lot, but it does mean that parents' income is the *largest* factor in predicting one's economic success. Still, as John Marsh points out, almost everyone thinks that education will help their own children to achieve more, and there is some truth to this. Educational attainment does play a role in any given individual's success. Of people who are born in the poorest quintile (the two in ten families with the least income) 6 percent "make it" to the top quintile (the richest two in ten). Another 11 percent of those born poorest make it to the top 40 percent of the population in terms of income.[5] For those, and in cases of more modest social mobility, education is the most common means by which people rise up the social ladder.

But what works for some cannot, by definition, work for a majority or for society as a whole. John Marsh uses the analogy of someone standing up in a crowded theater. While one person may be able to better see the stage by doing so, if everyone did it, we'd be back to where we started (except the taller people would be at an even bigger advantage). The only way for education to be a social elevator for all (or most) kids would be if there were enough decent jobs waiting for them once they finished their education. Yet, one in ten college graduates was working in a minimum wage job in 2005.[6] The Georgetown University Center on Education and the Workforce released a study in 2010 showing that one in four workers in America has a job that pays poverty-level wages.[7] According to this same study, more jobs being created today (think service sector) are jobs that require less than a bachelor's degree.[8] Seven of the ten jobs that have the most openings right now pay less than 150 percent of the official poverty threshold.[9] The problem for most people in America is not lack of education, it is a lack of decent jobs. Any *one* student has a chance of getting herself ahead by going to college, but it's not irrational that the majority of American adults don't earn a BA. Why would a majority of people make the sacrifice of getting through college when most new jobs in this country don't require it?

Education is such a useful ideological tool for the rich for two reasons. First, a plethora of studies correlate one's lifetime income to educational attainment.[10] There is evidence that the higher one's level of schooling, on average, the higher one's income. Pointing this out is both an old favorite of newsmagazines that recycle this "finding" frequently and also a staple lecture for high school teachers to "motivate" their students to study harder. However, what these studies obscure is that parents' educational background is a significant factor in predicting their children's educational attainment. So, while it's often the case that the more education one has, the more one will earn, it's also true that children whose parents are more highly educated are much more likely to be highly educated themselves.[11] Since the children of the rich are much more able to pursue higher education irrespective of intellectual capabilities, perhaps education is not the social ladder that it appears to be. As this book is being written in the midst of the recession and budget cuts, this fact will be common sense to the millions of college students struggling to pay for school. Second, it's undeniable that a small minority of people do educate themselves out of poverty. Any parent has to hope that her child belongs to that group. It is based on this seemingly obvious connection between educational attainment and income, and the fact that a small minority of people are able to use education to climb the social ladder, that education becomes a powerful ideological weapon for the ruling class. On the one hand, the claim is that education is the key to solving the problem of poverty for a whole group or a whole country. On the other, if you're poor, it must be because you're lazy and didn't study hard enough.

Starting in the 1980s under Reagan, the federal government gave up on the comprehensive Employment and Training Administration, which had created almost two million jobs since 1978.[12] There was a paradigm shift—at that point, the government began to focus on job *training* programs (that is, education) rather than job *creation*. Behind this shift was the myth propagated by the Reagan administration that there just aren't enough skilled workers to fill high-end jobs. In fact, although this myth has become so pervasive that it is the unquestioned common sense even among progressives, quite the opposite is true. There are not enough highly skilled jobs to incorporate all the young workers with a college education. According to Jean Anyon, "as entry-level employees obtain more education, employers merely ratchet up the requirements."[13]

Thus, if our goal is to decrease poverty, we need solutions that would change the way that work is structured in our society. One could imagine forces capable of decreasing the poverty rate: a revival of the union movement in this country, so that workers can fight for living wages in sectors such as service, retail, and personal care; and, secondly, a federal jobs program (as opposed to a jobs-training program). Imagine what could be achieved in decreasing the chances of total environmental destruction if we put millions of young people to work in skilled and semi-skilled jobs designing and constructing green energy-generating sources.

Further, if our goal is to increase social *equality*, then we need solutions on an entirely different order. This chapter and this book are dedicated to a discussion about the meaning of the words "empowerment" and "democracy." I will argue that to transform teaching and learning at the most profound level, we need a society where people are collectively and democratically "empowered" to make economic decisions about the use of resources. In this context, knowledge and power would indeed be intimately connected.

So where does that leave progressive educators? We have a bit of a conundrum. Marx began to describe it in 1869: "On the one hand a change of social circumstances was required to establish a proper system of education, on the other hand a proper system of education was required to bring about a change of social circumstances; we must therefore commence where we were."[14] It seems like a catch-22 to say that society needs to change in order for education to be different, because who will change society if education is always a domesticating force? This chapter will argue, however, that there are contradictions inherent to our society. People's experiences in life sometimes expose these contradictions, and at certain times this leads to rebellions. These rebellions, then, connect knowledge to the pursuit of power and justice. It is at these times that knowledge comes alive, that people are transformed and can, in turn, transform society.

Capitalism and Knowledge

The very way that we understand *knowledge* is shaped by the realities of the world we live in and the systems we've set up to meet our needs. In a capitalist system, the way that work is organized has fundamentally changed people's relationship to understanding the world. At work, people experience "alienation," the separation of mental and manual labor. Alienation in Marxist theory describes the process by which we become "dehumanized." It happens when people become separated from that which makes us human—our ability to plan and control what we create. Unlike animals, humans developed the ability to think about how we meet our needs, cooperate with each other, and reflect on past experiences—in short, to bring creativity, forethought, and a collective effort to our work. Marx described the uniquely human connection between thought and work this way: "The spider carries out operations reminiscent of a weaver and the boxes which bees build in the sky could disgrace the work of many architects. But even the worst architect differs from the most able bee from the very outset in that before he builds a box out of boards he has already constructed it in his head. At the end of the work process he obtains a result which already existed in his mind before he began to build."[15] But under capitalism, most workers are totally divorced from the mental processes involved in planning their work, and lose all control over what they produce. That which made us human in the beginning is stripped away.

In addition to the rift between mental and manual labor, there is an ever-increasing division of labor. Most workers perform increasingly narrow and compartmentalized tasks all day. This is obviously true in the realm of manufacturing, as workers on assembly lines use specialized machines to perform one tiny task over and over again all day. But it also applies in service-sector jobs, office jobs, health care jobs, and so on. At McDonald's, one person works the french fry station, another (usually whiter) set of people staffs the cash registers, another fills the orders, and another keeps the eating area clean. In the medical field, doctors and nurses become increasingly specialized. As work becomes ever narrower, "expertise" becomes ever narrower. As a result, "knowledge" is broken into smaller and smaller chunks.

This is reflected in schools. Here we begin to learn how *not* to see the whole picture of the way the world works—the interplay among politics, economics, science, technology, language, and so on—because in school everything is divided into discrete "subjects." Each of these topics is in turn broken down into tinier and tinier subcategories or "units." Imagine that students are studying global warming. They study the chemical reason that carbon traps heat in the environment in science class. But rarely do they study concurrently the industrial production process that puts the carbon there, or the political processes for making decisions regarding regulations. Will these students be able to describe the real cause of global warming?

Teachers are artificially "specialized" by state credentialing processes. Teaching "special education," or "English as a second language," is seen as a specialized skill and not as a normal part of the learning process. The very fact that "special education" exists as a category is a reflection of the rigidity with which knowledge is seen as divided into different boxes; in fact, no two learners are alike in the modalities with which they learn. "Literacy" is a subject taught in isolation from others; sports and art are seen as "non-academic" subjects.

Another attribute of capitalism that affects the learning process is that everything is "commodified," or assigned a numeric value based on what it's "worth" in the marketplace. Everything—even one's body, sexuality, and ideas—is capable of being bought and sold on the marketplace in our current economic system. Even time, that elastic and free-flowing dimension, is assigned a numeric value based on hourly wages and how much each minute is "worth" based on how much we can get done. There is a drive to quantify and commodify what one knows. The international move toward standardized tests that has accelerated in the last thirty years is an attempt to impose business models onto knowledge. The latest and sharpest edge of this sword is the invention of value-added measures (VAM), the attempt to measure a teacher by his or her students' test scores.

The idea that we can quantify the value of knowledge leads to a style of teaching that Freire called "banking education," a pedagogical approach in which teachers deposit knowledge into the "banks" of students' brains, "the teacher teaches and the students are taught," and where "the teacher is the Subject of the learning process, while the pupils are the mere objects."[16] That administrations are now pushing to use VAM to assess teachers is a strange admission on their part that they expect teachers to implement exactly the model Freire criticized.

Dialectical Materialism: An Alternative View of Knowledge

Schools have the potential to help us see reality more clearly. They also have the potential to obscure it, to make it *harder* for students to see the big picture by reinforcing social norms and justifying the way the system works. Marxism presents an alternative way of looking at the world, an alternative view of knowledge based on the concept of "dialectical materialism." The alternative to compartmentalization of knowledge is not to ignore details. Rather, while we study things in greater and greater detail, the goal should be to use those details to construct a greater understanding of the whole. Applying dialectics to education, Paulo Freire states: "My question is how to make clear to the students that there is no such thing named biology in itself."[17]

In *Socialism: Utopian and Scientific*, published in 1880, Friedrich Engels identified the tendency of capitalism to divide up and isolate the various parts of nature and knowledge into increasingly disconnected parts. He decried: "This method of work has also left us as legacy the habit of observing natural objects and processes in isolation, apart from their connection with the vast whole; of observing them in repose, not in motion; as constraints, not as essentially variables; in their death, not in their life."[18] Dialectical materialism is an alternative way of seeing the world and knowledge. "For the materialist," according to Marxist writer Paul D'Amato, "all of reality is based on matter, including mental activity, which is a result of the organization of matter in a particular way. . . . Minds cannot exist apart from the materialist world, and the material world existed long before any mind was able to experience it."[19] Further, materialists see the systems that people have set up to meet their needs, and the development of the "productive forces" (for example, what sort of technology societies have developed), as the driving forces shaping society. Just as the production of objects is a social phenomenon, so is the production of knowledge. The type of society that we live in shapes how we are as human beings, what we think about, and how learning is organized.

In the "dialectical" part of dialectical materialism, society and nature are in a state of constant change; we can only understand these changes if we look at the whole process, not at disconnected parts; and changes in things both natural and social are driven by contradictions within them. Capitalism, for example, teaches us to look at things as specific, static, disconnected parts. According to Engels, "We find, in like manner, that cause and effect are conceptions which only hold good in their application to individual cases; but as soon as we consider the individual cases in their general connection with the universe as a whole, they run into each other, and they become confounded when we contemplate that universal action and reaction in which causes and effects are eternally changing places, so that what is effect here and now will be cause there and then, and vice versa."[20] For example, changes in the environment, like a better agricultural system that creates an improved and more stable food supply, can have an impact on people's brains and thoughts. The development of thought and ideas can then help humans to further alter their environment. Changes to the physical brain and to the thought process can be affected by environmental change, and can also be the cause of further change of that environment.

The Marxist Lev Vygotsky, writing in the aftermath of the massive social upheaval of the Russian Revolution, applied dialectical materialism to the study of human learning. Vygotsky's views on psychology and cognitive development were so prescient and revolutionary that they are highly regarded and read widely in schools of education today. His *Thought and Language*, published in 1934 in Russian, wasn't translated into English until 1986 (other works of his had begun to be translated in the 1970s). Since they were translated during an era when people were questioning the dominant theories of learning, and since they were a revolutionary break with these formerly dominant theories, they became popular in schools of education. Here's how Vygotsky himself explained his differences with prior theories of cognitive and language development: "The [earlier] method analyzes complex psychological wholes into elements. It may be compared to the chemical analysis of water into hydrogen and oxygen, neither of which possesses the properties of the whole and each of which possesses properties not present in the whole. The student applying this method in looking for the explanation of some property of water—why it extinguishes fire, for example, will find to his surprise that hydrogen burns and oxygen sustains fire."[21] Vygotsky, on the other hand, used the dialectical concept that the different elements of thinking, communicating, and interaction with the material world are interconnected and influence each other.

The most revolutionary contribution that Vygotsky brought to the field of cognitive development was the idea that learning was a *social* phenomenon. This was a major advance on previous theories, such as those of Piaget, which saw psychological development as being fixed by the physical development of the brain in stages that were relatively constant across individuals and societies. Up until that point, psychologists argued that the brain's physical development preceded learning. Vygotsky saw these two as part of an interrelated process, one influencing the other. Vygotsky argued, "The very mechanism underlying higher mental functions is a copy from social interaction; all higher mental functions are internalized social relationships. These higher mental functions are the basis of the individual's social structure. Their composition, genetic structure, and means of action—in a word, their whole nature—is social."[22] Vygotsky's research on cognitive development was informed by, and in turn provided evidence for, the scientific method of dialectical materialism. Human beings are social animals, and knowledge is a collective process that is created as we as a human race attempt to use and alter the material world to meet our needs.

Vygotsky's concept of a "zone of proximal development" (ZPD), informed by the idea that learning is a social, interactive, collective process, is one of the most useful concepts in cognitive theory. Every learner finds herself at a certain base of knowledge and cognitive development. The ZPD is the area between where a learner is and where she can get to in a given period of time in terms of understanding and development. She moves through this zone between where she is and her potential with the help (or "scaffolding") provided by the experience and knowledge of others, and also through her own inquiry and life experience.

Radical educator Wayne Au, in an excellent paper on Vygotsky, writes, "In a way, it is commonsensical to say that, as individuals, we cannot know everything there is to know, and therefore we can learn more if we work together and share specific expertise and understanding."[23] While it may be commonsensical, it is also a fundamentally materialist conception of how knowledge works. Vygotsky's insights were no doubt informed by the space for freedom of human interaction and intellectual awakening created by the revolutionary society in which he was operating after the Russian Revolution of 1917. The impact of the Russian Revolution on learning and on Vygotsky's thought is described in chapter 7.

Among the most important radical/Marxist theories of learning, which became wildly popular on the heels of the global radicalization of the late 1960s, was *Pedagogy of the Oppressed*, written by Brazilian Paulo Freire. (Chapter 6 examines Freire's work and his legacy in greater detail.) According to Freire, learning is fundamentally about naming the world in order to be able to transform it and create a new one. There is a dialectical connection between these processes: as we develop our understanding and theory about the world, we will act on this understanding. These actions will transform the world and in turn, our theories will develop and change. "Men and women develop their power to perceive critically the way they exist in the world and in which they find themselves; they come to see the world not as a static reality but as a reality in the process of transformation."[24]

Potentially, educators can play a role in helping students see the whole picture. This is related to, as UCLA professor and Marxist Peter McLaren puts it, "transcending the existing antagonisms between manual and mental labor."[25] Schools teach students to focus on one aspect of something and not the whole. But, at work just as at school, individuals are capable of (and naturally inclined to) think about what they're producing, how they're doing it, and why. If the ultimate goal is to break down the wall between mental and manual labor, then both teachers and students have to "see the whole picture," understand the world, and practice thinking about work as a creative process.

We can focus on teaching students to pose critical questions, analyze the world and the way it works, set goals, access resources, use evidence to back up their arguments. and test theories about social change. Indeed, many teachers who think of themselves as "social justice educators" and "transformative intellectuals" help students to develop the skills that they need to practice this sort of critical inquiry. In addition, whole schools with progressive administrators and teachers, such as the social justice academy that I helped to design in the Los Angeles Unified School District, push back against "banking education" and the prescriptions of scripted curriculum driven by standardized tests. Often, these relatively progressive schools can be pleasant and enlightening places to be in an otherwise difficult world that students have to negotiate.

Nevertheless, in an era in which teachers' jobs and livelihoods are increasingly pinned to students' test scores, teaching against the system will be the exception rather than the norm, and we will find our space to do so increasingly restricted. The rest of this chapter, as well as chapters 6 and 7, argue that "enlightenment" and "empowerment" cannot be achieved individually, one classroom or one student at a time. They will be collective processes, achieved for the most part outside the walls of our institutions. Teachers who understand this will not limit their efforts to the classroom.

Capitalism and Schools

In 1976, Samuel Bowles and Herbert Gintis wrote *Schooling in Capitalist America*, which focused on the form of education in modern society. It's been a point of reference for radical and Marxist education theory since its publication. It argues that schools serve a particular function in our society, namely the reproduction of social relations of production. This means, in part, getting future workers ready for their jobs. Bowles and Gintis's most famous idea is what they termed "correspondence theory." According to this theory, the hierarchical relations of work and production are mirrored in the relations we see in schools. The hierarchies between administrators and teachers, teachers and students, students and other students *correspond* to boss-worker relationships and indeed prepare students to play those roles. Students produce work for external rewards (grades) in much the same way that workers work only for a paycheck, have no control over the product they make, and become divorced (or alienated) from their work. Students don't "work" for the inherent value of knowledge, but rather do the work they are told to for the purpose of earning a grade and eventually a diploma. Like workers, they jump through hoops. There's a lack of democracy and intellectual control over the content of our studies that's similar to workers' lack of control over what they produce.

However, in the process of being sorted into different jobs in the capitalist economy, students most often do *not* gain the job skills that they need for even menial jobs. If the role of schools is to get people ready to be workers, it does not follow that they are simply glorified skills-training programs. In fact, they do very little to actually teach useful skills. Rather, the predominant function that schools historically have served is to control the behavior of students and to assimilate them—whether forcibly or more subtly—into the dominant ideology, behaviors, culture, and ways of speaking and interacting desired by the US ruling class. The "utilitarian" value of schools, according to Bowles and Gintis, is not about producing skills or knowledge that directly correspond to those needed on the job.[26] Rather, most of our cognitive skills are learned through our interactions outside of school, and the vast majority of skills we need for any job are learned on the job.

One of the most infamous examples of this idea, addressed in greater detail in the following chapter, is the Hampton-Tuskegee model of schooling. Booker T. Washington is remembered as an early advocate of practical, vocational schools. But more often, those schools focused more on teaching "character" and "work ethic," and students often complained that they weren't being trained to use the tools they would need to get skilled jobs. Rather, they were being asked to do redundant and low-skilled work. Today, while school boards have philosophical debates about the relative merits of vocational skills training and "college-level" academic skills, the reality, in my experience as a teacher, is that students receive far too little of either. To genuinely prepare students for the world of work, as one obvious example, we would need more than two functioning computers in classrooms that house forty students at a time.

Moreover, according to Bowles and Gintis, "the reasons why most larger employers supported public education are apparently related to the non-cognitive effects of schooling—in more modern terms, to the 'hidden curriculum.'"[27] There are many aspects of the hidden curriculum. The educational system selects for and rewards certain personality traits. Bowles and Gintis cite a study that shows that in calculating a student's grade point average (GPA), personality traits are almost as important as cognitive skills. Some of these highly rewarded personality traits include: dependability, perseverance, consistency, willingness to follow orders, punctuality, and ability to delay gratification. Personality traits that have a negative association with GPA are creativity, aggressiveness, and independence. So, schools promote individuals with the personality traits most associated with "good workers."[28] In short: in some schools, students learn to rule. In other schools, they learn to be ruled. In these latter schools, success is associated with obedience.

Jean Anyon's influential 1980 study, "Social Class and the Hidden Curriculum of Work,"[29] is an empirical study of how schools socialize children from different backgrounds.[30] She studied class differences in elementary schools through the lens of pedagogy and looked at four different kinds of schools: working class, middle class, "affluent professional," and "executive elite." She showed how styles of teaching and learning in these schools reflected expectations of the future roles of their students.

In the working-class school, emphasis was placed on obedience and rote learning. In the middle-class school, getting the right answer and following directions were emphasized, and doing well in school (getting enough "right" answers) held the promise of access to decent administrative-type jobs. The "affluent professional" schools, by contrast, emphasized student-driven, independent, and creative work, and afforded students a great deal of freedom. Curriculum at the "executive elite" school was similarly rigorous and inquiry based, but with more of a sense that there are "right" and "wrong" answers than at the more creative affluent professional school. Children there were being prepared to be excellent, powerful leaders.

Most moving from Anyon's study is the description of how children in each of the schools responded when asked what knowledge is. At the affluent professional school, many students responded to questions about knowledge by saying things like "thinking," "figuring stuff out," and "you think up ideas and then find things wrong with those ideas." When asked whether knowledge could be "made," the vast majority said yes. By contrast, at the middle-class school, only about half the students said that knowledge could be "made," and they said that to do it, they'd "look it up at the library" or "listen and do what they're told." At the working-class school, only one child interviewed thought that knowledge could be made, and none of the students used words like "think" to describe what knowledge is.[31]

Schooling in Capitalist America also argues that the form that education has taken—and the changes to it—have been driven by the changing needs of our capitalist economy. Since World War II there has been an increasing specialization of the workforce and a stricter division of labor. Capitalism has needed a massive expansion of middle-layer managers and bureaucrats to oversee increasingly technical work, and also to keep the workers below them in check, like service-sector retail managers in every store, mall, and fast-food restaurant. White-collar workers like software engineers, computer programmers, administrative assistants, and the office workers of corporate America, however, have little more control over the conditions of their work, over what they're making, or the allocation of resources in our society than do their blue-collar brothers and sisters.

Thus, the postwar expansion of higher education was driven by the increased need for a huge white-collar workforce, even as white-collar work became simultaneously more specialized and less skilled.

The expansion of higher education, of course, dovetailed with the demands of an increasingly confident working class, particularly people of color, for access to education. The GI Bill, for example, both satisfied demands made by soldiers returning from World War II and helped to prepare a generation of workers for the increasing demand for white-collar professionals. According to US Census data, in 1947 only 6 percent of Americans in their twenties had earned a bachelor's degree; today about a quarter have.[32] Also, starting in the 1930s and '40s and continuing on through the 1980s, secondary education was geared to serve the needs of a capitalist system with a large manufacturing base. High schools were built to accommodate thousands. In appearance and in terms of how they functioned, they resembled factories.

Nevertheless, a more progressive pedagogy was born out of the struggles of the 1960s and '70s. Students organized for ethnic studies programs, teacher-intellectuals began to talk about educating the "whole child," and people pushed back against both the Great Man theory of history and methodologies of teaching that emphasized rote learning.

Since the quieting of the movements that opened up the space for a more free and critical form of education, there's been a concerted effort to roll back the liberalization of curriculum. Perhaps the opening shot was the 1983 declaration in *A Nation at Risk* that our educational system is "in crisis," which opened the door for an era of renewed efforts to control curriculum. Radical academic John Bellamy Foster, in his essay "Neoliberalism and the Structural Crisis of Capital,"[33] writes that this has been fundamentally about controlling teachers' labor. Central to the "neoliberal" plan that has ruled the US economy from 1973 to the present is the idea on the part of business owners that it is essential to get more out of each worker (in this case, teachers) and to limit workers' voice and power in the workplace. In this case, that means attacking aspects of teachers' collective bargaining rights and academic freedom, and standardizing and scripting curriculum.

The imposition of business models onto education was accelerated with the 2001 No Child Left Behind legislation. Business models began with an increased focus on standardized, multiple-choice testing as a way of measuring educational quality. Recently, there has been a move to use students' testing data to measure individual teachers, as in the previously mentioned "value added" evaluation systems. Schools are forced to "compete" with each other, in theory letting parents act like rational "consumers" in a market system. The way that the business model and neoliberal economics have been imposed on schools for the past forty years is explored in depth in chapter 5.

Is This Theory "Deterministic?"

One critique of Bowles and Gintis is that their ideas are "too deterministic" because they argue that the economic needs of the capitalist system shape schools. Their focus on social structures and the "system" does not allow any space for individual people to make positive changes in the here and now. In response to Bowles and Gintis's classic work, Mike Cole, a British radical academic, argues that "the theory *can* have reactionary rather than progressive implications."[34] In other words, when the system seems overly *determined*, it can leave radical teachers feeling like there is a lack of space for doing any good now. "Some of my student teachers," Cole says, "have even looked upon the principle as reassuring in its promise of stability and the maintenance of the status quo, while others, with a more radical mind, have despaired at the seeming lack of space for individual and collective action."[35]

Cole also charges Bowles and Gintis with "crude mechanistic economism."[36] He claims that the theories developed in *Schooling in Capitalist America* are too simplistic in arguing that the economic base (the way production is organized in the economy) determines the institutions of the superstructure (political and cultural institutions and norms—in this case, schools).

In *Schooling in Capitalist America*, Bowles and Gintis don't actually write much in terms of "base" and "superstructure"—they only use the term "superstructure" once. In that sense, the critiques leveled at them are somewhat unfounded. More important, however, their work is far from crude. They argue that the economic system is more dynamic—that it changes more quickly—than the educational system, which is notoriously slow to change. This produces periods of sharp debate about educational reform, like the one that we're living through now, in which elites try to retool the educational system to be more in line with current economic forms and needs (in this case, to align more to a neoliberal economic model—see chapter 5 for a description of the agenda that today's economic elites have for our schools). These periods of friction often also open up space for students, parents, and teachers to advance an alternative vision of what schools should look like. Again, we see this happening today.

Nevertheless, this critique of Bowles and Gintis for economic determinism is so widely held that it is important to address in greater detail. The base and superstructure theory, in its original form, is actually about the dynamic jostling back and forth between the economy and extra-economic institutions. It leads to the theory that schools can play a role in social change because of the contradictions between these schools and the economy, and also the contradictions that they expose within society as a whole.

Marx began to lay out the concepts of "base" and "superstructure" in *A Contribution to the Critique of Political Economy* with these words: "The mode of production of material life conditions the general process of social, political, and intellectual life."[37] The economic "base" is the way that production is organized. In this case, under capitalism resources are privately owned. Owners hire workers and organize their work, and—no matter whether their company is a retail store, a health insurance company, or a steel manufacturer—their driving motive is profit. These profits must accumulate and be reinvested faster than their competitors' or the company will fail. To understand how a society works, it is most crucial to understand the relations of production at the base. Who controls the resources? How do decisions get made? What is the relationship between the planners and the workers? Is work a collective process or an individual one? How are wealth and resources distributed?

"Superstructural" institutions are those that are not directly involved in the production process, but take shape to facilitate the smooth running of society. These institutions include governmental and also cultural institutions as they evolve over time. Each institution develops its own rules and takes on an internal logic (and therefore an ideology) and method of operating. Courts and schools are two examples of institutions that are superstructural branches of the government. According to Marxist analysis, the way that work and production are organized (the "base") is the motor that drives societies. The people who control the resources and organize production have the most power to organize society's institutions to meet their needs. However, throughout the *Critique*, Marx also emphasizes how the economic base and superstructural institutions influence each other.[38]

Here's one way that the interplay between base and superstructure can play out with schools. The education system is set up to deliver obedient workers with the right skills and behaviors to the capitalists. The needs of the economic base shape what schools will look like. But then an ideology develops around the public school system, and it's one of equality, and one of "critical thinking." People hang their hopes on education. This ideology and these expectations can lead people to organize and fight for better schools. As in the case of the US South, the struggles for desegregation and access to quality education lead to legislative changes, like federal antidiscrimination laws, in society as a whole. These laws end up acting as regulations on businesses as well as the public sector. Furthermore, those student organizers carry their ideas and their experience, as well as the taste of victory from their struggles against desegregation, into their workplaces with them. Some of them become organizers for economic justice in society at large.

The logical implication of the theory of base and superstructure is that the economy must be changed, along with schools, in order to fundamentally transform education. For radical educators, this would mean that, rather than trying to change society solely (or mostly) through our pedagogy, we need to be involved in struggles for economic justice and democracy in our communities, in our unions, and in solidarity with other workers who are fighting back.

Many education and "New Left" writers have built on the critique of base and superstructure advanced by Louis Althusser, who argued that the base and the superstructure enjoy "relative autonomy."[39] In addition, he asserted that the original base and superstructure theory was too wooden and deterministic. Bowles and Gintis have acceded to this critique in important ways. In *Bowles and Gintis Revisited*, they grant that schools could be "sites of social practice," which they define as "a cohesive area of social life." The state, family, and capitalist production are all seen as "sites of production." Schools "participate" in all these sites. The "sites" can operate autonomously from each other, and each has relatively equal importance.[40]

There is an obvious reason why it is appealing to many on the New Left and many teachers to essentially reject the idea that the economy needs to be changed to change education. If the theory is wrong, or at least too wooden, then we can do our social justice work in our classrooms. In other words, we can give up on the idea of revolutionary change to the economic power structure and just focus on the changes we can make within schools. This chapter is devoted to speaking back to that conception, and arguing to social justice educators that what we do in schools cannot be enough if our goal is empowerment and a greater degree of social equality.

Nevertheless, the stated objection to the base/superstructure theory is that it is deterministic, dogmatic, and reductionist. Marxists, it is charged, "reduce" everything to a question of class. Two essays shed much light on this debate, Chris Harman's 1986 essay "Base and Superstructure," and Wayne Au's 2006 "Against Economic Determinism: Revisiting the Roots of Neo-Marxism in Critical Education Theory." Both of these essays draw the same conclusion: a look at the original writings of Marx (and many subsequent Marxists) shows that the original theory of base and superstructure are anything but deterministic, mechanical, and dogmatic.

Marx and Engels, while they asserted the importance of the economic base in understanding the dynamics of a society, also emphasized the feedback and interaction between the forces of production and all the political institutions created by societies. As Engels wrote:

> The economic situation is the basis, but the various elements of the super-structure—political forms of the class struggle and its results, to wit: con-stitutions established by victorious classes after a successful battle, etc., juridical forms and even the reflexes of these actual struggles in the brains of the participants, political, juristic, philosophical theories, religious views and their further development into systems of dogmas—also exercise their influence upon the course of the historical struggles and in many cases pre-ponderate in determining their form.[41]

The theory of base and superstructure is still one worth defending. Do schools serve the needs of the economic elite, the "shot-callers"? Does the economy play a decisive role in shaping our schools? I've argued that it does.

While teaching for justice is an extremely valuable thing, if educators see that as their main and only job, then some of our most justice-minded and talented individuals won't be helping where their help is needed most—in organizations fighting in workplaces and communities for a bigger slice of the pie and ultimately more power on the job for working-class people.

Nevertheless, Marx himself never said that schools, or any other "superstructural institutions," didn't have a role to play in helping to shape fights at the base—nor have most Marxists since. That's a caricature.

Racism, Oppression, and Schools

The other main critique among education theorists of Bowles and Gintis's work, and indeed of Marxism overall, is that Marxists don't pay enough attention to racism and oppression in the functioning of schools. Racism, of course, is a central defining feature in our educational system. A higher percentage of Black children attend segregated schools now than in 1968.[42] The teaching force in most cities is majority white (although in many places it's a slim majority and growing slimmer). When thousands of teachers were laid off in Los Angeles in 2009, Black and Latino teachers were disproportionately affected because many of them were young and newer to the job.

In the era of austerity, the trend toward a more integrated teaching force may be reversed because a new generation of young teachers of color are the last hired and first fired. In many segregated urban schools, then, nonwhite students face white teachers all day and often come to see them as part of the structure of authority of the state, reaching from the government to the courts, the police, and finally into schools.

Schools are rife with racism, sexism, and homophobia. Black students are three times more likely than whites to be expelled or suspended for some offenses, such as disrespectful behavior and public displays of affection.[43] They are disproportionately placed in special education classes and classified as having "behavior disorders." Bilingual education has been formally outlawed in three states, California, Arizona, and Massachusetts (see chapter 3), and is disappearing in many others, although educators committed to research-based best practices have found some small ways to buck these trends. Girls are called on less in class, sexually harassed, and regularly subjected to judgment and ridicule based on the most rigid gender stereotypes. Homophobia manifests as constant and ubiquitous mocking of lesbian, gay, bisexual, and transgender (LGBT) students and "gayness" in general by the most sexually insecure and scared segment of the population—adolescents. Often, homophobia means actual violence. And LGBT teens have the highest suicide rate of any group. Schools are an amplified microcosm of all the oppressions that exist in society: it's where some learn to oppress, and where many more learn to live with oppression, and in rarer instances, how to fight it.

At the same time, the social struggles of the past decades have brought an arsenal of federal antidiscrimination laws to the public schools. Schools are subject to stricter laws than the rest of society—they can be sued for failing to prevent hate speech, for example, and legally (although often not in practice) have to be proactive in preventing discrimination. Contests over discrimination in schools have been central to every struggle from the civil rights movement to the gay liberation movement. In short, schools are a battleground between the forces of discrimination and the forces of equality.

Fighting oppression is central to the Marxist strategy of getting rid of structural and institutional inequality. Yet, there are certain assessments of Marx's politics that have been repeated so many times that they have been accepted as orthodoxy. The idea that Marxism ignores oppression—expressed most often in terms of racism—is the intellectual starting point for both postmodernism and critical race theory in education; it is even conceded by some Marxists. In fairness to the critics: what gives this assessment any traction is the uneven historical record of socialist and Marxist groups in fighting racism. These movements at times produced inspiring moments of struggling for racial equality, and at others, outrageous instances of ignoring racial oppression or worse.[44] In fairness to Marxists, however, the critique is rarely based on critics having read anything in the Marxist tradition or knowing anything about its history.

Capitalism is a system founded on the exploitation of the vast majority by the few. Because this inequality is at the heart of the system, the few who rule over it need all sorts of ways to keep the exploited majority divided. Oppression—whether based on racial, ethnic, gender, sexual, religious, national, or other categories—is the central tool used to do this. Worse still, oppression functions ideologically both to justify and explain how society is set up. Here I'll draw out just one example, that of racism, and leave the parallels about other especially oppressed groups—in particular women and LGBT people—to the reader.

To justify the enslavement of Africans, racism developed as an ideology that relegated slaves to being something less than human and thus not worthy of freedom or liberty. In current times, the criminal justice system exposes this same dynamic. The racism used to whip up fears of crime means that more than two million people are behind bars in this country—with vastly disproportionate numbers of people of color locked up. But that same racism also ensures that enormous amounts of public funds are diverted into the prison system instead of being spent on schools, housing, health care, and other social needs in our communities—a diversion that affects us all.

Oppression, though, does not only function at an ideological level. It also produces material economic benefits for those at the top of society at the expense of everyone else. This claim is directly opposed to the notion of "privilege" that dominates most discussions nowadays about oppression, whereby those who do not experience a given oppression are privileged. Framing oppression as a question of privilege focuses almost exclusively on how individuals perceive or experience oppression. This analysis comes at the expense of a broader understanding of how oppression functions in society, and who really benefits.

Above all, it is the few who sit atop the pyramid of power and wealth in society who benefit materially from oppression. This is not to deny that material differences exist between and among oppressed groups under capitalism. In the United States, for example, according to a Pew Research Center study, the median wealth of white households is twenty times that of Black households and eighteen times that of Hispanic households.[45] On every other measure of the quality of life—longevity, health, infant mortality, educational attainment, and so on—whites on average fared better than Blacks. In no way does the Marxist understanding of oppression deny these differences or the inescapable conclusion that some people are worse off than others.

The question remains, though, of what actually causes those differences in the first place. That is, do white families earn more *because* Black families earn less? Marxist historian Keeanga-Yamahtta Taylor argues:

> To accept this explanation [that whites benefit directly from the oppression of Black workers] means to ignore the biggest beneficiary in the disparity between wages—employers and bosses. That employers are able to use racism to justify paying Black workers less brings the wages of all workers down—the employers enjoy the difference. This is not to deny that white workers receive some advantages in US society because they are white in a racist society. If they did not get some advantage—and with it, the illusion that the system works for them—then racism would not be effective in dividing Black and white workers.[46]

Marx made a similar argument in *Capital* in the most concise terms: "In the United States of America, every independent workers' movement was paralyzed so long as slavery disfigured a part of the republic. Labor in a white skin cannot emancipate itself so long as it is branded in a Black skin."[47]

Of course, school is one of the key institutions where we see and experience this oppression. The history of this oppression—and the struggles to end it—are at the heart of chapters 2 and 3. In genuine, dialectical Marxism, economic exploitation (that is, the way that bosses take advantage of our work for their own profit) and the oppression of people based on race, gender, and sexual orientation are related. We won't win economic demands like the struggle for more resources for schools without taking on issues of racism. The reason why many urban segregated schools are left to languish without resources is in large part the legacy of racism; "those kids" don't deserve what kids in the suburbs have. As long as Black youth can be painted as a "criminal" or "unemployable" element, people can continue to pretend that everyone has an equal opportunity for an education and those who don't get ahead must have themselves to blame. Just as we won't win more resources for our schools without taking on racism, we also can't beat segregation and other forms of oppression without a struggle for economic justice for our schools and against the economic system where the few dominate the many. The two are intimately and directly related.

Contradictions and Struggle as the Key to Change

Here we return to the base/superstructure theory to help us to understand how change happens. As Marx points out in the preface to the *Critique of Political Economy*, it is in the "superstructure," the realm of politics and ideas, where people "become conscious of [social] conflict and fight it out."[48] Schools help to expose society's conflicts in many people's minds. One of the contradictions, according to Bowles and Gintis, is that in order to grow (to accumulate more profits and develop the means of production), capitalists need a workforce that is more highly trained, more educated, and more self-directed. In the words of Andre Gorz, people's "human capabilities need to be developed."[49] This means education, and developing people's abilities to *think*, so that they can innovate—and have the management skills necessary to keep the capitalist system growing.

However, by grouping future workers together in schools, it is inevitable that some of the tools that are given to them will be used against the capitalist class itself. You cannot teach people to read and then control the content of all the books that they read. And you cannot encourage innovation without encouraging creative thinking. The inventors of new technology will, at certain points, question how their ideas are being used. Furthermore, you cannot stuff enormous groups of young people together into crowded, degrading conditions and not expect them, at some point, to organize for the equal opportunities that the system is promising. Humans are not machines—and herein lies the inherent vulnerability of capitalism.

There are ideological conflicts that help to expose the true nature of what's going on. There's a conflict between "democracy" in the political realm and dictatorship in the workplace. The concepts of "one person, one vote," equal protection under the law, and democratic decision making apply only within the narrow limits of the political sphere (and even here these concepts are mostly ideological and often violated). But no one ever promises that there will be any democratic control over decisions about the economy—that is, what gets produced and how it gets distributed. Political democracy is, in a sense, the perfect illusion of equality and equal participation in decision making. But its ideology, when carried to its logical conclusion, creates friction with the undemocratic nature of work and resource control. This contradiction is only apparent when people can zoom out their internal cameras far enough to look at how decisions are made about big-ticket items: what to produce, how much to pay people, how to organize transportation, whether to go to war.

From the contradiction between political democracy and economic dictatorship follows another: the gap between what we are promised in public education and the reality of what schools are. The rest of the chapters in this book are dedicated to exploring such instances, like the fight for bilingual education that arose in part from the contradictions in the migrant experience. Most people who cross the border into the United States report that their biggest motivator is to afford their children better education and opportunities than they enjoyed themselves. Their hopes are often frustrated. Likewise, the self-activity of former slaves in achieving their own literacy was fundamental to the establishment of public education in the South. When it became clear that this education reinforced the divisions in society, schools became crucial sites of struggle. New pedagogy was created that would influence future public school practice and access. Even today, education promises to be the antidote to inequality and poverty. And now, like always, the educational system disappoints.

The decisive conflict in our society is the one between those who own and control the wealth, on the one hand, and those who do all the work, on the other. These two groups have interests that are exactly opposite of each other—the main goal of those who control the wealth is to make profits. The less they pay the workers, the more profits they make. Herein lies the contradiction that drives social upheavals, struggles for power, and contests over the distribution of wealth—work is a *collective*, *collaborative*, and *social* endeavor. In almost every workplace, from manufacturing to the service sector, many people have to cooperate and communicate to get the job done. And yet ownership over productive resources is *private* and *individual*. We workers make and do things together, and yet wealthy individuals make decisions and control productive resources privately. Schools can help to expose this but cannot, by themselves, change it.

What We're Fighting For

In a few short sentences, Paulo Freire summed up a way of looking at an educational program for teachers who are committed to the transformation of society. He pointed out the

> distinction between systematic education, which can be changed by po-
> litical power, and educational projects, which should be carried out with
> the oppressed in the process of organizing them.
>
> The pedagogy of the oppressed, as a humanist and libertarian peda-
> gogy, has two distinct stages. In the first, the oppressed unveil the world
> of oppression and through the praxis commit themselves to its transfor-
> mation. In the second stage, in which the reality of oppression has already
> been transformed, this pedagogy ceases to belong to the oppressed and
> becomes a pedagogy of all people in the process of permanent liberation.[50]
> [emphasis in original]

Freire asks us to recognize that there is a difference between what we
can achieve as educators in a society based on the oppression of the few by
the many—he calls these "educational projects"—and the type of pedagogy
that we would be able to engage in if society were to go through revolutionary change. In the former, education can be liberatory only if it is connected
to struggle for change. This is what Marx meant when he said in the *Contribution to Hegel's Philosophy of Right* that "the weapon of criticism cannot,
of course, replace criticism of the weapon, material force must be overthrown by material force; but theory also becomes a material force as soon
as it has gripped the masses."

Myles Horton was one of the founders of the Highlander School in
Tennessee. Highlander educated generations of civil rights and labor leaders
starting in the 1930s and founded the Citizenship Schools that helped hundreds of thousands of African Americans to pass their literacy tests (then a
requirement for voting) in the Jim Crow South. Horton reflected, "It's the
structures of society that we've got to change. We don't change men's
hearts. . . . It doesn't make a great deal of difference what the people are; if
they're in the system, they're going to function like the system dictates they
function. . . . I've been more concerned with structural changes than I have
with changing hearts of people."[51] Coming from someone who changed a
lot of hearts, his advice is worth considering.

The second type of education described by Freire will be the kind of
truly liberatory education that many teachers dream of when they sign up
for the job, but which is largely impossible now. Here I'm referring to an
enlightening, engaged, and transformative process where the antagonisms
between teachers and students are erased. In this "utopian" type of education

(which I think is possible in a changed set of circumstances), there would be genuine collaboration between teachers and students in the mutual pursuit of knowledge driven by curiosity about the way the world works and essential questions that engage both teacher and student. The final section of this essay will return to the question of a genuinely liberatory education.

Envisioning an End to Racism, Segregation, and Poverty

Jean Anyon's 2005 book *Radical Possibilities* is dedicated to describing systemic reforms that would improve educational achievement, even if we take a capitalist economic system as a given. All these solutions reach outside the walls of schools. Most of the job creation for the past thirty years has been in the suburbs, as well as the highest corporate tax bases, even though unemployment is concentrated in the cities. Little to no public transportation exists to take displaced urban workers to jobs in the suburbs. What about a massive public transportation overhaul, revenue sharing between a city and its suburbs, or publicly subsidized housing in the suburbs? When this experiment was tried on a small scale, such as the Gatraux Program in Chicago and the larger-scale Moving to Opportunity program begun by HUD in 1994, it not only led to participants living in much more racially mixed neighborhoods, but participants earned 73 percent more income than a control group of inner-city residents who did not participate in the program.[52] This is probably the most viable way to desegregate our schools: through federally subsidized and voluntary desegregation of our neighborhoods.

Our schools were more segregated as this millennium opened than they were in the 1960s.[53] Desegregation is crucial to improving the quality of our schools. In Raleigh, North Carolina, in the 1980s, a school integration plan proved this. As chronicled by Gerald Grant, the school board merged Raleigh's schools with those of neighboring Wake County. Then they used race as one criterion to assign students to schools. This program became not only a national model for integration but also a national model for academic achievement. Of parents, both Black and white, surveyed, 94.5 percent were satisfied with the schools. Now, though, Tea Party conservatives have taken over the local school board and are trying to dismantle the program. Students, parents, and community members know instinctively that schools that are mixed racially and by social class will not be allowed to rot the way that poor urban schools are and have begun to use civil disobedience tactics to defend them.[54]

While there is very little evidence that the "reform" prescriptions of the Bush and Obama administrations of the past ten years (increased reliance on high-stakes standardized tests, "accountability," and charter schools) have raised educational achievement, there is evidence that relieving families of some of the stresses of poverty does help to raise educational achievement in students.[55]

A redistribution of income would help the academic achievement of children living in poverty. The stresses upon low-income families, and related problems like poor nutrition, have tremendous negative impact on children's cognitive development. Helping families out of poverty decreases parental depression and stress, improves access to "richer learning environments," and decreases behavior problems that can stand in the way of children's educational achievement.[56] Of course, to win these concessions we will need a movement at least as broad, deep, and sweeping as the civil rights movements of the 1960s and 1970s.

Revolutionary Restructuring of the Economy
Bowles and Gintis argued:

> Many modern progressive educators have seen a more equal and liberating school system as the major instrument for the construction of a just and human society. . . . The reader will not be surprised to find that we are more than a little skeptical of these claims. The social problems to which these reforms are addressed have their roots not primarily in the school system itself, but rather in the normal functioning of the economic system. Educational alternatives which fail to address this basic fact join a club of venerable lineage: the legion of school reforms which, at times against the better intentions of its leading proponents, have served to deflect discontent, depoliticize social distress, and thereby have helped to stabilize the prevailing structures of privilege.[57]

In 1976, as *Schooling in Capitalist America* was being written, the reforms to which they were referring were considerably more ambitious and progressive than the "reforms" that are most often talked about today. They were: racially integrated schooling, compensatory education (funding for schools with students of low socioeconomic status), open enrollment (allowing all students to attend college, specifically community colleges and state schools), and vouchers. All these came about as a result of the justice movements of the fifties, sixties, and seventies. The fight for racially integrated schooling in particular was one of the most inspiring movements for social justice of the last century. And yet Bowles and Gintis point out the limitations of these movements. These limitations have become clearer today as levels of segregation have slid back to levels similar to the sixties.

Vouchers, the idea that some public funds should be given to parents who choose to send their children to private schools, were an early back-door route to privatization. That's why they were so popular among conservatives like Milton Friedman and also among the religious right, which saw an opportunity to gain funds for parochial schools. The political problem of funneling public monies to private schools is thus fairly clear.

And yet, even more positive reforms such as Title I are politically complicated. "When special programs for 'disadvantaged' youth [Title I] were created," according to historian and author Lois Weiner,

> they were based on a "compensatory model" subsequently used for other groups, like students with disabilities and immigrants requiring instruction in the school language. From the start this model had serious political and educational limitations, including the way "success" was measured, through students' scores on standardized tests (Bastian et al. 1986). . . . Another flaw in the compensatory model was the implicit acceptance of its educational theory about why some children do not succeed in school, that children of historically oppressed groups are underachieving because they have problems, deficits, that needed remediation. Compensatory programs in the United States provided much-needed but relatively small funding increases for the education of minority students while ignoring systemic inequalities resulting from the structure and organization of schooling.[58]

Today, in the absence of a real social movement, the "reforms" have either been co-opted by pro-corporate forces, as in the case of charter schools, or are modest (some might even say timid), as in the case of the 2003 ACLU lawsuit *Williams v. California*. That lawsuit, for which I gave testimony, demanded simply that all students have access to clean restrooms, textbooks to take home, and highly qualified teachers (even if the teacher-to-student ratio is 40:1). The reforms of today make an even stronger case that schools cannot be "*the* major instrument for the construction of a just and human society."

Nevertheless, if Bowles and Gintis intended to say that reforms *only* "deflect discontent, depoliticize social distress, and thereby have helped to stabilize the prevailing structures of privilege," then that view is too one-sided. The correlation between winning real reforms and positive changes to social services, on the one hand, and revolutionary transformation on the other, can be a positive one. So, for example, the fight to integrate schools in the 1950s and '60s encouraged people to demand *more* rights, not fewer. It raised expectations and convinced people that if they stood up, they could win. It brought people of various ethnic backgrounds into the same spaces, which in turn helped (in many cases) to break down stereotypes. The gains of the early civil rights movement, around busing, school, and restaurant desegregation led to more radical systemic analysis for many, both Black and white.

To use another example from a different region of the world: the Arab Spring of 2011 was born out of years of ongoing struggles for political liberalization, the right to political association, and an end to repression. The street vendor in Tunisia who immolated himself in protest against state repression of the informal sector of the economy may not have foreseen that he would fan the flames of a movement that would topple dictators. More to the point, the resignation of Hosni Mubarak in Egypt in February 2011 does not appear to have put a damper on the organization of the Egyptian working class and youth. On the contrary, at the time of the publication of this book it appears as though organization to hold the military-led government to the promises of the new constitution persists. People tasted their power and want *more*. The struggle for reforms can inspire rather than dampen the struggle for revolutionary change when this struggle raises people's expectations, gives them confidence, and leads to questions about the organization of society.

The more important type of structural change, then, in the words of Bowles and Gintis, is the "revolutionary transformation of the educational system, integrated with a dramatic re-ordering of control of power in the economic realm." We need a "comprehensive intellectual reconstruction of the role of education in economic life."[59] Many would call this socialism: democratic control over economic resources.

This book is dedicated to propagating two key ideas. First, new societies are born out of struggles against the old ones; a new education system would probably be shaped by the things that people most want to change about our current system. Every year, at activist meetings and in my class, I am part of discussions with students about what an ideal school would look like. Some of the same themes always come up: there would be field trips everywhere. Learning would take place by doing; there would be robotics clubs and music clubs. There would be lots of green space, either in the yard or on the roof. There would be medical care on campus, the class sizes would be tiny, the students could choose and shape their own electives, all students would have laptops, and everything would be clean. Even our imaginations are conditioned by what we *don't* like about schools today. And yet if we think that schools should be democratically controlled, then it is impossible to pre-plan what education would look like in a more liberated society. Many teachers reading this book may be frustrated because we have been conditioned to want a "road map" for how to do things—how to teach social justice in the classroom, for example. This chapter has argued that such an approach to creating a more just society is too limited. So what should we do then?

The second idea that drives this book was articulated best by the emancipated slave and freedom fighter Frederick Douglass, that "power concedes nothing without a demand." So teachers need to participate in struggle. We need to build solidarity with our working-class brothers and sisters internationally and domestically. When other workers are attacked, we need to defend them, and when they strike, we need to walk their picket line. Workers who stand up and fight for good contracts or union representation will help to create the kind of living-wage jobs that our students need. We should participate in struggles for legalization of undocumented workers and against foreclosures. Through our participation in these and other struggles, we need to talk with communities about a vision of a society worth living in and fighting for. Lastly, we need to recognize that vision is necessary. But it can't come to fruition without organization.

The hardest question to figure out is how to organize to win. We cannot wait for future generations to do so. As Waseem Wagdi, a protester at the Egyptian embassy in London, said on January 29, 2011: "I had hoped, and I think with millions of people, that our children will live in a more humane society. But in this society we are lucky enough that the heroes in Egypt are not waiting for our children to dream, they are bringing all of our dreams true today in Suez, in the factories, in Tahrir Square. The biggest square in the Arab world is being liberated today from this regime. . . . I am proud to be Egyptian today." We cannot wait for the next generation to figure out how to fight for change; that's shirking responsibility. If teachers are not to be missionaries, we need to realize that we, too, need to be liberated alongside our working-class brothers and sisters. We need to defend ourselves against the attacks that are coming down on us, at the same time that we need to fight to better the conditions in our classrooms and our own pay and working conditions. Our unions are potential weapons in this fight, but they need to be retooled.

Rank-and-file teachers need to take control of these unions and make them less bureaucratic and more geared for struggle. That is the theme of chapter 5.

Schools are interconnected with the way that our economy is organized. They promote the growth of capitalist productivity in one way—especially in the realm of very specific scientific developments. But they stunt human capabilities in other ways, because they function as one tool of social control. "From forms of development of the productive forces, these relations turn into fetters," Marx argues in the preface to the *Critique of Political Economy.* "There begins an epoch of social revolution."[60] The capitalist organization of society has become a barrier to the development of the human race. If profits continue to be the driving motivation behind production, then industry will continue to spew catastrophic levels of pollution into the environment. Half of the world's population will continue to live in want, and competition will continue to hinder the kind of intellectual cooperation that could provide us with the inventive force to improve human living standards. A more rational and cooperative system would be in the interests of all but the tiny group of elites who benefit from the current arrangement.

Ultimately, an alternative society in which teaching and learning would be truly liberatory would be based on two principles: democracy and empowerment. "Democracy" should be defined not in the narrow sense of electing representatives every four years, but as economic democracy: collective control over society's resources. If we had economic democracy, we could harness our available resources to meet human needs instead of for profit. Imagine the incredible intellectual engagement that would require of whole communities of people. This is related to the second concept of "empowerment." Empowerment is not something that happens in our minds, nor is it an achievable goal for any individual who doesn't have the opportunity to command major resources. It occurs when people have real decision-making power about what is produced in the community, how it is produced, what type of services we provide for ourselves and each other, and society's priorities. If these decisions were made in a truly democratic fashion, then learning, teaching, debating, arguing, convincing, in short, intellectual engagement with the world and each other would be much more profound than most of us can even imagine today.

2

The Struggle for Black Education
Brian Jones

[P]robably never in the world have so many oppressed people tried in every possible way to educate themselves.
—W. E. B. Du Bois[1]

The Second Coming of the Civil Rights Movement?

The longstanding struggle of African Americans for equal access to quality education in the United States is a matter of great concern on all sides of the current debate about education reform. The call for racial justice in education has been raised, on the one hand, by seasoned educators and activists who have catalogued and protested the increasing resegregation of US schools and the racial isolation of urban communities, and who have led the fight for desegregation and for parity in school funding. On the other hand, the mantle of racial justice has been claimed as well by current education reformers who advocate for privatization, charter schools, greater usage of standardized tests, and the endless gathering of data on teacher effectiveness; in fact, many of these reformers boldly describe their efforts as the second coming of the civil rights movement.[2]

The arguments by current education reformers: that too many Black parents do not value education and are not transmitting the proper values to their children; that teachers' unions are an obstacle to racial justice in education; that philanthropists are Black parents' best ally in the struggle for equality; and that racial justice is not synonymous with desegregation or equitable funding, but rather with market-oriented changes that foster competition and encourage private-sector management of schools are based on a dubious set of propositions about racial politics today. The actual history of the Black struggle for education in the United States challenges every one of those propositions.

Before casting aspersions on parents for not teaching the proper values, it is vital to step back and consider the heroic efforts of successive generations of Black parents and students to educate themselves. In so doing, we see that these attempts were repeatedly frustrated by violence, repression, and subterfuge that took a variety of forms. Nevertheless, the very fact that this struggle has continued virtually uninterrupted in American history leads one to ask not what's wrong with Black parents, but rather what forces today are serving to thwart their aspirations. This pattern of struggle and repression begins with the heroic efforts of slaves and former slaves to become literate, against all odds.

Slavery and Compulsory Ignorance

> *Be it enacted, That all and every person and persons whatsoever, who shall hereafter teach, or cause any slave or slaves to be taught to write, or shall use or employ any slave as a scribe in any manner of writing whatsoever, hereafter taught to write; every such person or persons shall, for every offense, forfeit the sum of one hundred pounds current money.*
> —South Carolina law, enacted in 1740[3]

Generally, one does not have to legislate against something that cannot happen. Thus, the passage of laws such as the one quoted above betrays the understanding—and fear—held by white colonial planters of the intellectual potential of the human beings they held in chains. Africans, who of course were brought against their will to the New World, carried with them a great deal of knowledge, including technical and agricultural skills and understanding from their home societies. Moreover, as a significant proportion of enslaved Africans were Muslim, they brought with them Arabic literacy, as well—one estimate suggests that 10 percent of Africans brought to the United States in the eighteenth century could read Arabic.[4]

But in the United States, their lot was to be worked to death to grow and harvest cotton and tobacco. Thus, their ability to maintain, develop, and pass on that knowledge was violently constrained. Compulsory igno-rance for them—and especially for their children—flowed not from irra-tional prejudices of the master class, but from a quite rational understanding of what was necessary to maintain Africans in a subjugated status.

"Schooling," the saying went in the South, "ruins a nigger."[5] But the desire to know and understand the language and the ways of the strange, cruel New World was essentially unquenchable. The story of the struggle for Black education begins with the first Africans to set foot in the New World.

It is a story of self-determination and self-organization, not of charity. Much attention has been given to the kindhearted master here or there who taught his slaves to read. While this did occur, the ignorance laws and the slave owners' own self-interest were enough to keep this phenomenon marginal.[6]

In a few northern cities, free Africans and their allies established schools through churches and mutual aid societies. Around the time of the Revolu-tionary War, such schools were established in Philadelphia and New York.[7]

It was much more common for enslaved Africans to teach themselves and each other to read, despite the personal risks. As the result of one such attempt: "a slave by the name of Scipio was put to death for teaching a slave child how to read and spell, and the child was severely beaten to make him 'forget what he had learned.'"[8]

Slaves and free Negroes (who were also often barred from sending their children to school) risked their lives to organize secret schools. One historian notes how "schools . . . were secretly maintained" in Virginia: "The colored aspirants after knowledge were constrained to keep their books and slates carefully hidden from every prying eye, and to assume the appearance of being upon an errand as they hurried along and watched their chance to slip unnoticed into the sedulously concealed schoolroom."[9]

Another clandestine school existed, amazingly "unknown to the slave regime," from 1819 to 1865 in Savannah, Georgia.[10] A slave named Eliza-beth Sparks was part of a group of both slaves and free Blacks who met in slave dwellings for literacy instruction. They called these secret sessions "stealin' the meetin'."[11]

Where Black education did manage to creep into the open, it was often quickly shut down. Thus, in the aftermath of Nat Turner's 1831 slave re-bellion, even the Sabbath schools were closed to Black children in the Dis-trict of Columbia. In the same year, a law in Virginia banned even free Negroes from school. Black parents who could afford to do so sent their children to other states to be educated. In response, the legislature passed a law stipulating that any child who left the state to receive an education could *never* return. Georgia passed a law prohibiting Blacks from working in print shops, because they were receiving too much education through their apprenticeships; South Carolina banned Blacks from working in any kind of office or store for the same reason.[12]

In the North, where Blacks had more opportunity to advocate in their own interest, education was at the top of their agenda. But as more and more states moved to create free public schools, they often banned Black children. Nevertheless, Black parents were still expected to pay taxes and thus help to underwrite whites-only education.

Ohio established its public school system in 1829, but the law specifically excluded Blacks. African American parents scraped together $40,000—an enormous sum, considering a "good" monthly income could be $10—to support a network of about fourteen schools statewide. With this experience under their belts, the parents began lobbying the legislature for public schools. By the late 1840s they had won the right to build publicly funded Black-only schools, elect their own school boards, and later to admit a number of Black children to white schools.[13]

The struggle to be allowed to establish Black schools quickly transformed into a struggle against segregated schools, and against segregation within schools. The great abolitionist Frederick Douglass was furious when he received a letter from his daughter, who was attending a seminary school in Rochester, New York. "I get along pretty well," she wrote, "but father, Miss Tracy does not allow me to go into the room with the other scholars because I am colored." Douglass "remonstrated and the principal asked the girl's white classmates where the girl could sit. All shouted 'by me!' Then parents were asked whether they agreed. Except for one, they did. The only parent who refused to countenance desegregation was H. G. Warner, editor of the *Rochester Courier*. Douglass reminded Warner in a letter: 'We are both worms of the dust, and our children are like us.'"[14]

In many northern towns, Black parents organized boycotts against segregated schools. In towns where Blacks had greater numbers (and therefore, greater political influence) they were able to win their demands. Antislavery organizations provided crucial support to these struggles. In some places, abolitionists won control of local school boards and moved immediately to integrate the schools. Boston, Salem, and Nantucket, Massachusetts, as well as Rochester, Buffalo, and Lockport, New York, all experienced boycotts where 70 percent of Black parents (or more) kept their children out of school to win desegregation. In Boston, one parent explained how they won their demands through unity and protest action: "We went round to every parent in the city, and had all the children removed from the Caste Schools; we made all our people take their children away. And in six months we had it all our own way—and that's the way we always should act. Let us be bold, and they'll have to yield to us."[15]

In the South, Black parents—free and slave, and often risking death—pursued every opportunity to educate their children. Meanwhile, in the "enlightened" northern states, Black parents had to wage a determined struggle to secure equal access to the schools their tax dollars were building for white children.

The American Civil War created a situation in which Black education could be organized in the open in the South for the first time and could be enormously expanded in the North. As we shall see, Black parents and students seized the opportunity with both hands. While they often funded their own independent schools out of sheer necessity, newly freed Blacks understood that the *right* to education was most secure in the form of free, public schools open to all.

Black Reconstruction

Public education for all at public expense, was, in the South, a Negro idea.
—W. E. B. Du Bois[16]

The American Civil War became a revolutionary war to abolish slavery and led to the economic ruin of the slave owners as a class. What is often overlooked in discussions about this process is the role of the *slaves themselves*—some two hundred thousand fought in the Union army—in securing their own emancipation.

Fighting for—and importantly, *winning*—their freedom, ex-slaves and their children transformed their own consciousness. "The children had only to heed the evidence of their eyes," historian Meyer Weinberg writes, "to know that great events had transpired and that their parents had played a large part in bringing them about." He continued: "Such a realization undoubtedly deepened the self-confidence of countless black children. It was a common experience during the years 1865–1970 to see the young teaching the elderly or both attending school together. . . . [A] traveler, reporting from Memphis the same month, described the scene in a classroom: 'Six years and sixty may be seen, side by side, learning to read from the same chart or book. Perhaps a bright little Negro boy or girl is teaching a white-haired old man, or bent old woman in spectacles, their letters.'"[17]

Booker T. Washington described it as a "whole race trying to go to school."[18] A journalist in Charlottesville captured the ferment: "And then the whole colored population, of all sexes and ages, is repeating from morning to night, a-b, ab; e-b, eb; i-b, ib; c-a-t, cat; d-o-g, dog; c-u-p, cup; etc.—through all the varieties of the first lessons in orthography. There are some four or five colored schools, and little negro chaps darken every door, with primers in their hands. If we pass a blacksmith's shop, we hear a-b, ab; if we peep into a shoemaker's shop, it is a-b, ab; if we pass by a negro cabin in the suburbs of the town, we hear the sound, a-b, ab; if the cook goes out to suckle her infant, it is a-b, ab."[19]

But the slaves did not wait for emancipation to begin their instruction. They *demanded* it in the midst of the war. Slaves escaping to Union army camps insisted on receiving literacy instruction. For example, during the war Blacks in Memphis asked teachers from the North to come down immediately: "We recommend the teachers to bring their tents with them, ready for erection in the field, by the roadside, or in the fort, and not to wait for magnificent houses to be erected in time of war."[20]

After the war, the Freedmen's Bureau was established to govern the affairs of the ex-slaves. In the fall of 1865, the bureau sent John W. Alvord throughout the South to study the condition of Black schools and to begin drawing up plans for a system of education. What he found astonished him. Everywhere he looked, ex-slaves were teaching themselves to read: "In the absence of other teaching they are determined to be self-taught; and everywhere some elementary text-book, or the fragment of one, may be seen in the hands of negroes."[21]

Anyone who could read easily attracted students and formed what Alvord called "native schools": "Two colored young men, who but a little time before commenced to learn themselves, had gathered 150 pupils, all quite orderly and hard at study."[22] By Alvord's estimate, there were "at least 500 schools of this description . . . already in operation throughout the South."[23]

But the newly freed Blacks took things a step further. After the war, they used every means at their disposal to press for the creation of a system of public schools. At times they were able to secure this concession at the point of arms with assistance of Union soldiers. But they also had a new weapon in their hands: their labor power. Emancipation meant the labor supply dropped to two-thirds of its prewar level.[24]

When the ex-slaves contemplated a return to harvesting cotton, they brought their newfound economic power to bear. "In 1866 and 1867," historian James D. Anderson writes, "Freedmen's Bureau officials observed the widespread emergence of the 'educational clause' in labor contracts between planters and ex-slaves." Such clauses dictated that the planters set aside funds and/or materials for the construction of schools.[25]

In the space of a handful of years, Blacks and their allies created something the southern states had never seen: a system of public education available to *all* children. Anderson explains: "Under the Military Reconstruction Acts passed in 1867, Congress empowered the generals of the armies of occupation to call for new constitutional conventions in which blacks were to participate along with whites. Black politicians and leaders joined with Republicans in southern constitutional conventions to legalize public education in the constitutions of the former Confederate states. By 1870, every southern state had specific provisions in its constitution to assure a public school system financed by a state fund."[26]

In hindsight, we know that Radical Reconstruction was overthrown and a racist terror returned Blacks to a subjugated, near-slave status. But that was not a foregone conclusion, and it is inspiring to consider the transformation of consciousness—white and Black—that took place as an immediate result of the war. For example, by the end of 1870, Florida had a public school system serving fourteen thousand students, of whom approximately one-third were Black. In 1872, a Black man was appointed as the system's superintendent of public instruction.[27]

Likewise, in 1868, North Carolina set up schools available to students of all races. One critic of the system at that time wrote, "The only error with which one may charge them is that they did not set up a system calling for separate schools for Negro and white children, and many people there are, who would not class this as an error."[28]

In 1865, a remarkable editorial in the Charleston, South Carolina, newspaper, the *Tribune*, made its peace with interracial schooling:

> So the thing is done. The loyal white people—the Irish and German population, have shown that they are quite willing to let their children attend

the same school with the loyal blacks; although it is true, that no attempt to unite them in the same room or classes would have been tolerated at the time. But in the play-grounds, white and black boys joined in the same sports as they do in the public streets; and there can be no doubt that now that this great step has been made, all the prejudice against equal educational advantages will speedily vanish, and indeed, it is the veriest hypocrisy in the city where very old families have aided in obliterating all the complexional distinctions by mingling their blood with that of their slaves.[29]

That such prejudice did not "speedily vanish" was not a necessary conclusion of this era, but rather, the fruit of the specific alignment of class interests that developed in the aftermath of the Civil War.

With the threat of secession safely behind them, the Northern industrial class now looked upon the South as an open field for investment and development. At first, industrialists considered Blacks to be an important ally in their struggle against the planter class. As such, it had been useful to assist in the expansion of their rights and opportunities. But once that struggle was won, the northern business class lost interest in the project of Black equality and became more concerned with figuring out how to ensure a stable system of southern agriculture and industry. This led the northern business class toward a policy of reconciliation with the planters, and consequently, accommodation to their backward ideas on race. This reconciliation resulted in, among other things, the infamous "rotten compromise" of 1877, in which southern electors agreed to cast their ballots for a Republican president in return for the removal of northern troops from the South.

The impact of this betrayal was tremendous. Blacks were abandoned to deal on their own with the now-unchecked campaign for "Redemption" led by southern planters. The Redeemers used violence, intimidation, and murder to prevent Blacks from voting or exercising any of their newfound rights and powers. The Ku Klux Klan—effectively a terrorist arm of the Democratic Party[30]—was an essential weapon in this struggle. The Klan terrorized Blacks and poor whites—making it life-threatening for whites to show any kind of solidarity with Blacks, or even to be members of the Republican Party. Historian Jack Bloom recounts: "An Alabama planter told a congressional committee that the Klan was necessary because Blacks 'are told by some . . . that planters do not pay sufficient wages for their labor.' The Klan often went out of its way to cooperate with the planters: during planting season, blacks were left alone. Sometimes planters used the

Klan against the poor whites. 'These bands are having a great effect, in inspiring a nameless terror among Negroes, poor whites, and even others,' a Republican editor wrote," [emphasis in original].[31]

The Klan targeted the South's fledgling public schools in particular. While there is anecdotal evidence of planters—in desperate need of labor—protecting Blacks from the Klan,[32] the overwhelming attitude of the plantation owners was that "learning will spoil the nigger for work."[33] Frederick Douglass spoke of how the "schoolhouses [were] burnt, teachers mobbed and murdered, schools broken up." In Georgia, the Klan threatened to whip any parent who sent their child to school. In York County, South Carolina, one school had to be rebuilt four times. Whole school districts closed in Mississippi and Georgia out of fear for the lives of students and teachers.[34]

By the late 1870s, the Black vote was effectively lost in the South, and the Republican Party was all but destroyed. The planters used the bogeyman of Black supremacy, combined with the terror of the Klan, to separate whites and Blacks and enforce a new "Jim Crow" system of strict segregation. Wherever possible, public education was uprooted. As the governor of Virginia put it: "Free schools are not a necessity. . . . They are a luxury, adding . . . to the beauty and power of the state, but to be paid for, like any other luxury, by the people who wish their benefits."[35]

Blacks certainly fought to maintain public education but, abandoned by the federal government, they were unable to turn the tide in their favor. The defeat of Radical Reconstruction was a reversal of historic proportions. The struggle for Black education had taken gigantic leaps forward in a relatively short period of time only to suffer a devastating setback.

Segregation, Philanthropy, and "Industrial" Education

Of course I know that this characterization of the Hampton philosophy is largely a matter of personal interpretation, and yet, in an institution where the President of the United States can with applause tell young men not to hitch their wagons to a star, but to a mule . . . it seems to me no infringement of the rights of hospitality to say that I believe that this doctrine is so fundamentally false as to call for a word of warning.

—W. E. B. Du Bois, speaking at the Hampton Institute, 1906[36]

A full discussion of the early twentieth-century struggles to establish and develop higher education for African Americans is beyond the scope of this essay. However, given the prominence of philanthropy in the current debates about public education, a brief word on the topic is appropriate. Additionally, the historic debates about the nature of Black colleges were intimately bound up with the question of the aims of grade school education, since the former was designed primarily to produce teachers for the latter.

It is commonly assumed that Northern philanthropy saved Black education (especially higher education) from the prospect of outright destruction at the hands of the Redeemers. There is more than a grain of truth to this. The overthrow of Radical Reconstruction was perilous to the project of defending—let alone extending—what had been achieved after the war. Wealthy, liberal industrial magnates from Northern states certainly did play an important role in building and promoting schools for Blacks in the South. In his 1935 masterpiece, *Black Reconstruction*, Du Bois praised the northern philanthropists as an essential element in helping to preserve Black education. He wrote: "The movement that saved the Negro public school system was not enlightened Southern opinion, but rather that Northern philanthropy which at the very beginning of the Negro education movement contributed toward the establishment of Negro colleges. The reason for them at first was to supply the growing demand for teachers, and was also a concession to Southern prejudice, which so violently disliked the white teacher in the Negro school."[37] But even this limited praise should be viewed in context. The movement to build and support schools for Blacks was fiercely independent. Black parents considered it of vital importance that *they* directly control the governance of the schools their children attended. The seriousness and extent of this commitment comes through in the simple fact that from 1865 to 1915, Blacks themselves contributed $25 million to support their schools while philanthropists contributed $57 million.[38] Relative to their respective resources, Blacks contributed their flesh and blood while the philanthropists contributed pocket change.

One of the most famous sources of northern philanthropy, the Rosenwald Fund, frequently raised the ire of Blacks for never putting up the entire cost of a school. In fact, they never even provided half of the money; frequently they only gave about one-sixth of the cost, expecting the local residents to pay the rest.[39] When the fund dispatched an emissary named Griffin to Bexar, Alabama, to tell the residents they had to raise $700 to get a Rosenwald school, the audience was despondent. "That sounded like a million to them," writes Anderson, "[because] in Bexar, $700 equaled the combined annual incomes of about seven black male adults." But they did eventually raise the money—and more—in part inspired by one of Bexar's oldest residents. Just as one of the parents was reduced to tears in frustration, an old man "who had seen slavery days" came forward, "with all of his life's earnings in an old greasy sack, slowly drew it from his pocket, and emptied it on the table. Griffin recalled that the ex-slave said: 'I want to see the children of my grandchildren have a chance, and so I am giving my all.'"[40]

The reason that Black parents, with almost no financial resources to speak of, contributed so much more proportionately to their wealth than the industrialists is that they understood all too well the importance of controlling their own schools. The logic behind this was twofold. On the one hand, the new Jim Crow social system erected by the white southern ruling class physically excluded Black children from the public schools. Thus, Blacks had little choice but to build and support their own schools. On the other hand, their rich, white northern "friends" often did not share their priorities. With money came an agenda. The only way for Black parents to guarantee that *their* vision of education was carried out was to finance and govern their own schools. Free, interracial public schools were the ideal, but barred from the public schools and prohibited from participating in their governance (or from voting at all), Black parents were forced to develop independent schools. Despite their precarious position, they remained wary of northern philanthropy, for reasons discussed below. Some white observers even complained of the Negroes' "lack of gratitude."[41] One white educator, describing the feeling among Black parents in Savannah, Georgia, said, "What they want is assistance without control."[42]

Furthermore, Du Bois's comments about northern philanthropy should be balanced by his very different assessment of the role of the philanthropists during the first two decades of the twentieth century. This is an important subtext to his famous debates with Booker T. Washington. Du Bois is well known for these polemics against Washington and the "Hampton-Tuskegee" model of education Washington advocated.

This model is (and was) known as *industrial education*, something that many equate to what today is known as vocational education. In reality, however, the Hampton-Tuskegee model as it was designed in the early twentieth century was more akin to menial education. At institutes built on the Hampton-Tuskegee model, students learned ironing, washing, scrubbing, sewing, hoeing, and picking. Many students had ten hours of daily drudgery followed by a few hours of moral instruction. Students who attended the school to gain genuine industrial skills were greatly disappointed, and often wrote letters of protest at the low level of training. Those who enrolled to learn blacksmithing got very little time heating metals. Students who wanted to learn carpentry instead spent years learning to be handymen—instructed in the use of the same tools over and over.[43]

Samuel Armstrong, a white man who helped found the Hampton Institute and served as its principal from 1868 to 1893, believed that Blacks were mentally capable but morally weak. He intended the Hampton Institute to be a place where Blacks would learn certain lessons: that capitalism was the natural state of humanity, that class distinctions were meaningless, that labor and capital were fundamentally harmonious parts of society.

The reality of this educational model contradicts the usual framing of the debates between Du Bois and Washington, with Du Bois advocating a classic liberal arts education and Washington calling for vocational education. In fact, Du Bois *did* support industrial training—real industrial training, not the menial labor as described above—as quite valuable, and often argued that it should be combined with liberal arts education.

As for Washington, he did not finance the model he advocated. The real interests that lay behind the drive for menial education for Black youth were northern (and southern) industrialists. Whereas Black parents pursued education as a means of liberation—a way to give their children a chance to escape the conditions that stifled past generations—northern industrialists saw education as a means of socializing the Black workforce and preparing them to accept their role in the southern economy as agricultural workers and domestic servants, especially in the context of the increasing Black flight to urban areas. Hampton trustee Robert Ogden stated it plainly: "Our great problem is to attach the Negro to the soil and prevent his exodus from the country to the city," since "[t]he prosperity of the South depend[ed] upon the productive power of the black man."[44]

Indeed, Booker T. Washington was a star pupil. He absorbed the fundamental message of the Hampton-Tuskegee idea: that Blacks were culturally inferior and were better off making the best of segregation rather than challenging it. He told a church audience in 1900: "My friends, the white man is three thousand years ahead of us, and this fact we might as well face now as well as later, and that at one stage of his development, either in Europe or America, he has gone through every stage of development that I now advocate for our race."[45] Washington even went so far as to publicly argue that slavery had been a net benefit to Blacks.[46]

The philanthropists focused their attention on training Black teachers who, imbued with the Hampton-Tuskegee values, could spread them across the South wherever they taught. Said Armstrong, the principal of the Hampton Institute: "Let us make the teachers, and we will make the people."[47] Du Bois actually had a similar perspective. He was focused on developing an elite "talented tenth" that would help uplift the rest of the race. Du Bois advocated academic education, but did not think that it was feasible for the vast majority. But Du Bois was highly aware of the efforts of private philanthropists to limit the horizon of Black education. At a speech to a Fisk University audience, he warned: "And so today this venerable institution stands before its problem of future development, with the bribe of Public Opinion and Private Wealth dangling before us, if we will either deny that our object is the highest and broadest training of Black Men, or if we will consent to call Higher education that which you know and I know is not Higher Education."[48]

Increasingly, southern teachers came from Black colleges or "normal" schools (teacher-training schools). But these Black-sponsored institutions and state schools were too academically focused for the northern philanthropists. By throwing their tremendous wealth behind Black schools that followed the Hampton-Tuskegee model, they hoped to undermine the spread of classical liberal curricula.[49]

Still, Black parents and students had different aspirations. Again and again they protested and resisted the Hampton-Tuskegee model. Du Bois represented the growing consensus among Black parents and students that there had to be opportunities for Blacks to get a real higher education. In 1927, students at the Hampton Institute went on strike to protest the low academic standards. Anderson quotes Robert A. Coles, a leader of the student revolt: "Hampton's new students possessed a 'Du Bois ambition' that would not mix with a 'Booker Washington education.'"[50] By the 1930s the philanthropists had more or less conceded this demand, and the Hampton-Tuskegee model was altogether revamped.

In the meantime, a new technique to limit Black higher education was devised: accreditation. In the name of "raising standards," a national system of accreditation began taking shape in the early 1900s, and was formally in place by 1928. To receive official designation as an institution of higher learning, accreditation required having a certain level of financial endowment and certain facilities and resources. Thus, schools that were independent, Black-financed institutions were almost always denied accreditation, while those favored by philanthropists had the means to pass.

In sum, Black colleges—many funded through churches and other independent Black organizations—had created thousands of teachers who fanned out all over the South. They had provided some kind of education to millions of children for the first time. But there was still a long way to go. White philanthropy, unfortunately, was a part of the problem. In the decades that followed, Black life in America went through tremendous changes that opened up new opportunities to fight for equal access to education. Once again, Black families mounted a struggle to take advantage of the changed situation. They found new allies in the course of this struggle, and once again, new obstacles were thrown in their path.

Fighting Jim Crow Schools

We want mixed schools not because our colored schools are inferior to white schools—not because colored instructors are inferior to white instructors, but because we want to do away with a system that exalts one class and debases another.
   —Frederick Douglass[51]

Over the course of the twentieth century, African Americans underwent a profound transformation as a people. Through migration from the countryside to the southern cities, and through migration from the South to the North, they transformed themselves from a rural people into an overwhelmingly urban one.

From 1940 to 1950 alone, the Black population outside the South grew from 2.4 million to 6.4 million.[52] Blacks fought for inclusion in the vast expansion of industrial production—and, despite efforts to exclude them, made huge strides. The median annual Black family income jumped from $489 in 1939 to $3,088 in 1963.[53]

Black families had high expectations for urban life. Above all, they expected that their children would be able to get a better education. But wherever Blacks moved—to the northern cities, to the West, or even to the southern centers of industry—they were crowded into ghettoes and forced to send their children to segregated schools. In New York in 1924, a study found that the students in "Negro high schools lagged about one-quarter behind . . . white students." Interestingly, the study also observed, "Black students were more persistent than their white classmates, however, and dropped out less often."[54]

Harlem parent William Delmar had one child in a mostly white school, and the other in an all-Black school. He characterized the differences between his children's experiences: "We notice the difference in the content of the curriculum, in its quality and the amount of enrichment. . . . We notice the difference in the quantity of guidance. In the mixed school, guidance counselors try to be imaginative, to be in guidance with the aspirations and potentialities of the students. In my daughter's school, guidance is limited to channeling the children to be [beauticians] or nurse's aides."[55]

The few students who did enter northern desegregated schools experienced a profound and persistent isolation and degradation. Teachers would not call on them for months or would tell them to "go back where they came from." In addition, they were excluded from the schools' social, cultural, and athletic activities.

In 1939, Malcolm X was the only Black student in his high school in Mason, Michigan. He told his English teacher that he wanted to be a lawyer. The teacher replied, "Malcolm, one of life's first needs is for us to be realistic. Don't misunderstand me, now. We all here like you, you know that. But you've got to be realistic about being a nigger. A lawyer—that's no realistic goal for a nigger. You need to think about something you can be. You're good with your hands—making things. Everybody admires your carpentry shop work. Why don't you plan on carpentry? People like you as a person— you'd get all kinds of work."[56]

No matter their social status or personal success, northern Black students could still be treated as second-class citizens. For example, a Brooklyn high school informed six Black seniors—one of whom was the daughter of W. E. B. Du Bois—that they were disinvited to the prom. Du Bois promptly met with the superintendent and won re-invitation for all six girls.[57]

The terms *de jure* and *de facto* are often invoked to explain the difference between segregation in the South as compared to the North. De jure indicates that segregation was a matter of law. But in the North, we're often told that segregation was merely de facto—a matter of custom, *not* of law. But historians have begun to interrogate the concept of de facto segregation. What they have found is that Blacks who migrated to the North encountered a web of racial restrictions on their housing and school options—more often than not backed up by government agencies and the force of law.

For example, in 1917 the Chicago Real Estate Board ruled that whites could sell their homes to a Black person, but only if he or she was not the *first* Black person on the block.[58] Federal housing policy, the actions of real estate agents, and the lending practices of banks were among the forces consciously enforcing segregation in housing and education.[59]

Moreover, in 1924 the California Supreme Court ruled that segregated schools were constitutional: "It is not in violation of the organic law of the state or nation . . . to require Indian children or others in whom racial differences exist to attend separate schools."[60] Other strategies included the use of intelligence tests (Philadelphia) or classifying Black students as "retarded" (Chicago).[61] The use of such tests, whose roots are in the eugenics movement, gave scientific cover to segregation. In 1940, Du Bois recalled, "it was not until I was long out of school and indeed after the (first) World War that there came the hurried use of the new technique of psychological tests, which were quickly adjusted so as to put black folk absolutely beyond the possibility of civilization."[62]

In the face of all this, Black parents waged a heroic struggle to end segregated schooling. The famous 1954 Supreme Court decision *Brown v. Board of Education of Topeka*, which declared segregated schools unconstitutional, is often perceived as the starting point for this movement. In reality, it began much earlier. From the 1920s to the 1950s, large desegregation battles took place in northern suburbs and industrial towns in Pennsylvania, Ohio, New Jersey, New York, and Michigan.[63]

Parents and teachers also fought to challenge the substandard conditions in the schools and the use of explicitly racist textbooks. In 1936, a group of Black parents formed the Committee for Better Schools in Harlem (CBSH). They pressed their demands directly to school officials. Their efforts contributed to the city's decision to construct four new schools in Harlem between 1937 and 1941.[64] The Communist Party–led (and mostly Jewish) Teachers Union worked with the CBSH in these fights. "They developed close working relationships with black teachers in almost every school in Harlem," historian Mark Naison explains, "and had begun to lobby for physical improvements, free lunches, and better conditions for teachers."[65]

The degrading treatment of Black students in northern schools was a sore point. When a 250-pound white principal, Gustav Schoenchen, was alleged to have physically assaulted a fourteen-year-old Black student, the CBSH teamed up with Harlem's best communist organizers to set up picket lines outside the school. Their protests attracted thousands of people, including elected officials and leading NAACP activists. In the end, the city caved to the pressure and transferred Schoenchen out of Harlem.[66]

The New York Teachers Union organized conferences on challenging racism in the city's curriculum, and protested the way Black students were guided away from academic careers.[67] In 1951, the group produced a study entitled "Bias and Prejudice in Textbooks in Use in New York City Schools: An Indictment." It showed how widely used textbooks contained factual errors about the Civil War and outright racist lies about Africans and African Americans. Furthermore, the union created its own antiracist curriculum, "The Negro in New York, 1626–1865: A Study for Teachers."[68]

Unfortunately, the Teachers Union was destroyed in the postwar anti-communist witch hunts. The Second World War—ostensibly a war against a racist regime in Germany—made segregation at home all the more intolerable. Furthermore, in competition with the Soviet Union, Jim Crow laws were an embarrassment to the US ruling class. This created an ideological opening for Blacks to challenge those laws. But the Cold War cut another way as well, providing a pretext for repression. Starting under the Truman administration, the anticommunist witch hunts that later became known as "McCarthyism" served as an important check on postwar militancy. All progressive movements—especially those aimed at challenging segregation— were demonized as part of a vast communist conspiracy.

As an example, the NAACP mushroomed from just fifty thousand members before the war to three hundred and fifty thousand after.[69] But liberals, labor leaders, and even civil rights activists, in too many instances, caved to the pressure and even participated in the witch hunts. When W. E. B. Du Bois declared himself a communist, the NAACP forced him out of the very organization he had helped to found. NAACP leaders advised against civil disobedience and instead focused on battling segregation in the courts.

As a growing political and economic unit, African Americans and their demands could not be ignored forever. In the courts, legal segregation was losing ground. "The *Brown* decision," writes socialist author Ahmed Shawki, "in fact, only confirmed the basic thrust of the Court's rulings since the 1940s. A May 1946 Supreme Court decision, for example, ruled that laws requiring segregation on interstate buses were unconstitutional. In April 1944 the Court ended, by an eight-to-one majority, the use of all-white primary elections."[70]

In many cases, it was activism that led to the lawsuits in the first place. In 1951, Barbara Johns, a high school junior, organized a student strike at her all-Black high school in Virginia to protest the poor conditions and overcrowding. Students contacted the NAACP for help, but the lawyers advised them against striking. The strikers' determination won the lawyers over, and their claim became part of the basis of the famous 1954 *Brown v. Board of Education* case.[71]

Seen in this light, the *Brown* decision was just as much the *result* of Black agitation as the *cause* of it. That the decision was a watershed event is not in doubt. While *Brown* did not immediately end segregation, it did give Black parents and students a tremendous boost in confidence. For decades they had struggled against segregated schools. Now, the highest court in the land ruled that such segregation must end.

But the limitations of *Brown* need to be understood as well. The first issue is how the court defined the problem: "Segregation of white and colored children in public schools has a detrimental effect upon the colored children. The impact is greater when it has the sanction of the law, for the policy of separating the races is usually interpreted as denoting the inferiority of the negro group. A sense of inferiority affects the motivation of a child to learn. Segregation with the sanction of law, therefore, has a tendency to [retard] the educational and mental development of negro children and to deprive them of some of the benefits they would receive in a racial[ly] integrated school system."[72]

Rather than addressing the problem of residential segregation or inferior resources or facilities—the fact that separate schools in a racist society would *never* be equal—the court hung its decision on the narrower issue of psychology (the "sense of inferiority"). By contrast, Black parents on the whole did not believe that their children needed to sit next to white kids to improve their self-esteem. The reason for putting their kid in a "white" school was primarily a strategy for getting access to better resources. As Detroit parent Vera Bradley put it: "We were upset because they weren't getting as many materials as some other schools. We figured if it was desegregated, we would get the same."[73]

The psychological angle of *Brown* had the perverse effect of stigmatizing Black schools (and consequently, Black teachers) as necessarily inferior. Black kids were to be "integrated" into white schools—but never vice versa.

Reacting to *Brown*, Du Bois cheered, "I have seen the Impossible happen. It did happen on May 17, 1954." But he also cautioned that Blacks were now confronted with a "cruel dilemma." On one hand, sending their kids to white schools meant getting access to what they had been denied for so long. But on the other, "with successfully mixed schools they know what their children will suffer for years from southern white teachers, from white hoodlums who sit beside them and under school authorities from janitors to superintendents who hate and despise them. They know, dear God, how they know."[74] Furthermore, the court set no timeline for desegregation. A year later, in what is widely known as the *Brown II* ruling, it called for desegregation to take place "with all deliberate speed." In the opinion of one NAACP lawyer, this really meant "movement toward compliance on terms that the white south could accept."[75]

In the years following, Blacks took advantage of *Brown* and pressed to make its promise a reality. They faced stiff resistance. Petitions for desegregation were rejected in dozens of Southern cities. In one case, fifty-three Blacks signed a petition in Yazoo City, Mississippi. After weeks of retaliation—firings, evictions, and other harassments—every single signature had been retracted.[76] In 1956, Alabama outlawed the NAACP altogether. In 1957, when the Reverend Fred Shuttlesworth tried to enroll his children in an all-white school, he and they narrowly escaped with their lives: "A mob of people armed with chains, brass knuckles, pipes and knives set upon us . . . Mrs. Shuttlesworth was stabbed in the hip, Ruby Fredericks, our second daughter, had her foot hurt in a car door by one of the men and I was beaten with a chain and brass knuckles, knocked several times to the ground, had most of the skin scrubbed off my face and ears, and was kicked in my face and side as members of the mob really set out to kill me."[77]

Famously, when Black students tried to integrate Little Rock Central High School in September 1957, they were driven back by the Texas Rangers and by racist mobs. President Eisenhower tried to avoid the conflict, but eventually was forced to send US troops to escort the students—the first time federal troops had been sent into the South since Reconstruction.[78]

Southern racists dug in their heels to preserve the Jim Crow system. Defenders of northern segregation did the same. By 1962 the NAACP was participating in legal challenges to school segregation in sixty-nine northern and western cities.[79] But the courts increasingly leaned toward the view that plaintiffs had to prove that school districts were segregated *intentionally*— the fact of segregation was not sufficient to hold them responsible.

The legal strategy was not enough. A decade after *Brown*, 90.7 percent of the South's Black children still attended all-Black schools—*four hundred thousand more than in 1956.*[80] The same was true, unfortunately, in the North and West. After *Brown*, schools in Los Angeles became more segregated. The *California Eagle* reported that more Black children attended all-Black schools in Los Angeles than they did in Little Rock.[81] In New York City, the number of Black and Puerto Rican segregated schools climbed nearly fourfold, from fifty-two in 1955 to 201 in 1965.[82]

By this point, however, there was no going back. Black parents and students were determined to secure what the courts deemed theirs by right. Legal victories were to be rendered meaningless unless Blacks were willing to take the struggle outside the courtroom. The fight against segregated schools—especially in the northern cities—became a mass movement.

In New York, Viola Waddy was a part of a group of Harlem parents who, defying the law, kept their children out of school in 1958. The "Harlem Nine" won an important victory when a judge ruled that the New York City Board of Education was offering inferior education to Black children.[83] In Boston, moreover, nearly 2,500 Black students stayed out of city schools in 1963 to protest racial segregation. A second boycott saw 20,000 participate and led to the passage of the Racial Imbalance Act of 1965, which "forbade the commonwealth from supporting any school that was more than 50 percent white (although the act considered majority or all-white schools racially balanced)."[84]

In the Midwest, Blacks in Chicago formed a multiracial coalition that led boycotts against segregation in 1963 and 1964 (with 224,000 and 172,000 children participating, respectively).[85] In 1964, 20,000 students boycotted segregated schools in Gary, Indiana, and more than 75,000 did so in Cleveland, Ohio.[86]

Taken together, the years 1963 to 1965 represented the apogee of this movement. In New York City, almost 500,000 students stayed out of school in February of 1964, and more than 350,000 did so a second time to press for integration. In the latter action, interestingly, Malcolm X marched with them.[87]

Just as in the South, northern officials claimed that the problem was not segregation. Instead, they insisted that the problem was Black students themselves. Rather than condemning the pervasive structures of racism and segregation, they tended to pathologize Black students. A study of the Watts riot even claimed that this pathology *caused* segregation. It read in part: "[T]he very low level of scholastic achievement we observe in the predominantly Negro schools contributes to de facto segregation in the schools. . . . We reason, therefore, that raising the scholastic achievement might reverse the entire trend of de facto segregation."[88]

The movements described above brought increased attention, resources, and in some cases, desegregation to public schools. The high point of desegregation corresponded to the high point of the Black civil rights movements: the tail end of the 1960s. Overall, desegregation was most successful in the southern states. In eleven southern states, the number of children in all-Black schools plummeted from two-thirds in 1968 to one-sixth in 1970, to one-eleventh in 1971–72.[89] In the North, by contrast, there had been progress since 1954, but after 1960—outside of a few locations where desegregation orders stuck—segregation worsened.[90]

Once again, Black parents and students had waged a historic struggle to overcome racial isolation and to win equal access to education. At times, they found allies in teachers' unions—especially those that contained within their ranks a significant contingent of organized radicals. The Black movement was powerful enough to destroy legalized segregation, but racism persisted in other forms. Furthermore, this struggle proved that racial and educational justice was bound up with broader questions of social justice—questions of economic inequality, employment, and housing.

From Desegregation to Community Control

Despite the claims of its defenders, northern segregation was not the result of the "natural" inclinations of individuals or of the invisible hand of the free market. Rather, segregation was engineered. In the post–Second World War years, the federal government built interstate highways nationwide and subsidized home loans for sixteen million veterans. Through these policies, the Federal Housing Administration encouraged middle-class residents to leave the inner cities and discouraged the development of city neighborhoods.[91] Furthermore, the terms of those loans *mandated* that new housing developments remain racially homogenous. Meanwhile, only 5 percent of new housing construction between 1949 and 1964 was for low-income residents.[92] In other words, the federal government underwrote segregation. The Black movement, powerful as it was, did not succeed in untangling this web of institutional racism—especially federal housing policy and localized school funding.

The 1965 Elementary and Secondary Education Act of 1965 (ESEA) stands out as a tragic example of how federal policies passed in response to rising civil rights movements could be turned into defeats. The ESEA was part of a number of Great Society policies from the mid-1960s and promised billions of dollars in federal support for "educationally deprived children." However, it left the actual distribution of the money in the hands of local officials. Consequently, the funds were rarely used for impoverished inner-city schools; more often they were diverted to the development of schools in the growing suburbs. ESEA money, intended to help urban Black and other historically oppressed students, was frequently used instead to benefit suburban white students.[93]

As the social movements waned, federal housing and education policies ensured that some white families would enjoy a degree of mobility unavailable to Blacks, and thus served to enshrine the system of separate and unequal schooling. While polls showed whites increasingly in support of desegregation, in practice the opposition was much stronger.[94]

White resistance to desegregation took a variety of forms. "White flight" was the most basic. When Black families moved into a neighborhood or sent their children to a school, white families often moved to another neighborhood or sent their children to a different school. When their school districts were ordered to desegregate, some white parents complained that this violated the free-market principle of "choice." One white Detroit parent wrote in a local newspaper: "We believe 'forced busing' is depriving us of our Constitutional Rights and our Freedom of Choice."[95] Or they argued that busing was destroying the foundation of American society by forcibly separating children from their neighborhood school. But, as historian Jeanne Theoharis argues, in this context the very term *neighborhood schools* "brings to mind a close-knit, small-town (if imaginary) America that diverts attention away from who gets to be part of the neighborhood in the first place."[96]

The busing issue was always a canard. In 1970, half of students in the US went to school by bus, but fewer than 5 percent of those students did so because of desegregation plans.[97] In fact, busing had long been an instrument of segregation. In Boston, for example, where white parents used the bogey of "forced busing" to oppose desegregation, thousands of white students were already being bused every day *past* their neighborhood schools to attend all-white ones further away.[98]

That the tremendous efforts of Black parents and students yielded so little progress—especially in the urban school systems in the North—created an atmosphere of frustration. In 1969, the *New York Times* reported: "Increasing numbers of young Negroes are tiring of the steady abuse that comes with integrating white schools. Many . . . believe that integration has been too nearly a one-way street with Negroes always leaving their schools to go to white schools."[99] Desegregation remained a popular demand, but the intransigence of white racist reaction sent many Blacks looking for other means to secure quality education. "When 10,000 Queens [New York] white mothers showed up to picket at city hall against integration," Doris Innis remembered, "it was obvious we had to look for other solutions."[100]

In this context, some Black parents and activists began to raise the demand of "community control." For them, community control meant becoming empowered as effective co-managers of the schools. Of particular concern was the selection of staff. Black parents did not necessarily demand an all-Black teaching staff for their children, but mistreatment at the hands of racist teachers was a long-standing complaint. "My son was two years ahead in his southern school," Reverend Herb Oliver recalled. "When we moved to New York he started flunking math. His teacher told me, 'He's doing fine.'"[101]

Detroit, Newark, and Chicago had a substantial population of Black teachers by the late 1960s, but in New York there was an unmistakable racial divide between teachers and students. During the 1950s, approximately eight hundred thousand whites left the city, and roughly seven hundred thousand Blacks and Puerto Ricans moved in. By June 1960, Blacks and Puerto Ricans were 40 percent of all New York City students, but 75 percent of students in Manhattan. New York City public school teachers, meanwhile, remained 90 percent white for the next ten years.[102]

Reverend Oliver lived in the Ocean Hill–Brownsville section of Brooklyn. The prominent junior high school in the neighborhood (JHS 271) had among the lowest reading and math scores in the city, and typically sent only 2 percent of its graduates to any of the specialized high schools (which required entrance exams).[103]

The Ocean Hill–Brownsville district became the site of the most heated battle. In 1968, when the community-elected governing board decided to transfer out nineteen white educators (thirteen teachers and six administrators whom the board felt were hostile to the idea of community control[104]), the United Federation of Teachers (UFT) took its members out on a series of strikes, claiming that the members' right to due process had been violated. The teachers were only transferred, though, not fired or dismissed as the union claimed.[105] Critics at the time charged that UFT president Albert Shanker used the pretext of the "termination" of the teachers in Ocean Hill–Brownsville as an excuse to challenge community control.[106] Indeed, apart from a brief period of collaboration with the local board, the UFT turned against community control and began lobbying aggressively against it in the state legislature two months before the teachers at JHS 271 were transferred.[107]

In a profoundly divisive turn, the union portrayed *itself* as the victim of racism. When, during the conflict, UFT teachers at JHS 271 received an anonymous, threatening, anti-Semitic letter, Shanker made half a million copies and distributed them throughout the Jewish community to solidify support for the union.[108]

But the real question was not anti-Semitism against the union, but rather whether or not the union would side with Black parents in their fight for self-determination. Tragically, the UFT leadership remained implacably hostile to community control. While many rank-and-file teachers, Black and white, crossed the picket lines in solidarity with the Black parents, the vast majority of teachers—some fifty-four thousand out of fifty-seven thousand—walked off the job during the first strike.[109]

Members of the Black community made vigorous efforts to break the strike. Some radical groups, such as the Socialist Workers Party and the Independent Socialist Clubs, also came out against the strike and crossed the picket lines.[110] Steve Zeluck, then-president of the New Rochelle Federation of Teachers, put his finger on the heart of the matter when he argued that the urban teachers' unions faced a choice: "genuine, not token, close cooperation with the insurgent forces of the ghetto on a wide range of issues . . . or . . . alliance with the status quo, the educational bureaucracy, against the ghetto community."[111]

That the UFT chose the latter course was not inevitable. As we have seen, the organization's predecessor, the left-wing Teachers Union, took a different approach. But so did some of the UFT's contemporaries. In cities such as Chicago, where there were greater numbers of Black educators, parents and unionized teachers in some schools joined together to fight for community control.[112]

At the very moment it needed to embrace a radical perspective on the persistence of racism, the UFT was led instead by liberal cold warriors. Shanker had marched for civil rights with Martin Luther King Jr. But whereas King moved to the left and spoke out against the war in Vietnam,

Shanker moved to the right and proudly supported it.[113] Shanker was part of a conservative wing of the labor movement. To this group, the defeat of Jim Crow heralded the end of racial barriers. Thus, they were unsympathetic to Black radical arguments about institutional racism and were predisposed to view "ghetto insurgents" as extremists who were "going too far" rather than as necessary allies. When the UFT drafted a volume of *Lesson Plans on African-American History*, Shanker personally intervened to cut out radical ideas. He removed two chapters on Malcolm X and even the words of Frederick Douglass that "power concedes nothing without a demand."[114]

Historian Jerald Podair's contention that community control is a perilous demand—because white communities will wield it in a racist manner to exclude Blacks—shows a similar limitation in the liberal approach to racism.[115] There is a critical difference between oppressed groups using community control over their schools as a strategy to fight racism and oppressor groups using local control to maintain the racist status quo. Furthermore, there is a difference between color-blind policy and antiracist policy. Equal, "color-blind" treatment of two groups at unequal starting points does not lead to real equality. Genuine equality requires antiracist policy—such as affirmative action or reparations—and requires supporting the right of *oppressed* groups to self-determination.

The bitter fruit of the UFT's strike ripened in the 1970s. The city used the recession to strip residents of crucial public services and the union of jobs and protections on the job. The two groups should have been natural partners in a united struggle against such cuts, but the bad blood of 1968 made such an alliance unthinkable.

The limitation of community control (like other "localist" schemes) is that it does not necessarily change the larger societal factors—such as segregation and the availability of financial resources or jobs—that are decided elsewhere, but that play a huge role in determining local outcomes. In the decades that followed the high points of the Black struggle for education described above, it is precisely these broader societal conditions that have deteriorated. The material gains of the civil rights movement have mostly been hollowed out or outright destroyed. In education, this has led to a perverse situation in which Black parents and unionized teachers are blamed for the shortcomings of the schools, while powerful politicians and billionaire philanthropists are lionized as champions of racial justice.

Resegregation and the Achievement Gap: Where Do We Go from Here?

American schools have become resegregated. More than fifty years after the *Brown* decision, they are profoundly separate and unequal. This is not to say that *Brown* and the social movements that preceded and followed it had no impact. "American society as a whole was dramatically transformed by *Brown*," writes education historian Diane Ravitch. She continues: "It is almost impossible to imagine the election of a black president in 2008 without that decision, which opened doors on campus, in the workplace, in politics, and in popular culture. And yet . . . there is a curious conundrum. The *Brown* decision was about public schools, but it seems to have had a large impact upon every aspect of American life except the public schools."[116]

Still, as Jonathan Kozol has pointed out, it is ironic—and tragic—that the most segregated schools nowadays are often the very ones named for the leading lights of the desegregation struggles. In San Diego, a school named after Rosa Parks is 86 percent Black and Hispanic. In Milwaukee, a school bears Dr. Martin Luther King's name, but is 99 percent Black and Hispanic. In New York City, the Thurgood Marshall School is 98 percent Black and Hispanic.[117]

In 2007, Gary Orfield and Chungmei Lee, writing for UCLA's Civil Rights Project, summarized how various branches of government have conspired since the early 1970s to dismantle desegregation. "The fact of resegregation," they wrote,

> does not mean that desegregation failed and was rejected by Americans who experienced it. Of course the demographic changes made full desegregation with whites more difficult, but the major factor, particularly in the South, was that we stopped trying. Five of the last seven Presidents actively opposed urban desegregation and the last significant federal aid for desegregation was repealed 26 years ago in 1981. The last Supreme Court decision expanding desegregation rights was handed down in 1973, more than a third of a century ago, one year before a decision rejecting city-suburban desegregation.[118]

The 1973 *San Antonio v. Rodriguez* decision upheld the localized system of school funding, primarily through property taxes. Thus, schools in wealthy district were guaranteed larger school budgets than those in poorer neighborhoods. The next year, the 1974 *Milliken v. Bradley* decision essentially stated that desegregation plans could not force students to cross school district lines unless there was evidence that multiple districts had conspired to deliberately segregate students. For the next two decades, court orders to desegregate could not stop northern whites from using the *Milliken* "escape hatch" to avoid integration by moving across district lines.[119] Predictably, the gap between the wealth of Black and white neighborhoods grew during the 1970s and 1980s, as did the gap in the quality of education in their respective schools.[120]

Rodriguez and *Milliken* set the pattern for the decades to come: segregation was given a pass, and localized funding was declared constitutional. The results should not be surprising. As of 2005, thirty-five states were spending less on the districts with the most minority students than they were on the districts with the fewest.[121] Nationwide, this amounted to a differential of approximately $1,100 per child. New York had the highest racial differential: $2,200 per child.[122]

Tragically, there is very little political will to do anything about segregation or economic inequality. Instead of *equity*, the current policy discourse is focused on *excellence*. Despite the hope that many invested in President George W. Bush's "No Child Left Behind" (NCLB) initiative, which highlighted the persistence of the racial "achievement gap" and set the goal of closing it by 2014, progress toward that end has been incremental at best.[123]

Obama, in fact, has doubled down on Bush's emphasis on high-stakes testing. Concurrently, he is promoting the idea that Black education is not thwarted by institutional racism, structural inequality, or segregation, but rather by a failure of personal responsibility. When his presidential campaign stops brought him before Black audiences, then-candidate Barack Obama hardly missed an opportunity to chastise Black parents. On one occasion, Obama said that Black absentee fathers were "acting like boys instead of men." He continued by advising Black parents to make better choices about what their children eat and to supervise their studies. "Buy a little desk or put that child at the kitchen table," he said. "Watch them do their homework."[124]

While the idea that Black parents as a whole just don't take an active role in the education of their children is widespread, it is simply not true. "Black parents are more likely than white parents to place their children in educational camps," professor Michael Eric Dyson writes, citing the work of a 2003–04 study, and "[more likely to] attend PTA meetings, check their children's homework and reward their children for academic success."[125] Furthermore, the centuries-long struggle of Black parents—briefly recounted in this chapter—shows just how wrong this idea is. That it retains widespread acceptance is a product of just how much the discussion has been turned on its head. In the absence of an alternative perspective, the victims blame themselves.

History helps us to take a different view. In 1933, the great African American historian and educator Carter G. Woodson wrote that the problem with the system of education is that it is steeped in the perspectives of the dominant group. "For example," he argued, "the philosophy and ethics resulting from our educational system have justified slavery, peonage, segregation, and lynching. The oppressor has the right to exploit, to handicap, and to kill the oppressed. Negroes daily educated in the tenets of such a religion of the strong have accepted the status of the weak as divinely ordained, and during the last three generations of their nominal freedom they have done practically nothing to change it. . . . When you control a man's thinking you do not have to worry about his actions."[126] Today, the "religion of the strong" goes a step further: it attempts to co-opt Black history for its own purposes. For example, Secretary of Education Arne Duncan called the release of the pro–charter school, anti-union *Waiting for Superman* "documentary" a "Rosa Parks moment."[127] When a group of hedge fund managers organized a charter school fundraiser, one of the attendees—a banker from Goldman Sachs—described his and their efforts as the "civil rights struggle of my generation."[128]

Here, Black history is stripped of its real content. In the eyes of those on Wall Street, this is to be a "movement" for racial justice in education, but with no aspiration for social justice. They want us to believe that there can be excellence without equity. The struggles summarized below suggest otherwise. In fact, they indicate four key points for moving the current struggle for Black education forward.

First, we must face the fact that there can be no progress toward racial justice—in education, or in any other sphere—without progress toward social justice. Again and again, the history of the Black freedom struggle demonstrates this point. As we saw, the struggle for public schools during Reconstruction ran up against the labor needs of the new southern economy; likewise, the fight to desegregate Jim Crow schools ran up against the government's racist housing policies and the shifting patterns of industrial development. The institutions of racism are so bound up with the economic system that the one cannot be unwound while leaving the other intact. Thus, there can be no genuine long-term solutions for Black education without addressing Black unemployment, the prison-industrial complex, environmental racism, and the housing crisis.

Second, instead of viewing Black students and parents as pathologically deficient or apathetic, we should start from the fact that they have waged an *uninterrupted* struggle for quality education for at least two hundred years. Then, we should investigate the specific historical circumstances that alternately have advanced and frustrated those aspirations and have led to our current predicament. It would be foolish from a historical perspective to think that this flame has been extinguished. Where we find students or parents alienated or disinterested in school, rather than trying to paint them as deficient, we should investigate what is going on in their lives (or in school) to stifle or suppress the desire for learning.

Third, instead of seeing philanthropists as likely change agents in a "movement" for racial justice, we should understand that they never operate purely on altruism (else they would hardly have been able to acquire such wealth in the first place). Rather, we should understand that philanthropic support *always* comes with strings attached. Historically, this has meant financial support for the business/corporate elite's vision of what Black education should be. Furthermore, history shows that genuine solidarity between parents and educators is a potentially powerful force for change. These groups have been divided and pitted against each other to the detriment of both.

Lastly, we should understand the fundamental difference between the aspirations of Black parents, who, out of sheer necessity, might look outside of the public school system in search of something better for their children and the growing cadre of wealthy and powerful backers of such alternatives.[129] The former group is merely seeking quality education where it has long been denied. The latter stands to gain tremendously from privatization. Since Reconstruction, Blacks have been the staunchest advocates of free public schools, not because they are everywhere superior, but because only such a system safeguards the *right* to an education for *all* children. Our struggle, going forward, should be to defend that right, and to fight to make sure such education is—for all children—of the highest quality.[130]

The Indian Boarding Schools
Michele Bollinger

From the 1870s to the 1960s, tens of thousands of Native American children attended Indian boarding schools—scattered across the country, both on reservations and off—run by US government officials or Christian missionaries.[1]

As a result, generations of Indian[2] children were traumatized by a number of barbaric practices employed by school officials: separation from family and community, child labor, physical torment, and sexual abuse. At the heart of these schools was a barbaric form of racism—one that aimed to strip American Indians of any semblance of cultural identity, tradition, and spirituality.

The most infamous of these schools was perhaps the Carlisle Indian Industrial School, which opened in 1879 under the direction of Lieutenant Richard Henry Pratt. Pratt's own words best represent the character of Indian schools and the so-called reformers who led them: "A great general has said that the only good Indian is a dead one, and that high sanction of his destruction has been an enormous factor in promoting Indian massacres. In a sense, I agree with the sentiment, but only in this: that all the Indian there is in the race should be dead. Kill the Indian in him, and save the man."[3]

It Was the Liberals
Unbelievably, the nineteenth-century leaders of the campaign to strip Indian children of their language and culture through education often identified as "friends of the Indian." Influenced by Helen Hunt Jackson's *A Century of Dishonor* and Lewis Henry Morgan's *Ancient Society*, they held that under the direction of white Christian leaders, "savage" Indians could shed their supposedly barbaric ways, assimilate into white society, and become "civilized."

Driven by Christian evangelism and upper-middle-class Republican morality, these "reformers" took great pains to distinguish themselves from the unseemly US Army generals who just wanted to collect scalps.

In 1891, Dr. Merrill Edward Gates, speaking to the Lake Mohonk Conference of the Friends of the Indian, claimed that "the time for fighting the

Indian tribes is passed."[4] But what he meant was that an equally insidious war of a different type was needed to reinforce and ensure total Indian subjugation. Gates called for an "army of Christian school-teachers," and argued: "We are going to conquer barbarism, but we are going to do it by getting at the barbarism one by one. We are going to do it by the conquest of the individual man, woman and child, which leads to the truest civilization. We are going to conquer the Indians by a standing army of school-teachers, armed with ideas, winning victories by industrial training, and by the gospel of love and the gospel of work."[5] As historian David Wallace Adams put it, "the war against Indians had entered a new phase. . . . The next Indian war would be ideological and psychological, and it would be waged against children."[6]

Complete conquest was necessary for the US government, as white settlers, big industrialists, robber barons, and rail and mining interests expanded westward. In 1885, Congress extended its jurisdiction over Indian reservations for major crimes; in 1887 the Dawes Act was passed, which destroyed communal ownership of land and forced "surplus" tribal lands to be sold to non-Indians and corporate interests.

Westward expansion came at an enormous price. Millions of Native Americans perished during the European conquest of North America— from disease, starvation, war, and forced relocation. The US Army's most notorious Indian killers, Andrew Jackson and William Henry Harrison, went on to become American presidents.

From Osceola and the Seminoles in what is now Florida to Crazy Horse and the Lakota in the northern plains, American Indian resistance has always been fierce. As late as 1876, under the leadership of Sitting Bull and Crazy Horse, the Lakota managed to kill George Armstrong Custer and defeat the Seventh Cavalry in the famous Battle of the Little Bighorn. Despite this, by the 1880s, as US domination of indigenous nations was imminent, some American officials began questioning the military approach. Adams explained, "Secretary of the Interior Henry Teller calculated that over a ten-year period the annual cost of both waging war on Indians and providing protection for frontier communities was in excess of $22 million, nearly four times what it would cost to educate 30,000 children for a year."[7] While complete defeat of the indigenous population seemed close at hand, US government officials remained insecure about the stability of their conquest.

They found the spiritual and cultural revival of the late 1800s known as the "Ghost Dance" so threatening that the US military occupied the Sioux Reservation, and in 1890 it slaughtered three hundred Indian men, women, and children during the massacre at Wounded Knee. Left to their own devices, Native Americans attempted to revive their culture by organizing a new wave of resistance. For the US military, violence alone was deemed insufficient. Instead, US officials became convinced that aggressive, forced assimilation through schools was necessary.

The Schools

If the common school is the glory and boast of our American civilization, why not extend its blessings to the 50,000 benighted children of the red men of our country, that they may share in its benefits and speedily emerge from the ignorance of centuries.
—Indian Board of Commissioners, 1880[8]

In 1877, Congress allocated $20,000 to the first Indian schools. By the 1920s, an estimated 80 percent of Indian children in the United States and Canada attended Indian schools at some point during their youth.[9] In 1879, Richard Henry Pratt, whose background not only included military service but also acting as warden of the Fort Marion military prison, opened the Carlisle Indian Industrial School in Carlisle, Pennsylvania.

The goal of these schools was to aggressively strip Indian youth of their cultural traditions, languages, and religious beliefs. The approach to education was not grounded in an understanding of child development or academic instruction—but rather racism, Christianity, and military discipline. Reformers preferred to call this approach "civilizing." David Wallace Adams notes the views of US Commissioner of Education William Torrey Harris: "Attributes of civilization included a commitment to the values of individualism, industry, and private property; the acceptance of Christian doctrine and morality, including the 'Christian ideal of the family'; the abandonment of loyalty to the tribal community for a higher identification with the state as an 'independent citizen'; the willingness to become both a producer and consumer of material goods; and finally, an acceptance of the idea that man's conquest of nature constituted one of his noblest accomplishments."[10]

The reality was demeaning, exploitative, and beyond damaging for Indian children. All children—including those as young as four or five years old—were forced to cut their hair or shave their heads, abandon traditional dress for military-style uniforms, relinquish customs and language in order to Anglicize their names, and use English. Students lived in barracks and each day was like boot camp—down to the military drills, regimented schedule, and orderly marching from work to prayer, class, and meals. The schools aimed to teach obedience, orderliness, and discipline above all else. Punishment was frequent, swift, and fierce as teachers and administrators treated the Indian children with brutal contempt.

Academic instruction occurred daily, but unlike white students, Native students spent only about two hours a day in class. The curriculum was laced with bigotry, emphasizing citizenship, patriotism to the United States, and "civilization." One Indian student essay from the 1890s exposes this dynamic: "The white people they are civilized; they have everything and go to school, too. They learn how to read and write so they can read newspaper. . . . The red people they big savages; they don't know nothing."[11]

One of the key strategies used to garner support for the boarding schools was a promise that they would provide Native children with useful technical skills for a world transformed by the Industrial Revolution. In almost every instance, the boarding schools broke that promise. Similar to the Hampton-Tuskegee model described in chapter 2, Indian boarding schools instead subjected Native children to a *menial* education, not a vocational—let alone academic—one.

Child labor was central and by most accounts took up over half the day. Girls worked in laundries, in kitchens, and on sewing; boys in metal, wood, or leather shops, or in agriculture. Under sweatshop conditions, Indian children were highly productive: girls, sewing and laundering thousands of garments a year; boys, mining tons of coal. However, they gained little skill from this work, as they tended to use methods that were increasingly out of date—and in some cases, the strain of the toil led to injury or death. Indeed, over the years, thousands died from hunger, disease, or escape attempts gone wrong.[12] Moreover, as generations of Indian children were taken from their families and placed under the direction and control of teachers, missionaries, and generals, many endured horrific physical and sexual abuse. To give but one example of the scale of this abuse, in 2011 the Catholic Church was forced to pay out a $166 million settlement to American Indian and Alaska Native survivors victimized by Jesuit missionaries teaching in village or reservation schools in the Northwest and Alaska between the 1940s and 1990s.[13]

Resistance

Ongoing parent and student resistance to forced enrollment in the schools presented school superintendents, Indian agents, and US officials with a constant crisis. Resistance to mandatory schooling was extensive. Native American children—teenagers in particular—ran away constantly. Those who remained rebelled by speaking their own language, meeting in secret, disrupting class, mocking teachers and staff, performing slowdowns while working, and committing vandalism and arson.

Many Indian parents refused to enroll their children in schools. They hid them, encouraged them to run away, fought off officials during roundups, withdrew their children from the schools, sometimes as a group, and re-taught them traditional ways when the children returned home. At times, entire villages would refuse to let US officials take their children. In response, US officials spared no expense to take the children. Starving parents were denied rations, others faced attacks by agency police during the roundups, and those who physically interfered with children being taken were detained. It took a massive effort to get Indian children into the boarding schools, both on and off the reservations.

For example, in 1892, after the Fort Hall Boarding School in Idaho sat underenrolled for more than a decade, US Indian agent S. J. Fisher—who, earlier, had reported to the commissioner of Indian Affairs that he had to "choke a so-called chief into subjection" to get him to enroll his children—faced a complete breakdown of authority when both Shoshone and Bannock police refused to bring children in by force.[14] After years of the commissioner begging the government to take action, the US Army forced students to Fort Hall at gunpoint.

Closure

Renowned American Indian Movement activist Leonard Peltier, who has been wrongfully incarcerated since 1977, once referred to his years at Wahpeton Indian School in North Dakota as his "first imprisonment." In 1928, the federal government commissioned the Meriam Report, which exposed the treacherous conditions at federal Indian boarding schools. The report states:

> The survey staff finds itself obliged to say frankly and unequivocally that the provisions for the care of the Indian children in boarding schools are grossly inadequate.

. . .
At a few, very few, schools, the farm and the dairy are sufficiently productive to be a highly important factor in raising the standard of the diet, but even at the best schools these sources do not fully meet the requirements for the health and development of the children. At the worst schools, the situation is serious in the extreme.

. . .
Nearly every boarding school visited furnished disquieting illustrations of failure to understand the underlying principles of human behavior. Punishments of the most harmful sort are bestowed in sheer ignorance, often in a sincere attempt to be of help. Routinization is the one method used for everything; though all that we know indicates its weakness as a method in education.[15]

In many ways, the Meriam Report marked the beginning of the end of the Indian boarding schools. The specific injustices highlighted in the report contributed to a set of legislation in 1934 known as the Indian New Deal. It included the Johnson-O'Malley Act, which authorized federal subsidies for local agencies to provide education and health care to Native children. In effect, the act allowed public school systems to collect federal monies for Native children attending school.[16] The combined impact of the Meriam Report and public schools opening their doors to Indian children led either to outright closure of many boarding schools or to their transformation into different institutions. Many other boarding schools, however, remained open for decades. There should be no confusion over their legacy. The US government committed reprehensible crimes against Native peoples and owes, at the very least, a historically accurate reckoning to the many victims of Indian schools.

3

Linguistic Justice at School

Jeff Bale

The greatest barrier to the Mexican-American child's scholastic achievement . . . is that the schools, reflecting the dominant culture, want the child to grow up as another Anglo. This he cannot do except by denying himself and his family and his forebears, a form of masochism which no society should demand of its children.

—A. Bruce Gaarder, specialist in foreign languages with the US Office of Education, El Paso, Texas, November 13, 1965[1]

One of the most urgent—and misunderstood—issues facing US public education today is meeting the needs of students who are not yet proficient in the English language. The quote above comes from *The Invisible Minority*, a 1966 report by the National Education Association task force on education in the Southwest. This report both was shaped by and contributed to the struggle for Chicano civil rights that would lead to passage of the Bilingual Education Act (BEA) of 1968, touching off a decade of education reforms meant to improve the educational experiences of emergent bilingual[2] students. Despite many important limitations, the BEA represented a significant advance in two ways. First, it consolidated the gains in bilingual and bicultural programs that were often fought for school by school, especially in the Southwest and West. Second, as part of official federal educational policy, the BEA legitimized what educators and activists long had known and advocated: that students learning English had specific educational rights, including the right to be educated in their home language. The ink had hardly dried on the BEA, however, when attacks on the legitimacy of bilingual education began. That the quote above still applies to the vast majority of schools highlights how far the clock has been turned back on the gains made in bilingual-bicultural education in the late 1960s and 1970s.

To be sure, plenty of educational and linguistic research has helped us better understand how youth learn additional languages and which classroom practices aid language learning. Likewise, we know a lot about which educational policies support language learning and which policies thwart it. But yet, the trend over the last decade has been toward English-only education. In some cases—in California, Arizona, and Massachusetts—bilingual education has been outlawed altogether. Clearly, all the knowledge that educational research has generated has had a limited impact on what *actually* happens in our schools. As renowned sociolinguist Joshua Fishman put it, somewhat desperately: when it comes to bilingual education, "why are the facts so useless?"[3]

This chapter addresses that question by making a basic claim: that the education of emergent bilingual students is above all a *political* question, not one that educational or language research alone can address. Specifically, when we look back at the history of US schooling, we can see a clear relationship between the state of US imperialism and the educational experiences of emergent bilingual students. At times when US imperialism was on the rise, the use of non-English languages at school was either restricted or repressed. These restrictions were rooted in intensely nativist and racist political climates. The opposite has also been true: when US imperialism has been beaten back or defeated, social space has opened up for using and teaching non-English languages at school. As I will argue below, a key factor in forcing open that social space has been the existence of militant movements against racism and for immigrant rights.

To back up this claim, this chapter is set up in four parts. First, I explain Marxist politics as they relate to the question of nationalism and imperialism and use them to argue the case for language rights at school. The next two sections describe specific historical periods as examples of this relationship between US imperialism, language, and schools. The final section discusses the return of English-only policies and practices at school, and suggests what can reverse that trend.

A Marxist Case for Language Rights

Clearly, this chapter takes for granted the benefits of multilingualism, both at individual and societal levels. The overwhelming balance of applied linguistic research on language learning has demonstrated that people who can use multiple languages tend to be more sensitive and effective in communicating with others, and that they are more flexible, creative, and divergent in their thinking. Moreover, the research is unequivocal that literacy in the first language makes learning additional languages—and becoming literate in them—much easier.[4]

Despite this consensus on bilingualism, however, bilingual education has been far more controversial. Table 1 below summarizes the most common models for emergent bilingual education. At first glance, it seems to be a hodgepodge of models—in fact, the alphabet soup of acronyms related to emergent bilingual education (such as ESL, ELL, BLE, LEP, and so on) and the different terminology for such programs are a key source of frustration for many teachers new to working with emergent bilinguals.

In making sense of these various models, two essential features help to distinguish between them more easily: whether emergent bilingual and English-only students are to be educated together in the same classes or separately; and whether the ultimate goal is proficiency and literacy in *English*, or in *both* (or multiple) languages. The shading in table 1 indicates which programs address which questions. The lighter shading indicates the only two models that educate emergent bilingual and English-only students together, although the latter is the result of denying emergent bilinguals any sort of language support at all. The darker shading indicates the few program models that have biliteracy and bilingualism as their formal goals.

As the table makes clear, even if a program goes by the name "bilingual education," the educational goal for that program is typically restricted to proficiency and literacy in English. At best, the child's first language is used as a tool to get to English proficiency and literacy; by the middle grades, any sort of instruction or development of the first language is left behind. Moreover, almost every model described above targets—and then separates out—emergent bilingual children for remedial or compensatory support. To be sure, such support is better than nothing. But the dominance of remedial or compensatory models exposes a widely held belief that not speaking English is a "problem" for schools to "fix." By contrast, dual-language or two-way programs stand alone in acknowledging that emergent bilingual

Table 1. Different models of bilingual education and their goals[5]

Model	Features	Main Audience	Goals
Dual-language or two-way immersion programs	English and the additional language are used in equal amounts	Emergent bilinguals and English-only students	Bilingualism and biliteracy in English and the additional language
Maintenance-bilingual programs	English and the additional language are used in equal amounts	Emergent bilinguals	Bilingualism and biliteracy in English and the additional language
Developmental or heritage bilingual programs	English and the additional language are used in equal amounts; "developmental" implies that students have only limited proficiency in the additional language when entering the program	Especially Native students in communities where the Native language is endangered	Bilingualism and biliteracy in English and the Native/additional language
Transitional bilingual programs	The additional language is used extensively in early grades, with little English. Those ratios reverse over the course of the program, until students exit into an English-only environment	Emergent bilinguals	English language proficiency and literacy
English-as-second-language programs	The English language is taught as a subject	Emergent bilinguals	English language proficiency and literacy
Sheltered English programs	Content areas (e.g., math, science, history) and English language development are taught simultaneously	Emergent bilinguals	English language proficiency and literacy
English immersion, or "Sheltered English Immersion" (SEI) programs	English language development using English only	Emergent bilinguals	English language proficiency and literacy
Null model	Submersion in mainstream classes with no language support	Emergent bilinguals and English-only students	English language proficiency and literacy

children possess a remarkable asset in speaking other languages, one that not only helps them learn English more efficiently, but also can benefit English-only students as well by broadening their linguistic repertoire.

Thus, what might appear as an "objective" choice of one program over another is, in fact, loaded with political content and the potential for conflict. This potential for conflict underlines the idea that emergent bilingual education is primarily a *political* issue. Specifically, any analysis of the political conflicts surrounding bilingual education needs to address two central questions: 1) what difference does it make in what language(s) children learn? In other words, why is language so often a "target" for oppressive practices at school? And 2) on what political basis can we challenge that oppression and establish language rights at school? This section explains the classical Marxist theories of nationalism and imperialism and uses them to understand conflicts over language and to frame the case for language rights at school.

Language and Nationalism

The starting point to understanding the political turmoil over bilingual education is the contradictory relationship between language and modern capitalism. On the one hand, creating national languages—and actually getting people to speak them—has been a key feature of dividing up the world into this or that nationality. As we will see, ruling groups within each nation-state have used national languages, like national borders, to help establish and maintain their power. On the other hand, because capitalism is a global, and not merely national, system, it brings multiple cultures and languages into contact—and often into conflict—with one another.

How this contradiction plays out varies over time and context. But it is rooted in capital's need for a specific infrastructure, which most often takes the form of the nation-state. In material terms, the state has served to pool resources to ensure successful capitalist development at the national level. Reaching a domestic market required a certain degree of political unity that could displace the old feudal or absolutist state structures that had stalled economic development.

In social terms, one consequence of the modern nation-state has been the invention and imposition of standardized national languages. Typically, defining the nation in terms of language required reaching far back into the past to cobble together a standardized language for modern use. As historian

Eric Hobsbawm has noted, such invention often came *after* the formation of the state, as was the case in Italy after unification in 1861. Hobsbawm quotes Italian nationalist Massimo d'Azeglio to illustrate the point: "We have made Italy, now it is time to make Italians."[6] An essential part of making Italians was to create "Italian," which the Italian ruling class did out of a Tuscan dialect.

The classic example of this process is what happened to "French" after the French Revolution of 1789. At the time of the revolution, a scant 4 to 5 percent of the population spoke the language that today is called French.[7] That language, based on a Parisian dialect, was introduced primarily through schooling across the new republic and imposed on people who spoke languages nothing like "French." Hobsbawm suggests the importance of the newly invented French language for the revolution: "There is little doubt that for most Jacobins a Frenchman who did not speak French was suspect."[8] At issue was not whether the new French citizen spoke "French" natively, but rather whether the citizen was willing to learn it as a loyal member of this new society.

This process of language standardization isn't just a relic of European revolutions from hundreds of years ago. Instead, debates over national languages have played a central role in nation-building in postcolonial Africa and Asia. For example, using Swahili was held up as a key way to show one's allegiance to the project of *Ujamaa*, or African socialism, under Joseph Nyerere in Tanzania from the 1960s onward. In fact, various Bantu peoples in East Africa have long spoken forms of the language. But the variety spoken in Zanzibar became the basis for a standard written form early in the twentieth century, and later a key tool for symbolizing independence.[9]

National languages don't just help identify who *belongs* to a certain national group; they are used just as much to *exclude* as well. Differences in grammar, vocabulary, or ways of writing can be used to define political rivals. In the former Yugoslavia, various nationalist movements have exacerbated tensions among Serbs, Croats, and Bosnians by reinforcing the differences in standardized versions of the Serbian, Croatian, and Bosnian varieties of what is essentially the same south-Slavic language.[10] The same was true in India at the time of Partition in 1947, whereby the cleavage of Urdu and Hindi—seen most clearly as two different writing systems—symbolized the supposedly immutable differences between Muslim and Hindu populations in Pakistan and India, respectively.[11]

In all these cases, the effect of this language invention has been the same: an almost-universal formula that Xians speak Xish in Xland.[12] However, merely standardizing languages has not been enough under capitalism. Instead, a whole set of beliefs about monolingualism has developed, especially in the West. These beliefs hold that Xians speak *only* Xish in Xland. Usually, full membership in Xian society is based, at least in part, on knowing and using the Xish language. And in almost every case, school is one of the main institutions in which monolingualism in Xish is enforced.

These dynamics create and reinforce powerful beliefs that speaking only one language is a natural and ideal human condition and a requirement to belong to this or that national group. These beliefs are especially absurd since—after three centuries of the modern nation-state—monolingualism in practice remains the minority human experience. Instead, the majority of the world's population grows up and lives as multilinguals, able to make their way through life using home languages, community languages, school languages, and official languages of government, media, and business, each at varying levels of proficiency. In other words, *monolinguals are in the minority.*

Language and Imperialism

If one side of this contradiction about language is tied to how capitalism developed *within* a given nation-state, then the other is about what happened in language terms as capitalism outgrew individual states. The drive to maintain and expand profits created an economic imperative to find raw materials and markets far beyond national borders. As Marx and Engels described it: "The need of a constantly expanding market for its products chases the bourgeoisie over the entire surface of the globe. It must nestle everywhere, settle everywhere, establish connexions everywhere."[13] Of course, the ruling elite of each nation-state is forced to take part in the same chase. The competition this creates—a competition among wealthy nations over who will control the rest of the world—has led to repeated economic, political, social, and ultimately military conflicts, a process Marxists refer to as imperialism.

In linguistic terms, there have been two specific consequences of imperialism. First, aggressor nations imposed their respective national languages on oppressed peoples. Second, Western colonizers with limited proficiency in the indigenous languages they encountered described those languages in formal terms by making grammars or developing dictionaries. This process of formalization often was used to invent ostensibly timeless divisions between indigenous societies—divisions that these societies generally had not recognized in the past.[14]

The linguistic legacy of colonization lives on to this very day. In most postcolonial societies the ex-colonial language (e.g., English, French, Spanish) is still used as an official language in school and government.[15] Beyond the prestige associated with knowing ex-colonial languages, official status generally means that attending university or getting a government job requires advanced proficiency. But even when indigenous languages are deemed official and used at school or in the government, they are often the standardized varieties invented through colonization that differ greatly from the language used in the daily lives of ordinary people.[16]

The linguistic consequences of imperialism have been just as profound *inside* aggressor nations as well. Marxist geographer David Harvey has written about the tendency of the US state "to mobilize nationalism, jingoism, patriotism, and, above all, racism behind an imperial project."[17] Understanding that each of the *-isms* on Harvey's list has its own unique features, for ease of discussion, I refer to them collectively as *chauvinism*. Of course, it is far easier to whip up popular support for specific imperial conflicts once a supposed enemy has been turned into an Other: a member of an inferior ethnicity or nationality, in need of liberation or civilization, or condemned altogether to annihilation by the aggressor nation. However, chauvinism has its own consequences at home. By enforcing a national identity defined by specific ethnic or racial, linguistic, and/or religious criteria, chauvinism functions to unite all members of the aggressor nation.

On the one hand, chauvinism masks the fact that the ruling class declares wars while ordinary people are the ones who fight them. In terms of economic competition, too, chauvinism helps conceal the fact that such competition enriches the employers at the expense of working people. On the other hand, chauvinism exacerbates a general feature of class society, namely the divisions created between working people of various ethnic, racial, gender, and sexual identities, among others. These divisions prevent the social and political unity that can challenge ruling-class oppression overall. At moments of imperialist conflict, chauvinism makes this oppression worse by targeting those individuals and groups at home who do not qualify as members of the dominant national group.

While Harvey's list of *-isms* implies the linguistic aspects of chauvinism, I will be explicit: a key part of US imperialism is enforcing English monolingualism in ideological and practical terms. The chauvinism fueled by US imperialism not only enforces a specific "American" national identity, but also requires that this identity be expressed *in English*. Furthermore, at times of overt war, proficiency in English is held up as patriotic and a sign of loyalty, while using—let alone teaching—"foreign" languages is deemed suspect.

Language Rights at School

The focus of this essay up to now has been on the impact of nationalism and imperialism on languages largely in the negative. Nationalism is the basis for a whole set of ideas that tie membership in a given nationality in part to the language one speaks. Thus, school becomes one of the main institutions to ensure proficiency in standardized national languages, almost always to the exclusion of stigmatized varieties of language (for example, African American or Chicano Englishes) or immigrant languages. Imperialism makes the situation even worse, not only by imposing the language of the aggressor nation on the colonized, but also by exacerbating at home the process by which language, like religion, ethnicity, or national origin, defines who does and does not belong.

However, nationalism is not only a consequence of the needs of the ruling class. Instead, nationalism can form the basis for resisting that class. The experience of imperialism generates struggles for democracy on the basis of national independence and freedom. Russian revolutionary V. I. Lenin wrote extensively on the relationship between nationalism and imperialism, in part because the socialist movement of his day was rife with political debate on the topic. The key question for him was how to combat national oppression in a way that could both end that oppression and lead in fact to greater unity among working people internationally.

The debate at the time centered on a specific slogan of "the right of nations to self-determination." At issue was whether an oppressed nation had or should have the right to secede from the oppressor nation and form its own state. While much has been written about that debate, the details of it are beyond the scope of this argument. What is relevant, however, about that debate is Lenin's distinction between the nationalism of the oppressor and the nationalism of the oppressed. Indeed, Lenin often clarified this distinction by way of concrete examples based on schools—how they functioned in tsarist Russia, and what they should look and sound like after the Russian Revolution of 1917.

Lenin's focus on school should come as no surprise. On a personal level, Lenin's upbringing exposed him to ongoing debates and discussions about language and school in tsarist Russia. His father, himself an educator and later a government official overseeing schools, was a close friend of I. Iakolov. Iakolov was a teacher of Chuvash[18] origin and an ardent supporter of an approach to native language instruction similar to transitional bilingual education. Language researcher Isabelle Kreindler argues that Lenin gained specific insights into the connections among language, school, and national liberation through observing the discussions between his father and Iakolov.[19] More important, because Russia was an empire built on the oppression of multiple national minorities, any strategy to win national liberation had to focus on the most concrete and specific details. Schools in tsarist Russia historically had imposed the Russian language and culture across the empire, a policy known as Russification. Thus, the questions of which language(s) a teacher should speak or in which language(s) a pupil's books should be printed were anything but academic. Chapter 7 recounts what the Bolsheviks did in practice after the revolution in 1917 regarding language and culture at school for national minorities; here, Lenin's arguments are described briefly.

The policy of Russification provides an excellent example by which to understand the dynamic approach to the national question that Lenin advocated. On the one hand, Russification was a direct result of colonialism and the Russian chauvinism that went with it. As such, he argued against the establishment of any official national language or the imposition of Russian on national minorities at school. On the other hand, Lenin was not indifferent at all as to whether national minorities had the opportunity to learn Russian. Access to the language was a practical component of the *freedom to integrate*. In an article entitled "Is a Compulsory Language Necessary?" Lenin argued:

> The liberals differ from the reactionaries in that they recognise the right to have instruction conducted in the native language, *at least in the elementary schools*. But they are completely at one with the reactionaries on the point that a compulsory official language is necessary. . . . [Socialists] desire more than [they] do that the closest possible intercourse and fraternal unity should be established between the oppressed classes of all the nations that inhabit Russia, without any discrimination. And we, of

course, are in favour of every inhabitant of Russia having the opportunity to learn the great Russian language. What we do not want is the element of coercion. We do not want to have people driven into paradise with a cudgel; for no matter how many fine phrases about "culture" you may utter, a compulsory official language involves coercion, the use of the cudgel. We are convinced that the development of capitalism in Russia, and the whole course of social life in general, are tending to bring all nations closer together. . . . People whose conditions of life and work make it necessary for them to know the Russian language will learn it without being forced to do so.[20] [emphasis in original]

Lenin was as insistent on the right of national minorities to linguistically and culturally relevant schooling as he was in rejecting an official or state language. His arguments addressed two different contexts: multinational urban areas, and regions throughout the empire where a specific national "minority" comprised the majority of the population. For example, in 1911 he conducted an analysis of the national origin of pupils in St. Petersburg as tallied by state officials, identifying almost forty different nationalities. Not only did Lenin attack the chauvinism of local education officials in counting Byelorussian and Ukrainian nationalities as Russian, but he called specifically for state provision of classes and materials in each national language and relevant to each nationality's history and culture. He wrote:

But we may be asked whether it is possible to safeguard the interests of the one Georgian child among the 48,076 schoolchildren in St. Petersburg on the basis of equal rights. And we should reply that it is impossible to establish a special Georgian school in St. Petersburg on the basis of Georgian "national culture," and that to advocate such a plan means sowing pernicious ideas among the masses of the people. But we shall not be defending anything harmful, or be striving after anything that is impossible, if we demand for this child free government premises for, lectures on the Georgian language, Georgian history, etc., the provision of Georgian books from the Central Library for this child, a state contribution towards the fees of the Georgian teacher, and so forth. . . . To preach the establishment of special national schools for every "national culture" is reactionary. But under real democracy it is quite possible to ensure instruction in the native language, in native history, and so forth, without splitting up the schools according to nationality.[21]

After the revolution in 1917, the context of the debate over self-determination shifted in large part to the eastern borderlands of the old empire, whose indigenous populations had long been oppressed by ethnic Russian colonizers. Lenin was often in the minority among the leadership of the Bolshevik party in insisting that each national minority in this vast region had the right to conduct local government, school, and so on according to national custom and language. Anything less, he maintained, would mean imposing the revolution on national minorities and bolstering Russian chauvinism. In 1919, he argued: "All our talk about Soviet power will be hollow so long as the toilers of Turkestan do not speak in their native tongue in their institutions. Soviet power differs from every bourgeois and monarchical power in that it represents the real daily interests of the labouring masses in full measure, but that is only possible on the condition that soviet institutions work in the native languages."[22]

With respect to school, this meant using the native language for instruction; paying a 10 percent bonus to teachers who spoke the respective language (given the privation caused by civil war and the general economic underdevelopment in these regions, such a bonus stands out as particularly noteworthy); preferential hiring of teachers from the respective national minority; and a massive expansion in textbook production in the various languages.[23] As remarkable as these policies were—and far in advance, as we will see below, of anything going on in US schools of the day—by the end of the 1920s, the Russian Revolution had essentially been defeated. Stalin's rise to power led in general to the undoing of almost all the gains made in the first years of the revolution.

Nevertheless, how Lenin applied a dynamic understanding of nationalism, imperialism, and the principle of national liberation to the most mundane details of school is instructive in terms of understanding language rights and public education today. If schools in general are one of the main venues where national oppression is carried out—that is, used to impose a specific national identity expressed in a specific national or official language—then combating that oppression has to include explicit language rights, namely the right to use and be taught in one's language at school. The basis of this right is not that there is something inherently oppressive about English, in the case of the United States, or something automatically liberatory or special about a given oppressed language, be it Spanish, Arabic, or Ojibwe. Rather, the right to use one's native language at school is an integral part of combating national oppression: it both expands democratic rights for linguistically and culturally diverse youth, and challenges the chauvinist or racist ideas held by some Anglo students and teachers. However paradoxical it may seem, expanding language rights at school is in fact a central component of *overcoming* national divisions overall.

This chapter now turns to applying this discussion of the Marxist case for language rights to public schools in the United States. First, it looks at the history of struggles over language use and language rights in two distinct eras, namely Americanization at the turn of the twentieth century and the Chicano civil rights movement of the 1960s and 1970s. It then describes the rise of English-only education from the 1980s onward. Highlighted throughout both discussions is the general connection between US imperialism and language use at school. Specifically, at times when US imperialism has been on the rise, using non-English languages at school has been restricted or repressed. The opposite is also the case: popular movements to beat back US imperialism have helped open up social space to use and teach non-English language at school and in society at large.

The Americanization Movement

In fact, one myth about the turn of the twentieth century is pervasive in today's debates about emergent bilingual education. This myth rests on two points. First, immigrants from this era were all too happy to abandon their home language and culture in the "unfair exchange"[26] for opportunity. Second, Latinos today who insist on maintaining Spanish are an aberration and thus represent a threat. The reality is that then, just as now, immigrants and their descendents exhibited a pattern in which: 1) the immigrant generation learns little English; 2) their children are bilingual; and 3) the third generation is English-dominant.[27] When we consider the level of anti-immigrant racism and hostility toward non-English languages in schools at the turn of the twentieth century, it is no wonder that second- and third-generation students adopted English so quickly.

In the West and Southwest, nativist racism led to the establishment of a dual system of segregated schools that prepared some white students for their future roles as leaders and owners, while training most Mexican and Asian students for life as workers. One plan to Americanize Mexican Americans in California dates to 1928. The plan identified "the Mexican element" as "the greatest problem confronting Southern California today." To solve that "problem" the plan called for segregated schools to educate Mexican American children by teaching English "to replace the Spanish [language] as the medium of use."[28] In addition, boys were to receive instruction in the industrial arts and girls training as "domestic servants."[29]

In another revealing example, the San Francisco school board in 1905 reaffirmed its commitment to excluding Japanese and Chinese students from school. Part of the resolution read, "It is the sense of the members of the Board of Education that the admission of children of Japanese or Mongolian descent as pupils to our common schools is contrary to the spirit and the letter of the law and that the co-mingling of such pupils with Caucasian children is baneful and demoralizing in the extreme."[30] An editorial from the November 6, 1906, edition of the *San Francisco Chronicle* supported the board's position, arguing: "There is also the objection to taking the time of the teachers to teach the English language to pupils. . . . It is a reasonable requirement that all pupils entering the schools shall be familiar with the language in which instruction is conducted. We deny either the legal or moral obligation to teach any foreigner to read or speak the English language. And if we choose to do that for one nationality, as a matter of grace, and not to do the same for another nationality, that is our privilege."[31]

A similar fate greeted Native children. In the late nineteenth century, the federal government began to establish boarding schools for the education of Native children. The first of these opened in Carlisle, Pennsylvania, in 1879. Children from various Native nations were purposely schooled together to make communication in their native languages and the maintenance of their cultures more difficult. Of course, stripping Native children of their language and culture was portrayed as a civilizing mission by the federal government. J. D. C. Atkins, who was the federal commissioner of Indian affairs under the first Cleveland administration, described this project in an 1887 report: "In the difference of language to-day lies two-thirds of our trouble. . . . Schools should be established, which [Native] children should be required to attend; their barbarous dialects should be blotted out and the English language substituted. . . . The object of greatest solicitude should be to break down the prejudices of tribe among the Indians; to blot out the boundary lines which divide them into distinct nations, and fuse them into one homogenous mass. Uniformity of language will do this—nothing else will."[32]

As Atkins's report makes clear, an important goal of Americanization was not just that students learn English, but that English should *replace* the home language. As one example, Julia Richman, a New York City school district administrator, was particularly stringent in imposing English at school. Although Richman herself was a German Jew, she forbade Yiddish from the schools she administered and assigned teachers to monitor the lunch hall and playground to enforce the rule, even during breaks.[33]

As World War I approached, the political dynamics of Americanization shifted to equate learning English with loyalty. By contrast, to respect or embrace diversity was to be unpatriotic.[34] Language researcher and historian Terrence Wiley presented an extensive account of the hysteria surrounding Germans and German Americans during the war, which included purges of German-language titles from public libraries; dismissal of all German-language university faculty; public assaults, including tarring and feathering, on German Americans and German religious minorities such as the Mennonites; and support from the National Education Association for anti-German and English-only medium-of-instruction policies. German-language instruction was criminalized in two states, and the number of states with English-only medium-of-instruction policies doubled from seventeen in 1913 to thirty-four in 1923.[35]

The fate of German-language education during World War I is a clear example of the connection between US imperialism and language use at school. Along with the United States entering the war—what historian Sidney Lens described as "the big leap"[36] for US imperialism—specific and ongoing campaigns denounced all things German. Despite, or perhaps because of, the demographic prominence of German Americans, their culture, customs, and language were now branded not only foreign but also seditious. Of course, German Americans were not the only targets of this wartime panic, nor was linguistic difference the only battleground. Historian John McClymer catalogued the multiple facets of internal repression that resulted from US involvement in the war. Anti-German chauvinism connected with the rebirth of the Ku Klux Klan in 1915; the sedition and espionage prosecutions of 1916–17; the Red Summer of race riots against African Americans in 1919; the "American Plan" of anti-unionism, including the Palmer Raids in 1919, which mobilized anti-immigrant and anti-communist sentiment to deport thousands of immigrants suspected of radical left activism; and the 1920 trial and subsequent execution of Italian anarchists Sacco and Vanzetti.[37]

It is within this general context, what McClymer called a negative revolution in terms of the extent of the racism and reaction that characterized the period, that English language proficiency served as a proxy for loyalty to the United States and as a requirement for inclusion into US society in general. Public use of non-English languages, let alone formal education in them, was tantamount to an act of sedition.

High school foreign-language enrollments give a sense of the impact of this general wartime panic. Secondary-level German-language enrollments, until 1914 the most popular modern language studied in high school, plummeted in 1921 to 1.2 percent of all foreign language enrollments—and essentially never recovered. The attack on German affected foreign language study overall: as the number of youth attending high school rose throughout the 1920s—not until the 1930s did the majority of adolescents attend high school—the proportion of that youth learning additional languages at school continued to fall, reaching its lowest point just after World War II.[38]

However clear this particular case of wartime language panic may be, it is only the most obvious example of the relationship between imperialism and language learning. To get a fuller picture, we have to see imperialism as something bigger than just formal wars. Instead, we have to understand it as a process of economic, political, social, and at times military conflict between world powers. In this sense, then, World War I marked the culmination of a more complex process through which the United States grew into an imperial power.

This development was rooted in four dynamics. The first was the meteoric rise of the US economy: by 1900, it was the largest and most productive in the world.[39] Second, the Civil War allowed the federal state to consolidate its power. The abolition of slavery brought an end to noncapitalist economic relations in the South, and northern political power rooted in an industrialized economy imposed itself across the entire United States.[40] Third, westward expansion was complete by the turn of the twentieth century. It was a threefold process that included extermination or marginalization of Native nations; barter and extortion to acquire territory; and formal war with Mexico to push the border south to the Rio Grande. Fourth, the United States projected its power internationally for the first time in this era, with the Caribbean and Pacific Islands as its early targets. The Spanish-American War of 1898 was a turning point in terms of establishing military and naval power on two fronts and marked the first time the United States ventured into extra-continental colonialism.[41]

To be clear, US imperialism rose in fits and starts, not as a lockstep, linear progression. Important struggles—from Radical Reconstruction in the South, the antiracist organizing drives of the Wobblies across the West, and the Philippine Insurrection (1899–1902) against US occupation to the one million votes cast in 1920 for Socialist Party presidential candidate Eugene Debs *while he was in jail* for his stance against World War I—challenged the consolidation of US power. In other words, there was nothing automatic or predetermined about how US imperialism grew. But by expanding how we understand imperialism from merely this or that war to a much broader economic and political dynamic of conflict and competition among wealthy nations over who will control the rest of the world, we can make better sense not only of the *specific* hysteria surrounding the German language during World War I, but of the *general* trend toward cultural and linguistic homogenization imposed primarily through schooling.

That trend, in fact, takes hold far before the onset of World War I. Efforts to restrict non-English languages in education date as far back as the 1830s. Interestingly, in many cases those efforts not only failed, but instead actually resulted in formal policies *supporting* instruction in non-English languages, as was the case with German in Ohio.[42] Furthermore, it is irrefutable that anti-German hysteria during World War I marked the end of German as a prominent community language in the United States. However, German-medium schooling was already in decline from the 1870s onward, targeted as much on linguistic terms as it was for its association with Catholicism. Indeed, a second round of efforts to restrict German-medium schooling occurred after the Civil War, and this time, those efforts generally succeeded.[43] Therefore, just as US imperialism rose in fits and starts from the second half of the nineteenth century, culminating with World War I, Americanization and attacks on non-English languages unfolded in fits and starts, too. Specifically, the two trends developed in strikingly parallel ways: as *external* US power expanded (insofar as "external" includes conflicts with Native nations, Mexico, Spain, and the Central Powers), the *internal* enforcement of an "American" national identity—one expressed in English only—became ever sharper.

The Chicano Civil Rights Movement

By contrast, the Chicano civil rights movement of the 1960s and 1970s forced a radical shift in the education of emergent bilingual students. The Chicano movement developed in many ways as a rejection of the liberal agenda of as-similation that dominated Mexican American political groups after World War II.[44] Persistent segregation, poverty, and racism against Mexican Americans exposed the limits of assimilationist goals, as well as divergent political strategies between middle- and working-class Mexican Americans.[45] As Ignacio García described it: "In their [Chicano activists'] eyes, American institutions, such as the government, schools, churches, and social agencies, had failed. American institutions, as far as activists were concerned, were inherently racist."[46] Rediscovering and revitalizing Chicano history, including the Spanish language, became a primary goal. Importantly, this movement was made up as much of descendants of Mexicans indigenous to the territories the United States annexed in the nineteenth century as it was of immigrants.

Indeed, Chicano struggles over schooling were central to the movement.[47] Considering the schooling conditions Mexican American youth faced, it is no wonder why. Although the segregation of Mexican American students had been outlawed, it was the de facto norm. In 1960, only 13 percent of Mexican American students held a high school diploma and only 6 percent attended college.[48] The average Mexican American student had a seventh-grade education, and in Texas the dropout rate was 89 percent.[49] Mexican Americans were often pushed into remedial, vocational, and Reserve Officer Training Corps tracks or pushed out of school altogether. Speaking Spanish was outlawed almost universally, disciplined by paddling, soap in the mouth, and other forms of corporal punishment. Quotas were common for the number of Mexican American athletes or cheerleaders, even in schools where Mexican American students were in the majority.[50]

In response to these conditions, bilingual and bicultural education reforms became central demands of a movement comprised largely of local, school-based struggles. The first bilingual program began at the Coral Way Elementary School in Miami in 1963.[51] Of course, the context for this program (that is, serving the children of elite exiles from the Cuban Revolution) was entirely different from what Mexican Americans in the Southwest faced. Nevertheless, Coral Way served as a model for bilingual programs elsewhere, which increased by ones and twos before 1968 in Texas, New Mexico, Arizona, and California. Winning these programs, however, often required organized and intentional resistance. The history of this resistance indicates three points that characterized the impact of the Chicano civil rights movement on schooling and second language education, described below.

First, students were the primary actors in this resistance. In March 1968, for example, students walked out of five high schools in East Los Angeles. These actions followed efforts to use petitions at school board meetings to present a series of student demands, including a citizens' review board of schools with majority Chicano enrollment, an increase in Chicano teachers and staff in those schools, and authorizing the citizens' board to develop bilingual and bicultural programs based on a school-community partnership. A report in the March 17, 1968, edition of the *Los Angeles Times* described the protests as "a week and a half of walkouts, speeches, sporadic lawbreaking, arrests, demands, picketing, sympathy demonstrations, sit-ins, police tactical alerts, and emergency sessions of the school board."[52] Overall, some twelve thousand students participated in the walkouts,[53] which ultimately led to the enactment of many of the original demands, including the oversight board and the implementation of bilingual-bicultural programs. Not only did dropout rates fall dramatically but the East Los Angeles walkouts became a model that Chicano activists across the Southwest would emulate.[54]

Throughout 1969 in Crystal City, Texas, students organized in the hundreds to present petitions at a number of school board meetings, which the all-Anglo board routinely ignored. Students responded in December by leading a three-week boycott of the junior and senior high schools. The boycott began with demonstrations of hundreds of students in front of the high school and spread to target Anglo-owned businesses that were known for their racist practices against Chicano employees and customers.[55] A similar process played out in Houston in 1970. Although the student strike did not last as long, some 60 percent of students participated, a rate far greater than in Los Angeles or Crystal City.[56]

Second, while students were central actors in school-based struggles for bilingual and bicultural education programs, they did not act alone. Alliances formed between and across generations. Many of the organizations actively involved included university students in Chicano and other radical organizations, such as United Mexican-American Students (now known as MEChA) in East Los Angeles, and the Mexican American Youth Organization (MAYO) in Texas. Particularly in the case of MAYO, these organizations served as conduits to generalize experiences and lessons learned from one locale to the next. These partnerships existed across generations as well, in terms of parent organizations and other radical political organizations comprised largely of adults. In California, these organizations included the

Mexican American Political Association and the Brown Berets; in Texas, the Raza Unida Party, Ciudadanos Unidos and Las Familias Unidas.[57]

The aspect of these political partnerships most relevant here concerns their impact on bilingual and bicultural curricula. In Crystal City, Texas, for example, MAYO worked with Texans for the Educational Advancement of Mexican Americans to establish what were known as *liberation schools* during the school boycott. These liberation schools became the testing ground for a Chicano-centered, bilingual curriculum that would later be implemented as formal district policy. The boycotts themselves triggered the intervention of the US Office of Education, which worked with parents (organized through Ciudadanos Unidos), MAYO, and faculty from Chicago State University and San Diego State University to prepare bilingual teachers and develop a new curriculum centered on Chicano history, literature, arts, and bilingual education. The full curriculum was completed and approved by the school board on February 1, 1973.[58] A similar story played out in Houston, where several organizations merged to form the Mexican American Education Council (MEAC). MEAC helped to organize a two-week boycott as the school year began in 1970, as well as to establish *huelga* (strike) schools, in which some three thousand students participated.[59]

Finally, these school-based struggles intersected with the efforts of state policy makers and education advocates to improve the experiences of Mexican American and other emergent bilingual students. For example, in 1965 the National Education Association conducted a study to assess the needs of Mexican American students in the Southwest. They held a conference in Tucson on October 30–31, 1966, to present and publicize the results. Earlier that year, the Equal Employment Opportunity Commission (EEOC), created by Title VII of the Civil Rights Act of 1964, held a conference in Albuquerque, New Mexico, on discrimination against Mexican Americans. Chicano delegates walked out of the conference to protest the lack of Mexican American representation on the EEOC board.[60] In a context of growing resistance across the Southwest to racism and segregation, these two events pressured officials in Washington to heed the demands Mexican Americans were making on schools, as well as those arising from new antipoverty and civil rights legislation.

These developments were powerful enough to pressure politicians to codify them as formal policy reforms. For example, in January 1967 Senator Ralph Yarborough of Texas sponsored the Bilingual Education Act. The bill received tepid support from Democrats and President Johnson.[61] Thus, to help ensure the bill's passage, Yarborough tied it to reauthorization of the Elementary and Secondary Education Act (ESEA) of 1965 rather than have it stand for a separate vote. In 1968, the measure was passed as Title VII of ESEA. Many discussions of the Bilingual Education Act rightly highlight its deficiencies: it neither required school authorities to provide for bilingual education nor defined what bilingual education entailed. Reauthorization of the act in 1974 provided such a definition, but it focused on *transition* from the home language to English, not on *addition* of English to the home language.

The official policy part of this story is, in fact, well known. Specific policies, such as the Civil Rights Act, the Bilingual Education Act, the Lau Remedies as established by the 1974 *Lau v. Nichols* Supreme Court case, and so on are main characters in a narrative explaining the "early days" of bilingual education. Sometimes, a nod is made to the civil rights movements of the day. However, little attention is paid to that connection in any detail. One consequence of this narrow perspective is that it distorts history itself. The actions of Important People, such as President Johnson signing the Civil Rights Act or Senator Yarborough sponsoring the BEA, are framed as the key source of change in this era. Of course, their actions did matter in terms of codifying important civil rights and language accommodations as reforms. However, these individual moves would have been impossible without the pressure created by broader social forces demanding change from below.

It is real people who organized, fought back, and forced opened social space to make policies like the Civil Rights Act or the BEA possible. Indeed, the collective impact of what people did during this era imposed radical changes on a number of interrelated fronts. Taken together, these struggles represent a compelling example of the second part of the argument in this chapter: that setbacks and defeats for US imperialism help make education in non-English languages more viable.

The main US imperial adventure in this era, of course, was the war in Vietnam. In fact, 1968 and 1969 marked horrific high points in US aggression in Southeast Asia. But those years also represented a significant turning point in the movement to end the war. Not only did a majority of working-class Americans register their opposition to the war for the first time in polls, but soldiers returning from Vietnam began to join, and sometimes lead, important antiwar organizations and events. As labor historian Sharon Smith noted, "By 1971, Vietnam Veterans Against the War (VVAW) was at the forefront of antiwar struggle at home."[62]

Chicano resistance to the war was key to this deepening opposition. Given that almost 20 percent of US casualties during the war were Chicano,[63] their resistance is not surprising. In 1969, activists organized a National Chicano Moratorium as part of the broader moratorium movement. They held another moratorium rally the next summer in Los Angeles, where the police unleashed a barrage of violence, killing a fifteen-year-old boy and a news reporter for a Spanish-language television station. Both the size and strength of the rally and the degree of police violence deepened the already fast-growing resistance to the war.[64] To be sure, US defeat in Vietnam—brought about by a mass antiwar movement at home, open rebellion of US troops against their officers, and Vietnamese resistance—did not end US imperialism.[65] However, it represented a significant setback, popularly known as Vietnam Syndrome, which prevented the United States from directly intervening and imposing its military power abroad for the next decade. Equally important, this defeat taught a generation that collective resistance could stop even the mightiest military in the world.

In addition to the anti–Vietnam War movement and the US defeat in Southeast Asia, the US working class flexed its muscles during this era. Some of these struggles represented connections between the radical civil rights and labor movements, such as the Dodge Revolutionary Union Movement of African American autoworkers. On a much larger scale, however, the most important industrial unions at the time took action, leading to a high point of strike activity in 1970. This included a sixty-seven-day strike against General Motors; forty thousand coal miners striking to win benefits for disabled miners; an illegal postal workers' strike that shut down post offices in more than two hundred locales and resulted in a 14 percent pay raise; and a Teamsters' strike led by the rank and file.[66] Such labor struggles compounded significant economic challenges to US imperialism at the time. By the early 1970s, Germany and Japan had emerged as serious economic competitors to the United States. Moreover, the decade was bookended by two worldwide recessions. Taken together, these developments meant the postwar period of unprecedented economic expansion for the United States had come to an end, undermining the economic basis of US imperialism.[67]

These antiwar and labor struggles connected with and fueled civil rights struggles such as the Chicano movement described above. Moreover, the gains codified in federal civil rights, voting rights, and antipoverty legislation in 1964 and 1965 confirmed among activists that struggle bred success, thus increasing their expectations of what was possible. In understanding history in this way, we can reframe the Bilingual Education Act (BEA) not as the *high* point of formal federal policy regarding language accommodations, but rather as a *starting* point of educational reform imposed from the bottom up. Moreover, the Lau Remedies of 1974, which mandated a form of bilingual education where maintenance of the home language was part of the goal, were an extension of this reform process imposed from below and a much stronger expression of students' right to bilingual education.[68] Unsurprisingly, the advocates who helped the Lau family in their court case against San Francisco schools had their own activist roots in Asian American civil rights struggles in the Bay Area. These roots included cutting their political teeth as student activists in the Third World Student Strike at San Francisco State College in 1968.[69] Finally, while it was not about bilingual education rights per se, we should also include the influential 1979 court case *Martin Luther King Junior Elementary School Children et al. v. Ann Arbor School District* as part of this trend. The case was brought by three African American families against the district in response to the negative treatment their children had received. The decision recognized nonstandard varieties of English for the first time and required schools to make accommodations to bridge the gap between them and academic English.

None of these reforms can be held up as perfect expressions of language rights or the sort of aspirations for language maintenance that multiple civil rights struggles demanded. None of them, however, would have been possible in the first place without those same civil rights struggles. That is, their shortcomings are secondary to the social movements on the ground that made such reforms possible at all. As such, this era exemplifies the counterpart of the connection between US imperialism and language use at school. If rising US imperialism and a more sharply enforced national identity expressed in English only fit together in the period roughly from the Civil War to World War I, then we see an inverse parallel between the first significant defeat of US imperialism and the efforts of civil rights activists to force open social space for the practice of and education in languages other than English.

But the very sort of popular struggle that made these reforms possible faded over the course of the 1970s and early 1980s. Instead, movement activists shifted the primary arena for their organizing to Democratic electoral campaigns and away from social and labor movements or community organizing. Coupled with the beginnings of an elite offensive to beat back the movements of that era, *all* the gains of the sixties and early seventies, including bilingual and bicultural education, came under attack. As a case in point: despite the Supreme Court decision in *Lau v. Nichols*, the Lau Remedies were never implemented as formal federal policy. Ronald Reagan, who assumed office in 1981, not only continued the ruling-class offensive begun under Carter,[70] but also made the first formal move to turn back the gains made in bilingual education practice across the United States.

Anti-Immigrant Backlash and the English-Only Movement

Bilingual education—and the broader societal goal of maintaining non-English languages—has been under attack ever since. Five points explain the nature and intensity of these attacks. To begin, these attacks culminated at the turn of this century with the passage of several state ballot initiatives effectively outlawing bilingual education. The first, Proposition 227, was passed by large margins in California in 1998. Bankrolled by Silicon Valley millionaire Ron Unz, the initiative—subtly called "English for the Children"—outlawed home language use for instruction and mandated English-only "sheltered" programs for a period "not normally intended to exceed one year."[71] Two years later, Unz moved on to Arizona, where he bankrolled Proposition 203, which also passed and ended bilingual education in that state. In 2002, Massachusetts's voters approved Question 2, an initiative to replace transitional bilingual programs with English-only ones. That same year, Colorado voters narrowly rejected the most restrictive initiative of all, an amendment to the state constitution that actually would have made bilingual education illegal.

Second, these specific anti–bilingual education measures have been fueled in part by a broader anti-immigration backlash. Since the late 1970s, anti-immigration politics and the racism behind them have moved from the far-right fringe to the political mainstream in the United States. For example, the federal government responded to a series of economic downturns in the seventies and early eighties by stepping up attacks on immigrant workers. In 1982, with unemployment at around 12 percent, the Immigration and Naturalization Service (now known as Immigration and Customs Enforcement, or ICE) initiated "Project Jobs" to conduct workplace raids and round up undocumented workers.[72] Four years later, Congress passed the Immigration and Refugee Control Act, which increased funds significantly for border control and detainment centers. The bill further increased police and military presence on the border and in borderlands.[73] Of course, these measures actually did little to stop immigration. They merely criminalized immigration further and added a terrifying level of violence.

This era of anti-immigrant backlash culminated in the passage of Proposition 187 in California in 1994. The measure declared undocumented immigrants ineligible for any public services. In essence, the initiative would have turned teachers, nurses, and other public employees into border patrol agents, requiring them to report undocumented residents who tried to access public services.[74] The pro–Prop 187 campaign director, Ron Prince, said of the measure: "You are the posse and [Proposition 187] is the rope."[75] Although Prop 187 was overturned in the courts, it marked the first major move by the far right to shift the political terrain of immigration in its favor.

Third, the attacks on bilingual education aren't just the *result* of a broader anti-immigrant backlash, but also have been used to *fuel* that backlash as well. In many ways, bilingual education and the maintenance of non-English languages in the United States are low-hanging political fruit that can easily be picked and stomped on to make the ground more fertile for anti-immigrant sentiment. Even *supporters* of immigrant rights will often qualify that support with demands on immigrants and their descendants to learn English once here. These attitudes range from the seemingly pragmatic ("we need a common language so that government and business can function smoothly"); to the patronizing ("we've allowed them in and they are benefiting from life here, so the least they can do is learn English"); to the overtly nationalist ("this is America and we speak English here"); to the mythical ("my grandmother had to learn English when she arrived from Poland, so they should too!"). Each of these attitudes—again, often held by *supporters* of immigrants' rights—reflects the role that language plays in bolstering nationalism; specifically, how language helps to define who *does* and *doesn't* belong. However—and the anti-immigrant right knows this all too well—it's not that far a leap from complaints about an immigrant's language to complaints about the immigrant herself. In this way, bilingual education—and, more generally, efforts by marginalized groups to maintain their languages and cultures—makes an easy target to shift the overall terrain of immigration politics much further to the right.

The fallout from Prop 187 in California represents a compelling example of this. When Prop 187 passed in 1994, it was widely considered far outside the political mainstream. Once the measure had been overturned in the courts, it was no accident that anti-immigrant forces turned next to bilingual education. Just four years later, Prop 227, described above, made its way onto the ballot. Not only did it pass, it was also implemented, effectively ending a thirty-year tradition of bilingual education in California public schools. What anti-immigrant bigots were unable to pull off with Prop 187 they began to make up for with Prop 227 by outlawing bilingual education.

This dynamic is even clearer in Arizona. Arizona earned the scorn of much of the nation in spring 2010 when it passed Senate Bill (SB) 1070, a vitriolic anti-immigration bill that allows the police to stop any individual and demand proof of legal residency or citizenship. In effect, SB 1070 has legalized and legitimized racial profiling by police of all Latinos, who make up almost one-third of Arizona's population.[76] Much of the analysis explaining how SB 1070 became law has focused on the especially rabid anti-immigrant climate in that state and the influence of far-right organizations from elsewhere in the United States. However, a decade of attacks on bilingual education, and on immigrants in public schools more generally, played a critical role in making a bill like SB 1070 possible in the first place.

Prop 203 was the opening salvo in these attacks. As mentioned above, it passed in 2000 and marked the beginning of a decade of public panic over immigrants in Arizona schools. As with its older cousin in California, Prop 203 mandated that English learners be educated in English only, and that they receive English language services for two years at most. After the second year, school districts are cut off from additional state funding to support English language education for a given emergent bilingual student.

Moreover, Prop 203 required the state to develop a new model, called Structured English Immersion (SEI), to use for English language education. After much public deliberation and controversy, the SEI model took effect in the 2008–09 school year. It mandates that any student who qualifies as an English learner be segregated from mainstream programs for four hours per day to receive one hour each of grammar, oral language, reading, and writing instruction in English. This means that for two-thirds of the school day, emergent bilinguals are segregated not only from everyone else, but also from proficient speakers of English! And at the secondary level, they are effectively denied any other content area instruction because so much of their day is dedicated to English language development.[77] Finally, a particularly outrageous consequence of Prop 203 is its impact on public schools on Native lands. To avoid state sanctions, public schools in the Arizona portion of the Navajo Nation have had to reclassify Diné[78] as a "foreign" language in order to continue their developmental bilingual programs.

Still, Prop 203 was only the beginning in Arizona. In the 2004 election cycle, Arizona voters approved another set of ballot initiatives that attacked immigrant students at school. One mandated that all higher education programs require proof of legal residency before enrolling students.[79] The initiative exploited voters' fears that a "wave" of "illegal" immigrants was stealing spots at universities that otherwise belonged to "Americans."[80] By contrast, the experience at Arizona State University at the time is telling. The campus is home to around sixty thousand students. Yet, fewer than two hundred students were unable—or unwilling—to comply with the new law. The irony of this initiative is that its greatest impact was felt precisely by immigrant adults trying to learn English at night school. Many public school districts offer adult education in English and other subjects. These programs, too, were required to demand proof of legal residency from their students.[81] This experience gives lie to the claim that immigrants are welcome—as long as they learn English. As far-right, anti-immigrant politics have become ever more mainstream, it is clear that a willingness to learn English is not enough.

This helps explain why Arizona has gone the next step to outlaw ethnic studies at the K–12 level altogether.[82] House Bill 2281 was passed in 2010, just a few weeks after SB 1070. While it does not mention Chicano Studies by name, it is clear that Chicano Studies is the target. Much of the analysis of HB 2281 focused on its timing in relation to SB 1070. But the state Board of Education had been gunning for Chicano Studies—and particularly the program in the Tucson Unified School District—for years before SB 1070 became law. One reason for the ongoing campaign was sheer vindictiveness: officials from Tucson Unified have been among the most vocal in the state to challenge Prop 203 and the SEI model it mandated. But the broader message behind this attack is clear, and it brings us back to the epigraph that opened this chapter: "The schools, reflecting the dominant culture, want the child to grow up as another Anglo. This he cannot do except by denying himself and his family and his forebears, a form of masochism which no society should demand of its children."

Fourth, as despicable as this campaign by anti-immigrant bigots has been, to lay it solely at their feet would be to tell only one half of the story. The other half includes the tepid, accommodating responses to such attacks by liberal organizations as the terrain shifted ever rightward under their feet. For example, the "No on 227" campaign in California in 1998 refused to mount a specific defense of bilingual education. Its leaders claimed the issue was too complicated to explain. This stance reflected not only their conservative and condescending attitudes toward ordinary voters, but also flew in the face of the history of bilingual education, which was fought for and won in the United States from the ground up. Instead, they focused their efforts on swaying the opinion of "swing voters," namely Republican women over fifty.[83]

Most notorious, though, was the response in Colorado to the Unz-financed amendment in 2002 to criminalize bilingual education. As mentioned above, that initiative failed, with 56 percent of the vote going against it. But the victory was a bitter pill: the main organizers against the initiative appealed to the vilest racism to drum up support against it. One TV commercial claimed that the measure would "force children who can barely speak English into regular classrooms, creating chaos and disrupting learning." James Crawford aptly summarized this approach: "If you can't beat racism, then try to exploit it."[84]

This combination of overt anti-immigrant backlash and panic around non-English languages has had its most far-reaching effect through the 2001 reauthorization of the Elementary and Secondary Education Act, better known as No Child Left Behind (NCLB). The BEA was abolished in that reauthorization. Not only did mainstream Latino rights organizations, such as the National Council of La Raza, support NCLB in the hope that accountability would expose how poorly schools educate Latino children, but erstwhile supporters of bilingual education in Congress, such as the Congressional Hispanic Caucus, were silent on the abolition of the BEA and voted for NCLB in unison.[85] What they voted for, however, has rightly come under increasing scrutiny. Any mention of bilingual approaches to educating students learning English has been silenced, replaced by variations on the phrase "English language acquisition."[86] Although funding for English instruction has increased, it has been tied to English-only approaches to language education. Even where state or local policy may in fact still support bilingual education,[87] NCLB's mandates for high-stakes testing *in English* have produced a blowback, effectively pressuring local authorities to adopt English-only approaches, hoping against hope that their students pass the test.[88]

Fifth, and finally, we have to see the continued attack on bilingual education in relation to the ideological fallout of a decade of war and occupation in Afghanistan and Iraq. The events of September 11, 2001, unleashed a wave of bigotry against Arab and Muslim Americans and anyone assumed to be such. This has included FBI roundups of Arab and Muslim Americans in the days immediately following 9/11, violence (sometimes lethal) against individuals assumed to be Arab or Muslim, and a seemingly unending media barrage of hatred directed at Arab and Muslim Americans.[89] This media campaign at times has been laughable for its ignorance, such as a prominent NPR reporter's complaint of fellow airline passengers wearing "Muslim garb,"[90] and other times hateful and violent, such as the campaign against founding a Muslim community center in lower Manhattan in summer 2010.[91]

Moreover, the impact of anti-Arab and anti-Muslim bigotry *at school* has been as devastating. For example, New York City opened the Khalil Gibran International Academy, an Arabic-English dual-language school, in Brooklyn in 2007. From the day plans for the school were announced, the mainstream media attacked the school with calls for New Yorkers to "break out the torches and surround City Hall to stop this monstrosity"[92]; claims that teaching Arabic was synonymous with teaching "pan-Arabist and Islamist baggage"[93]; and an ongoing campaign to discredit the school's Arab American principal, Debbie Almontaser, ultimately leading to her dismissal.[94] Since its opening, the school has had to change locations twice, taking it a considerable distance from the neighborhood it was originally meant to serve, which is home to one of the largest Arabic-speaking populations in the country. Consequently, few Arabic-speaking students have enrolled. In a final insult, as this book goes to press, the Gibran Academy stands on the list for closure in the current round of budget cuts. It is the only one of New York City's sixty-plus dual-language schools currently on the list. Of course, the Department of Education has officially cited low enrollments as the primary rationale for closure.

In Dearborn, Michigan, the story has been similar. Dearborn is home to the largest concentration of Arab Americans in the United States and, along with southeast Michigan more broadly, is the historic heart of Arab America. Nevertheless, even in Dearborn, speaking Arabic at school has been deemed a threat. In 2009 the Dearborn public school district contracted an external review of its three high schools. The report, released in December of that year, had a specific recommendation for Fordson, the high school with the largest Arab American enrollment. It urged building administrators to forbid the use of non-English languages at school. While the report didn't specify Arabic, the rationale it used gave the game away: "To do otherwise reinforces a perception by some that Fordson is an Arab school in America rather than an American school with Arab students."[95] Likewise, the report never defined the "some," but did say its recommendation came from focus group interviews with staff who complained that their Arabic-speaking peers were in fact talking about them.

Taken together, then, the anti-immigrant backlash since the late 1970s has led to specific policies that have outlawed bilingual education. At times, the bigots behind this backlash have used attacks on bilingual education to inch their cause into the political mainstream, thereby shifting the general political climate further to the right. At the same time, a decade of war and occupation has poisoned the political climate for Arab and Muslim Americans in particular, but also for *any* group hoping to use school to maintain the home language and culture.

Conclusion

As grim as the situation has become for bilingual education, and more importantly for the academic and linguistic needs of emergent bilingual students in US schools, the potential exists today as at no other time since the Chicano civil rights movement to turn things around. The remarkable May Day rallies for immigrant rights in 2006, and the ongoing struggles against workplace raids and militarization of the border—as well as the struggle in Arizona—have laid the groundwork for a new mass movement against racism and for immigrant rights. Meanwhile, the resistance in Wisconsin—spearheaded in many ways by teachers—and the emerging "Occupy" movement have openly identified with the ongoing revolution in Egypt and the Arab Spring more generally. This sense of solidarity has the potential—*finally*—to break through and beat back a decade of anti-Arab and anti-Muslim hate in the United States. On both counts, we stand before an opportunity to create precisely the kind of generalized political atmosphere that can lead to renewed support for bilingual education and respect for multilingualism in the United States.

A key part of this, however, is that educators and others dedicated to improving the education of emergent bilingual students must broaden the scope of their work and be clear on what it is we are fighting for. First, the political basis for supporting bilingual education in a country formed by conquest, slavery, and mass immigration must rest on the linguistic rights of ordinary people. These rights must apply equally to immigrants and their children to be educated in the home language; to Native nations and their efforts to revitalize their languages; and to speakers of non-mainstream varieties of English, such as African American English, to receive academic and linguistic support for learning standard, academic English. Second, the fight for these rights will not lead to a single model for education in every school. Whether maintenance-bilingual, dual-language, or more individualized language support models are the most appropriate is an issue to be resolved locally. The central argument, however, is that basing the fight for language rights on a broader fight against racism and for immigrant rights is the most effective strategy for challenging the monolingual ideologies and practice that have dominated in the United States. The Chicano struggles of the 1960s and 1970s have made this clear. It is only in this context that linguistic divisions in the United States can be overcome on a basis of equity, not on the basis of imposed English monolingualism.

It is impossible to predict what may spark the next round of struggle for the movement—perhaps struggles against workplace raids, perhaps fights around NCLB reauthorization or the ethnic studies ban in Arizona described earlier. No matter what that spark may be, absent mass movements fighting for change from the ground up, the crisis facing emergent bilingual students will continue. Solving that crisis means recognizing that without the strength of broad social forces, such as dynamic mass movements against racism and in support of immigrant rights, efforts to effect change at the classroom or policy level will by definition be limited. By learning the lessons of past victories and defeats concerning language and education, and connecting them to current struggles, we can transform the hope engendered over the last several years represented in the slogan "*Sí, se puede!*" into "*Sí, se pudo!*"

4

Obama's Neoliberal Agenda for Public Education

Gillian Russom

Writing in March 2008, the editors of *Keeping the Promise*, a Rethinking Schools book on charter schools, held out hope that the end of the Bush administration would mean new possibilities for a progressive education agenda: "This country is on the cusp of a new political dialogue. The conservative stranglehold on political debate is ending, opening up new opportunities for progressives to regain the initiative. How this opening will affect public education in general and charter schools in particular is not yet clear, but it ushers in new possibilities not imaginable a decade ago."[1]

After several years, the direction of education policy under the Obama administration is indeed clear. The biggest economic crisis since the Great Depression has called into question whether our public schools will be funded at even the most basic level required to function. Eighty-four percent of school districts describe their funding as inadequate, and the number of teachers laid off since the economic crisis began is likely to top three hundred thousand without substantial federal assistance to states.[2] As a result, class size is likely to increase in at least 65 percent of school districts.[3] Students who make it through the K–12 public system and hope to attend college are now facing huge tuition increases—of 20 percent in the California State University system and 32 percent in the University of California system, for example.

These devastating cuts are being applied to a public school system that is already in horrible shape. Many schools are overcrowded and crumbling,

Special thanks to Jesse Hagopian for his contribution to this chapter.

lacking essential technology and materials; learning is often dull because teachers are exhausted or focused on preparing for standardized tests; and students rarely get experiences that connect what they are learning to the real world. These abysmal conditions have led to a high school dropout rate of nearly 30 percent nationwide and more than 50 percent in many major cities.[4]

Education should be at the center of a national debate on social priorities, led by a president who promised "change." Instead, the economic crisis is being used by the White House to dramatically accelerate a neoliberal agenda for education, going far beyond what George W. Bush's administration was able to do with its No Child Left Behind (NCLB) policy. With Arne Duncan as education secretary, the administration has aggressively promoted a program with three principal elements: using test score data to evaluate teachers; shutting down or "reconstituting" schools deemed to be failing; and expanding privately run, mostly non-union charter schools. Other elements include the standardization of curriculum and a longer school day.

The wealthiest members of the ruling class are playing an open and active role in promoting this agenda. Foundations controlled by America's richest billionaires—the Gates, Broad, and Walton Family Foundations—are working in sync to shape education policy dramatically by leveraging their collective assets of more than thirty billion dollars to push charter schools and undermine teachers' unions. Moreover, these foundations give large sums of money to nearly every think tank and advocacy group involved in education, so almost no one is willing to publicly challenge the policies they promote.[5] And in an era of massive budget cuts, schools and districts are willing to chase any recommended "reforms" that come with money attached. It goes without saying that these billionaires have no education expertise, nor were they ever elected to set education policy. Thus, policies in one of the last "public" institutions in the United States are being set by the nation's most powerful private interests.

In an era in which government spending on schools and social services is being drastically reduced, the blame for poor educational outcomes is placed squarely with teachers. Speaking before an audience of business executives at the US Chamber of Commerce in March 2010, Obama supported a Rhode Island school board's decision to fire all seventy-four teachers and nineteen other school employees at Central Falls High School. "If a school continues to fail year after year after year and doesn't show sign of improvements, then there has got to be a sense of accountability," he remarked.[6] As the only high school in the poorest community in Rhode Island, Central Falls has been chronically underfunded. Yet it seems that the only people being held accountable are the teachers who have dedicated their lives to working with Central Falls students.[7] After weeks of protest by teachers, students, and parents, an agreement was ultimately reached to restore Central Falls teachers to their jobs—if they agreed to a longer school day and a new evaluation system.

The immense gap between the hope for a "new political dialogue" about education and the Obama administration's record begs an analysis that frames the individual, ongoing attacks in a broader understanding of neoliberalism—what it is and how it has set public education in its sights.

Neoliberalism and the Education Shock Doctrine

Neoliberalism emerged in the 1970s to become the dominant ideology of rampant free-market capitalism in the 1980s. Neoliberal policies seek to give free rein to business by deregulating markets (eliminating laws that protect workers, the public, and the environment), privatizing new sectors of the economy once thought to be the domain of the public sector, slashing government spending on social services, and promoting anti-union, "flexible" labor policies.

In *The Shock Doctrine: The Rise of Disaster Capitalism*, Naomi Klein shows how times of crisis have been used as opportunities to push through neoliberal policies.[8] Some people think of neoliberalism as the domination of the market over government, with a corresponding reduced role for the state. But Klein emphasizes that under neoliberalism, markets are not usurping the traditional role of government. Instead, governments are taking on an increasingly close partnership with the private sector, using public dollars and the strength of the state to implement policies that benefit business.

Chapter 1 of this book reviews the work of Samuel Bowles and Herbert Gintis, Marxist educational theorists. Returning to one of their main arguments about the relationship between capitalism and schooling helps us to better understand the impact that neoliberalism has had on public education. In general terms, Bowles and Gintis identify a dynamic relationship between the needs of capitalism in any given period and the way schools are structured and function. They argue:

> Major periods of educational change are responses to alternatives in the structure of economic life associated with the process of capital accumulation. The common school movement of the nineteenth century, we have

seen, developed to complement a burgeoning factory system increasingly rendering the family inadequate to the task of reproducing the capitalist division of labor. The Progressive Era accompanied the transition to corporate capitalism, in light of which the small, decentralized common school was manifestly anachronistic, both in its internal social relationships and in the degree to which it could be centrally controlled through enlightened social policy. . . . Crisis periods . . . appear in retrospect as the major turning points in U.S. educational history.[9]

Today, US capitalism is undergoing a period of major economic restructuring following the global meltdown of 2008. The neoliberal agenda for education is an attempt to meet the needs of capital in this period, and the crisis has given the ruling class increased leverage for implementing harsh policies. While neoliberal education initiatives were begun in the 1990s, they are both more urgent—and more possible—for the system today. It is important to clarify that even if we can identify various features of a broader neoliberal agenda, it is not the case that there is a clear consensus among the ruling class about a full plan, or even about each of these features. Privatization, discussed below in greater detail, is a good example. Typically, the term refers to the wholesale selling off of once-nationalized assets (for example, a utility company, an airline, a transportation network such as a rail system, and so on) to private companies. In the case of public schools, this is a bit more complicated. Even if some private corporations are chomping at the bit to get their share of the almost six hundred billion dollars spent on K–12 public education each year, there is not necessarily a wholesale agenda to cut all public funding of schools and turn them over to private corporations.

Whatever the political disagreements among the ruling class about how best to "reform" our schools, there are nevertheless five central features of the neoliberal assault on public education that we can identify. The first, austerity, is rooted in the scale of the economic crisis that engulfed the world economy in 2007–08. For a period of time between the economic downturn of the mid-1970s and the most recent crisis, capitalists were able to restore profitability and growth to the system by increasing productivity (that is, making fewer workers produce more goods), driving down wages, and attacking private-sector unions, deregulating huge sectors of the economy, and slashing taxes for corporations and the wealthy. The scale of the crisis this time, however, forced the state to step in and bail out the largest banks and corporations. The bailouts exacerbated a problem shared by every government around the world called the sovereign debt crisis, whereby government debt has begun to be a drag on capitalist productivity. Seizing on this opportunity, neoliberals have called for budget cuts in the name of "balancing the budget." That is, even after thirty years of cutbacks to public programs and the social safety net—which was always thin to begin with in the United States—the ruling class wants to get out of the current economic mess by making ordinary working people pay for its crisis.

The attacks in Michigan under Republican Rick Snyder, elected to office in 2010, provide a simple, if stunning, example. Governor Snyder has declared a budget crisis due to the state's $1.7 billion deficit. Exploiting this deficit, Snyder has demanded tax *hikes* for the poor and the elderly, a $270 cut in per-pupil funding for Michigan schools, an additional 15 percent cut to higher education, and that public employees be forced to pay 20 percent of their health care coverage. These cuts, according to Snyder, are the only way to cover the budget shortfall. And yet, instead of applying this new revenue to the deficit, Snyder instead has pushed through tax *cuts* for Michigan employers in the amount of . . . $1.7 billion. In other words, Michigan's poor, its elderly, its students have to do with less so that its employers can do with more. "Balancing the budget" has nothing to do with it—save for providing a convenient pretext to transfer wealth directly from ordinary people to the ruling class.[10]

Moreover, learning to live with less at school is not just about this or that budget cut. It is about a fundamental restructuring of the school system. Thus, austerity at school means sending layoff notices to every single teacher in a district, as the Detroit Public Schools' "emergency financial manager" did to 5,466 teachers and staff in April 2011.[11] It means closing schools—and selling the property—when class sizes are already at a ratio of thirty to one or higher. It means vilifying teachers and their "Cadillac" pensions and health plans as a pretext to break the union and drive down wages and benefits. This is what austerity at school looks like.

The second major feature of neoliberalism in public education is intensification of the "sorting machine" at school. This process—of separating out a small layer of youth who can move into white-collar, "knowledge economy" jobs from the rest of the students—may not be as apparent a feature of neoliberalism as are the financial attacks on education described above; however, it is just as consequential. This is especially true when political rhetoric focuses so much on fixing schools to improve US economic competitiveness and to produce workers for the "twenty-first-century economy." Take, for example, a line from President Obama's first major speech on education: "In 8th grade math, we've fallen to 9th place. Singapore's middle-schoolers outperform ours three to one. . . . It's time to prepare every child, everywhere in America, to out-compete any worker, anywhere in the world."[12]

We are told that restoring competitiveness requires standardized testing, closing "failing" schools, expanding charters, and making teachers work harder. But plenty of research has documented that such policies are not in fact capable of raising the skills of children overall to make them more "competitive."

In fact, that isn't really the point. Instead, the neoliberal approach further stratifies the education system to meet the needs of economic and political elites, because they hope to increase the skill levels of a *minority* of the population while investing as little as possible in the education of everyone else. Education is to be even more divided into distinct tiers, and access to it further rationed.

Increasingly, business accounting methods—such as test scores, value-added models to measure an individual teacher's impact on a student's test scores, and installing business executives to run schools and school systems instead of, say, educators—are used to identify some layers of the working class that can be funneled into higher education and employment as technical personnel, front-line managers, and professionals. Some schools may indeed improve scores as they focus on "test prep" at the expense of critical thinking and meaningful curriculum. Some charter schools may improve scores as they recruit out of public schools some higher-performing students with more stable lives. Those students who demonstrate the ability and willingness to fit into the mold of middle-level workers and supervisors can be afforded job opportunities.

But at a time when unemployment rates are triple those of the 1990s, significant numbers of working-class and poor children are relegated to the margins of the economy where they will be unable to find stable employment. And for many of those who do find jobs, education cannot in fact be the gateway toward a better future because there are just not enough living-wage jobs in the economy.[13] Thus, many students are being prepared for jobs where technical or critical skills don't matter—or for prison.[14]

Third, and directly related to the increasing stratification of public schools and their students, neoliberalism has upped the ante on using school as a mechanism of social control. This function of schooling is even more important in a time of crisis, when the living standards of students and their families are under attack and there are real dangers of rebellion. As Bowles and Gintis explain, neoliberal elites need schools to "help defuse and depoliticize the potentially explosive class relations" of our society.[15]

Part of this element of social control is an ideological shift in focus from education as a "public good" to education as "personal responsibility." In so doing, the crisis in education is no longer a public burden, but rather one for individual students, parents, and teachers to shoulder. One of the most profound reflections of this shift is the extent to which the term "educational equity" has all but disappeared from public conversations about reversing the legacy of racism in US schools. Instead, it has been replaced with a relentless focus on the "achievement gap." In other words, improving educational experiences and outcomes for youth of color is thus no longer a public, social, or systemic question, but rather a personal one measured above all by individual student performance on standardized tests.[16]

Moreover, charter schools and performance pay for teachers bring the ideology of competition into education, as opposed to the expectation that education should be a government-guaranteed right for all. Even when charters are nonprofits, this sends the message that we should trust privately managed entities instead of the public sector with our tax dollars. Sometimes, pushing free-market ideology is an explicit part of the plan: the original petition by Green Dot charter schools to take over Los Angeles's Locke High School required that students in history classes "demonstrate a belief in the values of democracy and capitalism."[17] A final, if crude, indication of this ideological shift is the ever-increasing amount of school time spent on testing and test preparation, which serves to further emphasize obedience over critical thinking.

Fourth, a critical feature of the neoliberal agenda for public education is privatization of one of the last major public assets in this country. It should come as no surprise that many private organizations and corporations are angling to get a piece of the almost six hundred billion dollars spent on K–12 education each year in this country—in 2009, the figure stood at $590.9 billion.[18] In an era when capital is desperate for avenues of profitable investment, privatization of public services becomes an attractive option—what David Harvey refers to as "accumulation through dispossession."[19] Of course, business leaders are excited about charter schools in particular because they are a mechanism for funneling public funds into private hands. And this dispossession is now formal federal policy: in order for states to qualify for any Race to the

Top (RTTT) money, they must increase the percentage of charter schools allowed to operate in that state. But privatization is occurring in other ways as well: textbook, curriculum, and testing companies have also been major beneficiaries of NCLB and RTTT, while many essential services that make schools function—from busing and custodial services to provision of substitute teachers and food preparation—have been outsourced to private bidders.

Fifth, and underscoring Klein's point mentioned earlier about government and private-sector collaboration to impose neoliberal policies, there has been a dramatic increase in the centralization of power over school systems, often placing control in the hands of one mayor or a state-appointed overseer.[20] As Bill Gates described it to the *New York Post*: "The cities where our foundation has put the most money is [*sic*] where there is a single person responsible."[21]

This feature of the attack on public education fits with the goals of local elites in urban areas who want to restructure their cities in ways that make them more hospitable to business investment (and consequently displace poor communities of color). For example, with Chicago's "Renaissance 2010" plan to "reconstitute" failing schools, "the mayor and Civic Committee are operating from a larger blueprint to make Chicago a 'world-class city' of global finance and business services, real estate development, and tourism, and education is part of this plan. Quality schools (and attractive housing) are essential to draw high-paid, creative workers for business and finance."[22] Moreover, in Chicago, as well as Washington, DC, replacing neighborhood schools with charter schools has gone hand in hand with the demolition of public housing.[23]

How Did We Get Here?

Current education policy in the United States is the result of a step-by-step erosion of the gains of the civil rights movement. The Reagan administration first sounded the alarm about a "crisis" in public education. Clinton brought in the private sector, paving the way for a major increase in the number of charter schools. George W. Bush's NCLB policy established state standardized tests as the determinants of school quality. And now the Obama administration is using federal funds in a time of economic crisis as a lever to increase privatization and pressure on teachers and to break teachers' unions.

As described in the previous two chapters in some detail, the civil rights movement held the government—and broader society—accountable for providing an equitable education to all children. As a result, the sixties and seventies saw federal laws that improved school funding, integration, bilingual education, and special education services. Those decades also saw a proliferation of experiments in pedagogy and demands for community control of schools.

The Reagan administration signaled the first major effort to beat back those gains with the 1983 publication of its now-infamous report, *A Nation at Risk*. The report claimed a "rise of mediocrity" in the nation's schools, citing dropping SAT scores and the increase in remedial classes being offered at community colleges.[24] It attacked the lack of "rigor" in the nation's schools, calling for higher expectations, more homework, national curriculum standards, and higher college admissions requirements. The report was also motivated by a fear that a poorly educated workforce would make the US economy less competitive. In the context of the Cold War, the report decried the way the United States was committing "educational disarmament." While *A Nation at Risk* focused on higher standards, it did not propose heavy-handed consequences for "failing" schools or "school choice" to undermine public schools. Nevertheless, it marked a turning point because it shifted the focus from supporting schools to placing higher demands on them, and from an emphasis on equity to strident calls for "excellence." These calls for excellence paralleled the shift in federal policy from jobs *creation* to jobs *training*.[25] As outlined in chapter 1, the blame for unemployment was shifted onto a lack of education as opposed to a lack of quality jobs.

The arguments in *A Nation at Risk* were carried through the standards movement during the administration of George H. W. Bush, which attempted to create a set of voluntary national curriculum standards for all public schools. While there is nothing wrong with a national discussion about what students should be learning, and in certain circumstances national mandates are needed against racist "state's rights" policies, it matters who is involved in the discussion and what they see as the purpose of schooling. In this case, the elder Bush administration saw this as a modernization effort to meet the changing needs of business by "align[ing] public education with the practices of modern, flexible, high-performance organizations . . . in the transition . . . to the postindustrial age."[26]

But it was under the Clinton administration that the private sector made its big entry into public schooling. Education policy fit in with the

"Reinventing Government" campaign through which Clinton hoped to prove his administration's commitment to big business's demands for cutting government bureaucracy. As Diane Ravitch explains: "The new thinking—now ensconced in both parties—saw the public school system as obsolete, because it is controlled by the government and burdened by bureaucracy. . . . With the collapse of Communism and the triumph of market reforms in most parts of the world, it did not seem to be much of a stretch to envision the application of the market model to schooling."[27]

The nation's first charter schools were established in Minnesota in 1991, and the Democratic Leadership Council endorsed charters early in the Clinton administration. In 1994, Congress established a program to give federal funds to charters as part of Clinton's education legislation. By fall 2001, there were 2,300 charter schools with nearly a half million students.[28]

Enter George W. Bush. Three days after his inauguration, Bush convened an education conference that led to his administration's NCLB policy. NCLB took another major step in distancing education policy from the civil rights era by making standardized test scores the primary measure of school quality. NCLB focused solely on measuring student achievement and imposing sanctions on schools that do not meet their Adequate Yearly Progress (AYP) test score targets. It also decreed that 100 percent of students would achieve proficiency on the tests by 2014, and mandated that states create timelines of how they would achieve this. The policy said nothing about how we might actually improve student achievement.

Under Obama, the neoliberal agenda has been accelerated primarily because of the scale of economic crisis—although it matters that as a Democrat, he faces far less opposition from unions and the left than previous presidents. Secretary of Education Arne Duncan is quite open about the fact that he is implementing a "shock doctrine" approach. In an interview with Roland Martin on the *Washington Watch* blog in January 2010, Duncan said, "I've spent a lot of time in New Orleans and this is a tough thing to say but I'm going to be really honest. The best thing that happened to the education system in New Orleans was Hurricane Katrina. That education system was a disaster. And it took Hurricane Katrina to wake up the community to say that we have to do better. And the progress that it made in four years since the hurricane, is unbelievable."[29]

The "unbelievable" progress Duncan referred to is about how after the hurricane, all New Orleans schools were closed and every teacher was fired.

Of New Orleans schools, 57 percent have now been reopened as non-union charter schools.[30] That half of New Orleans children are no longer in the public schools because they were driven from their homes doesn't seem to bother him.

Like a nationwide hurricane, the economic crisis has provided the "disaster/excuse" for pushing drastic changes to education policy nationwide. Speaking in San Francisco in May 2009, Arne Duncan said that California is facing a "moment of opportunity and a moment of crisis. . . . Despite how tough things are financially, it's often at times of crisis we get the reforms we need."[31] States have been plunged into such a deep budget crisis that they are rapidly revamping their education policies in hopes of attracting tiny portions of federal stimulus money from RTTT. Obama boasted about this in his January 2011 State of the Union speech: "That's why instead of just pouring money into a system that's not working, we launched a competition called Race to the Top. To all 50 states, we said, 'If you show us the most innovative plans to improve teacher quality and student achievement, we'll show you the money.' . . . For less than 1 percent of what we spend on education each year, it has led over 40 states to raise their standards for teaching and learning."[32]

The Obama-Duncan Agenda: A Race to the Bottom

Based on the outline described above of the main features of the neoliberal attack on public schools, and with some historical context of how these policies have come to dominate what "education reform" means, the remainder of this chapter looks in greater detail at the main tenets of the Obama administration's educational policies.

The Race to the Top Carrot and Stick

The best known and most ambitious is the RTTT program, announced in July 2009 as Obama's first major policy initiative on education. Bringing the spirit of free-market competition to the highest levels of government policy, RTTT asked that the fifty states plus the District of Columbia and Puerto Rico compete for a pool of $4.35 billion in stimulus funding for education.

RTTT's criteria for awarding grants are carefully calibrated to get states to do two main things: significantly expand charter schools and create data systems that allow teachers to be evaluated based on their students' test scores. In the selection process for RTTT applicants, fifty-eight points are awarded for "improving teacher and principal effectiveness based on performance" and forty points for "ensuring successful conditions for high-performing charters and other innovative schools," while only ten points are allotted for "making education funding a priority."[33]

To be eligible for a grant, states must link student test scores to individual teachers and principals for the purposes of evaluation. Applications are judged based on what percentage of a state's schools may be charters. RTTT guidelines suggest that "reviewers should give states high points if they have no caps [on the number of charter schools] or caps of 10 percent or more; medium points if they have caps of 5 to 10 percent; and low points if they have caps of less than 5 percent." Points are also earned for getting teachers' and other unions to sign memoranda of understanding agreeing to their "reform" plans.[34]

The RTTT funds are a tiny drop in the bucket compared to the scale of states' budget shortfalls. Yet the promise of these funds has been used to push through major changes to education policy: at least twenty-three states have overhauled teacher evaluation policies, lifted the cap on charter schools, or adopted punitive "turnaround" policies for their lowest-performing schools. For example, if California had been chosen in the first round, the state would have gotten at best seven hundred million dollars in one-time funds, scarcely 1 percent of its education budget. With these paltry funds as justification, the state passed a bill in December 2009 mandating "turnarounds" for the bottom 5 percent of schools and forcing schools to be converted to charters if 50 percent of parents sign a petition.[35] Obviously, politicians—from former Republican governor Arnold Schwarzenegger to liberal Democratic state senator Gloria Romero (who sponsored the new law)—pushed these policies not only to make California eligible for the grant money, but also because the policies coincided with some of their overall goals.[36]

The states chosen as winners of RTTT funds are those that have gone furthest toward implementing neoliberal policies. Florida was an early favorite because it already has a data system that tracks its students' test scores from preschool to college. Ohio was an early proponent of for-profit charter schools, which have had a horrible record in terms of student achievement.[37] Rhode Island was no doubt rewarded with RTTT funds for its dramatic attack on teachers at Central Falls High School. And five of the winners are southern "right-to-work" states with weak or nonexistent unions for teachers.

The administration is aiming to expand the program by $1.35 billion for 2011, and in July 2010 threatened to veto a House bill that would have redirected money from RTTT to save teachers' jobs.[38] "You could envision this going on until we felt like we've made significant progress across the country," one senior official said of the program. Without a major challenge, the competitive RTTT approach could shape school funding for many years to come.

Rebranding No Child Left Behind

When Obama took office, his administration signaled a desire to get rid of some of the negative connotations associated with NCLB. As the *Washington Post* reported, "The Obama administration has made clear that it is putting its own stamp on education reform. That will mean a new name and image for a law that has grown unpopular with many teachers and suburban parents, even though it was enacted with bipartisan support in Congress. 'It's like the new Coke. This is a rebranding effort,' said Joe Williams, executive director of Democrats for Education Reform."[39]

On March 15, 2010, the Obama administration released *A Blueprint for Reform: The Reauthorization of the ESEA*.[40] Despite whatever rebranding is going on (for example, Obama doesn't typically use the name "No Child Left Behind"), the *Blueprint* leaves all the basic pillars of Bush's law untouched. Like NCLB, the *Blueprint* focuses on "accountability" for teachers and schools based in large part on test scores.

The administration claims that the *Blueprint* changes the focus "from punishing failure to rewarding success," and schools that are improving will be granted more freedom from federal intervention. But the plan calls for increased consequences for low-performing schools. It sets up school turn-around grants which states can only receive if they choose one of four models for their most troubled schools: transformation (replacing the principal, extending the school day, and implementing new governance and "flexibility"); turnaround (replacing the principal and rehiring no more than 50 percent of the school staff); restart (closing the school and reopening it under the management of a charter operator); or closure.

These restructuring strategies are based on *The Turnaround Challenge*, the authoritative how-to guide by the Gates Foundation that Arne Duncan calls "the bible" for school restructuring.[41] Not surprisingly, studies by the Center on Education Policy have shown that these "federal restructuring strategies have very rarely helped schools improve student achievement enough to make Adequate Yearly Progress or exit restructuring."[42] Many of these strategies were first implemented in the Renaissance 2010 (Ren2010) program that Arne Duncan implemented as "chief executive officer" of Chicago Public Schools (CPS). Initiated by Mayor Richard Daley and the Commercial Club of Chicago—and with ninety million dollars in funding from the Gates Foundation—the goal of Ren2010 was to close sixty low-performing public schools and open one hundred new ones as small schools, charters, or "contract" schools by 2010. To date, Ren2010 has led to the closing of seventy-five schools and the opening of seventy new charters.[43]

The closing of neighborhood schools has caused great hardship for students who must relocate. On the one hand are the long commutes for students who need to connect to several train or bus routes just to get to school. On the other, there has been a spike in school violence in those neighborhoods in which students are forced to commute to schools in the territories of various gangs. For example, the number of students fatally shot on CPS campuses has nearly tripled since 2005.[44] Chicago parent Cheryl Johnson spoke at a CPS board meeting about the closure of her child's school: "Carver High School has been in our community ever since 1974. We should have a right to have our kids go to a school that is in the neighborhood, not to take two buses and to walk to a school that they've been fighting in for the last four or five years. . . . Renaissance 2010 is just an avenue for our kids to be killed on a regular basis."[45]

As Jitu Brown, Rico Gutstein, and Pauline Lipman explained in *Rethinking Schools*, "for affected communities who have longed for change, Renaissance 2010 has been traumatic, largely ineffective, and destabilizing to communities owed a significant 'education debt' (to quote Gloria Ladson-Billings) due to decades of being underserved."[46]

The problems of inner-city schools stem from poverty, inadequate funding and resources, underpaid teachers, and top-down control. It shouldn't surprise anyone that shutting these schools down or "reconstituting" them by firing dedicated teachers doesn't solve these problems. Moreover, in the *UCLA Law Review*, Andrew Spitser has argued that reconstitution is arbitrary, violates collective bargaining agreements, and has a negative effect on the quality of teachers and instruction. He wrote: "The loss of legitimacy and morale that would attend the labeling of a large number of schools as failing, and the upheaval caused by reconstitution in so many schools counsel further against reconstitution. . . . School officials need to take care that the methods used to hold schools accountable do not end up punishing the children that [they are] intended to help. . . . Reconstitution threatens to do just that."[47] By continuing to subject schools to these failed strategies, the Obama-Duncan *Blueprint* intensifies the stratification of schools and continues to mete out the harshest punishments to those with the greatest needs.

Like NCLB, the *Blueprint* also sets unattainable goals for school improvement, requiring all students to be on track to be "career and college ready" by 2020. As Monty Neill of the National Center for Fair and Open Testing explained, "If this reasonable goal is attached to an impossible timeline, it will simply become the new basis for continuing to castigate schools and teachers for not accomplishing what society has failed to provide the resources to accomplish."[48]

Teacher Quality and Value-Added Measures

To help make the blame on teachers stick and seem more credible, an "objective" measure of teacher quality is needed. School districts, politicians, and the media have largely championed value-added measures (VAMs), which apply corporate terminology and methods to judging teachers, despite voluminous research that proves their inaccuracy.

VAMs were developed mainly by William Sanders, a professor in the College of Business Administration at the University of Tennessee who had been a consultant for the agricultural, manufacturing, and engineering industries. In order to measure how much "value" a teacher has added to his or her student-products, students' test scores at the beginning of the school year are compared with those at the end of the year. Sanders found a wide range of "value added" by various teachers, and used his research to argue that "teacher quality" is more important than any other single factor in determining educational outcomes. He later argued that the racial "achievement gap" could be closed within three years if low-income students of color were simply assigned the teachers with high "value-added."[49]

Sanders contrasted his findings with what he called a "laissez-faire approach."[50] By claiming that funding, poverty, and broader societal factors have only a marginal impact on the educational process, the VAM ideology conveniently serves to absolve the powerful of blame and place all the pressure on education workers. Dozens of school systems, including those in Chicago, New York, and Washington, DC, are already using VAMs to measure the performance of schools or teachers. Many more are expected to join them, since school districts that do not use VAMs are ineligible for RTTT funds.[51]

In August 2010, the *Los Angeles Times* published the value-added ratings of six thousand elementary school teachers, rating them as "most effective," "more effective," "average," "less effective," or "least effective." The devastating impact of this stunt on teacher morale was immediately felt when dedicated LA teacher Rigoberto Ruelas committed suicide, shortly after he was listed as "less effective" by the newspaper.[52] Ignoring the meaning of the tragedy, the Los Angeles school board pushed forward with its demand that VAMs should constitute 30 percent of a teacher's evaluation (the percentage required by RTTT).

On the surface, VAMs might seem to be a fairer way of evaluating teachers, since they control for the question of which students are assigned to each teacher and simply measure whether those students have improved in that teacher's class. But what about the other things that affect how a student performs on a given test day—such as motivation, hunger, stress, problems at home, or absences during the year? VAMs place the results of all these problems at the feet of the individual teacher.

Because they don't actually measure all these "outside" factors, VAM teacher ratings are highly unstable from one year to the next. In a briefing report issued in August 2010, the Economic Policy Institute reported its survey of research on VAMs and concluded:

> One study found that across five large urban districts, among teachers who were ranked in the top 20 percent of effectiveness in the first year, fewer than a third were in that top group the next year, and another third moved all the way down to the bottom 40 percent. Another found that teachers' effectiveness ratings in one year could only predict from 4 percent to 16 percent of the variation in such ratings in the following year. A teacher who appears to be very ineffective in one year might have a dramatically different result the following year.[53]

The use of VAMs is not only devastating for teachers, but also contributes to the erosion of the quality of education for students. VAMs wrongly assume that standardized tests are an accurate way of measuring student learning. A teacher whose students are successful in critical thinking and project-based learning may not register as "effective" on the narrow measure of multiple-choice tests. The more that teachers' own evaluations are tied to these test scores, the more "teaching to the test" will replace authentic curriculum and assessments.

Another dangerous result of the value-added focus is that it creates a disincentive to teach the most disadvantaged students who may improve more slowly on tests. Moreover, it may exacerbate the bias in terms of which schools are labeled as "failing." In the *Los Angeles Times* study, the twenty-five schools deemed "least effective" were those in which African American and Latino students accounted for an average of 91 percent of the student population, while 84 percent qualified for free or reduced student lunch. In the twenty-five schools deemed most effective, however, African American and Latino students made up 59 percent of the population, and 62 percent of the students qualified for free or reduced lunch.[54] That a school's "effectiveness" is so strongly correlated with the racial makeup and economic status of its student population suggests that racism and poverty are what keep our schools unequal. Nevertheless, the ideology of VAMs is so useful to the ruling class that it trumps all research and evidence. As Diane Ravitch has argued, "the problem with using Value Added in any form is that . . . it has a pseudo-scientific aura about it, and in this climate, it will dominate all other forms of evaluation."[55]

School district administrations are hoping that test-score-based evaluations will help to weaken teacher tenure and seniority protections. Administrators want to be able to discipline and get rid of teachers more easily—especially those who are outspoken. Moreover, districts stand to save millions of dollars if they can reduce the number of veteran teachers who command higher pay and full benefits. Unfortunately, some teachers' unions are going along with this—American Federation of Teachers (AFT) president Randi Weingarten now proposes contracts in which teachers who are rated unsatisfactory would be given one year to improve or be fired within a hundred days.

Teacher Quality and Performance Pay

Not only are VAMs being used to determine ever-larger proportions of teachers' annual ratings, but those ratings are increasingly linked to how teachers are paid, known as *performance* or *merit pay*. In a March 2009 speech on education, Obama argued, "Too many supporters of my party have resisted the idea of rewarding excellence in teaching with extra pay, even though we know it can make a difference in the classroom." Duncan later clarified what "excellence in teaching" means: improving student test scores. "What you want to do is really identify the best and brightest by a range of metrics, including student achievement," he told the Associated Press.[56]

The push toward performance pay will be disastrous for three main reasons. First, it will tend to punish teachers in the most challenging schools in poorer districts, who must battle larger obstacles to improving their students' learning outcomes. Teachers in less challenging schools and districts with more affluent students will be rewarded. In one county in Florida where performance pay has been most fully implemented, three-fourths of the nearly five thousand teachers who received performance pay worked at more affluent schools, and only 3 percent worked at low-income schools.[57]

Second, performance pay creates an atmosphere of competition rather than collaboration among teachers. This will severely weaken union solidarity, and is poisonous to the kind of collaboration that is so essential for good teaching. As the creators of the website Teachers for CEO Merit Pay explain: "Performance pay structures in education force teachers to compete for a limited pool of merit-pay money, instead of collaborating to provide the best possible education. This creates a disincentive for teachers to share information and teaching techniques. Thus, the main way teachers learn their craft—studying from their colleagues—is effectively discarded. If you think we have turnover problems in teaching now, wait until new teachers have no one to turn to."[58] Even when monetary rewards are granted to whole schools instead of individual teachers, as is the case with union-supported performance pay schemes in New Haven and New York City, this can lead to finger-pointing within schools that don't get the money.[59]

Third, performance pay only raises the already-high stakes of testing, which has been proven to be both biased and a poor gauge of actual student learning. In its report, the National Center for Fair and Open Testing reviewed a range of research showing that performance pay leads to score inflation, narrowing the curriculum, flawed results from for-profit testing companies, and a distortion of the goals of education—and that it may not even raise test scores.[60]

If we want to improve the quality of education, we have to recognize the obvious fact that the conditions of students' lives play a huge role in their learning process. It is the high number of children living in poverty (at least 20 percent, highest among all industrialized countries) that accounts for the poor performance of the United States on international tests.[61] Even a report by the US Department of Education on the use of test scores to evaluate teachers argues that "more than 90 percent of the variation in student score gains is due to the variation in *student-level* factors that are not under control of the teacher."[62]

Charter Schools

The Secretary believes that high-performing charter schools can be an educational lifeline in communities with chronically low-achieving regular public schools. In such cases, charter schools . . . offer one of the most promising options for breaking the cycle of educational failure.
—"Race to the Top Program: Guidance and FAQs"

Leaders across the political spectrum are promoting charter schools as the magic-bullet solution for education. In 2009, Reverend Al Sharpton and right-winger Newt Gingrich toured the nation together as special envoys from the president to promote charter schools. "If we could come together on education, I think it's an example to the kids that some things should be above our differences," said Sharpton of this strange partnership.[63]

Charter schools are publicly funded but governed by institutions outside the public school system, including businesses, nonprofit organizations, universities, and groups of individuals who write a charter and get it approved. About a quarter of charter schools are run by for-profit companies known as Education Management Organizations (EMOs), while the majority are run by nonprofit Charter Management Organizations (CMOs) and other groups such as universities.

By 2010 charters grew from only a handful of schools in the early 1990s to some 4,600 enrolling 1.4 million children nationwide.[64] The National Alliance for Public Charter Schools boasts, "Today, a record 14 communities have more than 20 percent of their public school students enrolled in public charter schools, eight more than the number from just three years ago. Additionally, 72 communities now have at least 10 percent of public school students in charter schools, 27 more than three years ago."[65] Indeed, charter schools would not have been able to expand so rapidly in so many cities if they were not tapping into a widespread, genuine, and justified frustration with the state of our traditional public schools. But after a decade of significant charter school growth, research and experience from around the country shows that these schools are failing to serve students with the greatest needs, disrupting communities, increasing racial segregation of schools, and introducing new kinds of corruption into education, all while producing similar or worse educational outcomes than public schools. The evidence is mounting that placing education into the hands of unelected, privately run organizations is a disaster for students, teachers, and communities. Below is a brief overview of some of that research.

Equity and Access

On the surface, the existence of a variety of schools from which parents could choose would appear to provide more opportunities for disadvantaged students. In fact, quite the opposite is the case, as an important study from the UCLA Civil Rights Project explains. It is worth quoting the study at length:

> The ability to choose assumes ready exposure to available school options. Research suggests that families' access to the educational marketplace is unequally constrained by a number of factors, including contact with advantaged social networks, . . . language barriers, socioeconomic status and the ability of parents to arrange transportation for their schoolchildren. Education studies both in the U.S. context and abroad . . . all highlight a basic point. Unrestricted choice results in stratification.
>
> Take, for example, the application process for a new charter school. A parent or student must first hear about the charter program, which is dependent on the extent to which the new school has conducted outreach and advertising, whether materials were available in multiple languages, and/or if an encounter with another parent or contact provided information about the charter. The family must then navigate the application process, which often involves a lottery but also can mean a combination of other requirements like testing, teacher recommendations, parental involvement commitment or essays. If the student is accepted, then transportation to and from the school may have to be provided by the parent.
>
> On the other side of the process . . . significant private investment augments public support for charter schools. Targeted recruitment of students could help charter schools accomplish achievement promises made to these private funders. It follows that school choice . . . will almost always exacerbate inequality.[66]

One effect of charters' drive to improve their test scores is that students with disabilities are systematically marginalized. Moreover, the pressure to reduce costs means that they often do not employ the extra staff necessary to serve special education students. In 2009, students with disabilities attending charter schools in Los Angeles made up 7.6 percent of the overall charter student population, but 11.3 percent of the overall student population attending district-operated schools. During the 2008–09 school year, just 8.1 percent of LA charter schools offered special day programs for students with disabilities. In contrast, 87 percent of district-operated schools provided this same program option.[67] Charters also tend to enroll fewer emergent bilinguals. A 2009 *Boston Globe* study found that English learners were nearly one-fifth of Boston's public school enrollment, but just 4 percent of charter school students.[68]

Another serious concern is the increase in racial segregation associated with charter schools. UCLA's Civil Rights Project study found higher levels of segregation for Black students in charter schools than in public schools, even though public school segregation has been growing steadily for two decades.[69] Other studies have documented increased racial segregation due to "school choice" programs in North Carolina and New Jersey.[70] Unlike magnet schools that were established to further school integration by bringing together students from different parts of a city, charter schools tend to further segregation because they make enrollment decisions without regard to the impact on the school system as a whole. Thus the "market-oriented model of choice" tends to further segregate students based on resources, abilities, language, and race.[71]

Excellence

Charter schools aim to prove their success on the basis of test scores. And charters have a number of advantages that one might expect to lead to better scores than traditional public schools—"skimming off" better students, smaller class sizes, and additional resources from private sources. But even on the narrow measure of standardized testing, most charters are not achieving "excellence."

A 2003 national study by the Department of Education under George W. Bush found that charter schools performed, on average, no better than traditional public schools.[72] The study was initially suppressed because it hadn't reached the desired conclusions. A 2009 study by two Stanford economists involved an enormous sample, 70 percent of all charter students. It found that an astonishing 83 percent of charter schools were either no better or *actually worse* than traditional public schools serving similar populations. Indeed, the authors concluded that bad charter schools outnumber good ones by a ratio of roughly two to one.[73]

Why are charters unable to soar ahead of public schools in their academic results? For the quarter of charters that are run for profit, a focus on the bottom line compromises educational quality. In Ohio, where more than half of the state's charter money goes to for-profit companies, charters drastically lag behind traditional public schools. Only 8 percent of charters received a rating of excellent or effective, compared to 63 percent of public schools.[74] One recent exposé of charter schools in Ohio sheds light on why this is the case. Many of the charter schools included in the analysis have driven down costs by lowering teacher salaries while dramatically increasing class sizes and the administrator-teacher ratio. Because charter schools receive state funding on the same per-pupil basis as traditional public schools, upping these ratios leads directly to greater profits for the charter holders—often privately held corporations—at the expense of educational quality.[75]

And the quality of education at all charter schools is compromised by the fact that charter school teachers on average have far fewer years of experience than teachers at traditional public schools. Without the protection of strong unions, charter school teachers are more likely to burn out and leave the profession. In a 2009 study, researchers found a turnover rate of 25 percent among charter school teachers as compared with 14 percent among public school teachers. They found that the odds of a charter school teacher leaving the profession versus staying in the same school are 132 percent greater than those of a public school teacher. They found that the "turnover gap" was not a result of charter schools getting rid of "underperforming" teachers, but rather less experienced teachers voluntarily leaving the profession.[76]

Nevertheless, there will be instances where charter schools will be able to outperform traditional public schools due to their greater resources and more selective admissions. As Diane Ravitch explains, "The question for the future is whether the continued growth of charter schools in urban districts will leave regular public schools with the most difficult students to educate, thus creating a two-tier system of widening inequality. If so, we can safely predict that future studies will 'prove' the success of charter schools and the failure of regular schools. . . . As charter schools increase in number and able students enroll in them, the regular public schools in the nation's cities will be locked into a downward trajectory."[77] Regardless of test score results, charter schools' business model for education is not compatible with truly deep and meaningful learning. And the advantages that come with increased resources should be extended to all students—not just a select few.

Parent and Community Empowerment

The promise of parent empowerment has been one of charter schools' major tools in getting support for their agenda. Undoubtedly, parents have been mobilized to push for charter school expansion, and many charter school parents are involved in their children's schools. But truly empowering parents with a voice in the school system would run counter to the neoliberal goals of centralizing control over schools, introducing corporate forces into education, and gentrifying poor communities.

Before Arne Duncan's Ren2010 plan, Chicago public schools had a remarkable mechanism for parent and community input—Local School Councils (LSCs). LSCs have played an important role in resistance at several of the schools slated for closure under Ren2010. Because Duncan viewed the LSCs as an obstacle to his plan, he publicly stated in April 2007 that he wanted to break their "monopoly." In a speech to Chicago business leaders, Board of Education president Rufus Williams likened the relationship between LSCs and schools to having a chain of hotels being run by "those who sleep in the hotels."[78] If it is successful in dismantling the LSCs, Ren2010 will have destroyed what is "probably the most radical school reform in the country and . . . the largest body of elected, low-income people of color (especially women) in the United States."[79]

In Los Angeles, Green Dot charter schools organized the Los Angeles Parents Union (LAPU) to push for an expansion of charter schools. The LAPU renamed itself "Parent Revolution," yet parents who don't agree with their point of view are locked out of LAPU meetings.[80] In March 2010, Green Dot's unelected board of directors announced a decision to close one of its high schools, known as Ánimo Justice, in South LA. CEO Marco Petruzzi claimed that budget constraints made the closing necessary, and that Ánimo Justice was chosen "because it has not equaled other Green Dot schools in performance and enrollment."[81] In reality, Ánimo Justice had the highest percentage of emergent bilinguals of any Green Dot school.

In subsequent days, four hundred Green Dot students held a sit-in on their campus, and students and parents held a march and rally. Two students carried a sign that read, "*Tenemos el ánimo, dónde está la justicia?*" (We've got the spirit, where is the justice?) Exasperated parents demanded to talk with Green Dot's CEO and school officials but were turned away. The "Parent Revolution" group was nowhere to be found. "Green Dot promised us a quality education and a democratic school where our voice counts," said one parent. "So why is our school being shut down with no parent and student say?"[82]

Of course, the exclusion of parents' voices is a problem throughout the public school system. Most public schools are hostile and unwelcoming places for parents, where parents are only invited when there is a problem with their children's behavior. Giving parents a real say in their children's schools has to be a major goal of our struggle. But when schools are managed by unelected boards of directors obsessed with improving test scores, there will be an even stronger tendency to exclude parents from meaningful decisions.

While parents and teachers are marginalized, some people are feeling very much empowered by charter schools. A 2009 *New York Times* article showed the enthusiasm of New York's exclusive club of hedge fund managers for investing in charter schools. As the *Times* explained, "it is impossible to ignore that in New York, hedge funds are at the [charter school] movement's epicenter. The schools are 'exactly the kind of investment people in our industry spend our days trying to stumble on,' [hedge fund manager] Mr. Curry said, 'with incredible cash flow, even if in this case we don't ourselves get any of it.' . . . The reference is to the fact that New York State contributes 75 to 90 percent of the amount per student that public schools receive."[83]

The Attack on Unions

The following chapter discusses in greater detail the impact that neoliberal educational policies have had on teachers' unions. However, the central role that charter schools have played on attacking unions merits mention here, as well. Specifically, the growth of charter schools has caused a marked decrease in the number of teachers represented by unions. In the states where charter schools are expanding most rapidly, the density of teachers' union members is declining. In some places, like New Orleans, charter schools have been an integral part of the blueprint to obliterate whole bargaining units, like United Teachers of New Orleans.

These attacks have had a disproportionate impact on teachers of color. In Chicago, school closings have led to a 5 percent decline in the number of African American teachers since the beginning of Ren2010 in 2004, while the percentages of all other racial groups have increased.[84] The attack on teachers' unions is a major assault on the labor movement in a place where there is tremendous potential for "social justice unionism" to emerge through the organic connections between teachers and communities.

Grassroots Democratic Reform versus Top-Down Corporate Reform

The neoliberal assault on education has the potential to significantly dismantle public schools and teachers' unions within the next decade. Challenging it will require that we build a movement that is both militant and visionary about the future of public education. To create a broad movement of teachers, parents, and students, we have to continually tie the issues of reform, resources, and union rights together. We should fight to stop the privatization of our schools by unionizing charter school teachers—which will eliminate the advantage charters gain from paying teachers poorly—and ultimately bring those schools back into the publicly managed system.

We have to demand a dramatic influx of resources into our public schools on the scale of the hundreds of billions that have been wasted on bailouts for banks and imperialist wars in the Middle East. A movement for public education has the potential to lead the way and open up a much broader challenge to all the broken promises and conservative policies of the Obama administration: the attacks on all public sector unions, the budget cuts to all important social services, and the funding of banks, prisons, and war instead of people's needs for jobs with a living wage, decent housing, health care, and so on. We should demand that funds be used for hundreds of thousands of new teachers, rebuilding and upgrading buildings, reducing class sizes, and greatly expanding early childhood education. At the very same time as we demand a dramatic expansion of resources for our schools and communities, we must put forward our own solutions to transform the educational process in our schools.

We need to be part of the small struggles to improve schools in the here and now, because these will help build the community coalitions and the organized power to fight for the massive increase in resources that we need. To confront the dual attack of budget cuts and top-down reform, we need a dual strategy of community-driven reform combined with a constant and escalating fight for the resources our students deserve. Teachers, parents, and students know what is needed and are daily developing innovative curriculum and programs to make learning deeper and more meaningful for students. Increased parent input in schools, project-based learning, authentic assessments, constructivist literacy strategies, internships, projects that connect learning with students' communities, interdisciplinary instruction that fosters collaboration among teachers of different disciplines—these are just a few of the many types of teacher- and parent-driven school reform being developed by activists around the country.

At the same time, if we see that the attacks on public education are being driven by the needs of maximizing the profitability of our economic system, then we have to ask what the alternatives to this system are. The most important characteristic of neoliberalism is that it uses the power of the state to redistribute wealth from the bottom to the top of society. As Bowles and Gintis argued:

> What we demand of U.S. schools is perfectly straightforward. We envision an educational system which, in the process of reproducing society, vigorously promotes personal development and social equality. What we have shown is equally straightforward: The major characteristics of the educational system in the United States today flow directly from its role in producing a work force able and willing to staff occupational positions in the capitalist system. We conclude that the creation of an equal and liberating school system requires a revolutionary transformation of economic life.[85]

Students, Parents, and Teachers Nationwide Protest Gutting of Public Education

Rose Aguilar

The May 13, 2011, edition of Truthout *included this comprehensive roundup by Rose Aguilar of critical—and inspiring—struggles that students, parents, and teachers were waging.[1] Some of the struggles that she describes are larger and some are smaller. But each one is instrumental in rebuilding civil rights and labor movements that can beat back the sort of neoliberal attacks described throughout the previous chapter and lay the groundwork for a more liberatory education.*

When eighteen-year-old Tiffini Baldwin decided to take part in a peaceful sit-in to speak out against the possible closure of Catherine Ferguson Academy (CFA), a public school for pregnant girls and teen moms in Detroit, Michigan, she didn't think she'd be arrested. "What's wrong with standing up for education? When the cops actually showed up, I was afraid. I was more afraid for my three-year-old daughter," Baldwin said. "The cops were trying to intimidate us the entire time, saying they would take our babies away, but I knew that wasn't true because we met with lawyers before the action."

In an interview with *Voice of Detroit*, seventeen-year-old Ashley Matthews said the cop who arrested her slammed her down on her stomach on the floor. "All the girls went berserk, telling him to get off me, but he was just wiping up the floor with me. He pressed his thumbs in my neck, and he tightened the handcuffs so hard that I have bruises there. I cried at first, but then I made myself stop."

For most of the girls, the April 15 sit-in was their first taste of activism. "I've had political discussions every now and then, but this is the first time I've ever stood up for something I believe in," said Baldwin. "Since the action, I've become a lot more politically active."

Baldwin graduated from CFA last year and is now a freshman in college studying to be a physical therapist's assistant. She said enrolling in the school is the best decision she's ever made. "I learned how to interact with my child, how to handle outbursts, how to play with her and what questions to ask her. It would have taken me a lot longer to develop those skills without that education," she said. "The staff is so comforting and compassionate. They have the students' best interests at heart. I'm so proud I went to that school. It will always have a special place in my heart. It's like a second home to me."

CFA, which serves a majority Black teen population in one of the poorest cities in the country, has received national and international media attention and is the subject of the award-winning documentary *Grown in Detroit*. "Many of the teens come from underprivileged backgrounds and are faced with daily challenges that infringe upon their educational opportunities," according to the film's website. "The Catherine Ferguson Academy strives to provide quality education in order to ensure a bright future for each child. The goal of the principal and teachers at the academy is to prevent the pregnancy cycle from reoccurring in the next generation of infants. Lots used for farming and a barn built by the students lie adjacent to the school. The barn houses a variety of farm animals that the students help care for."

Nicole Conaway, a CFA science teacher who joined her students at the April 15 action, said that, in addition to receiving national attention, the action is waking young people up. "Students are responding," she said. "This is a major attack on the right to public education. It's the biggest attack of the century, and we're not going to sit back and let it happen."

According to Conaway, all of the sixty-five young women who graduated from CFA last year were accepted to postsecondary programs. No other public school that she knows of in the state can boast such an impressive record.

So, why would a school for pregnant girls and teen moms with a 97 percent average daily attendance rate and a 100 percent college acceptance rate be slated to either close or turn into a privately run, nonunion charter? CFA is just one of more than fifty Detroit public schools on Emergency Financial Manager Robert Bobb's list. "Robert Bobb's mission is to shut down the school district. He gets paid by various charter interests. It's a terrible situation," said Elena Herrada, an appointed member of the Detroit Public School Board whose district includes CFA. She also attended the April 15 sit-in. "It was so infuriating. The police wouldn't let me in, even though I represent that school in my district!"

When Bobb announced the plan in March, he said it would help cut the district's $327 million deficit. In April, he issued layoff notices to all of the district's 5,466 public school teachers. Calls to Bobb's office weren't returned. Herrada said she's been waiting to receive answers from her Freedom of Information Act requests for weeks. "They don't have to answer to anyone. All they have to do is deliver money to the state. In this case, they're taking the money that's intended for poor students and concentrating it into the pockets of the few."

According to *Forbes*'s E. D. Kain, Bobb is a recent graduate of the Broad Foundation's Superintendents Academy. The Broad Foundation, along with the Kellogg Foundation, pays Bobb $145,000 a year on top of his $280,000 government salary. For those of you not familiar with Broad, it is one of the leading foundations promoting school choice and privatization across the country. One might almost think that paying a public official hundreds of thousands of dollars a year might amount to nothing short of bribery, especially given the very specific agenda of a group like the Broad Foundation.

This is nothing short of a coordinated effort between the billionaire foundations pushing school reform and Tea Party conservatives intent on slashing benefits and ending collective bargaining rights. Public schools are under assault by the forces of privatization, and public school teachers face benefit and salary cuts while the very rich are promised tax cuts. Similar efforts are under way in Florida and Wisconsin.

"Detroit is the epicenter of this struggle, because if it can be done in Detroit, it can be done in every other major city," said Herrada. "The national media has created a narrative that we can't govern ourselves. We don't deserve to be in charge of our own resources." Herrada said government officials might cancel upcoming school board elections, claiming they're too expensive. "People are so angry. It's becoming an act of resistance to read. There are eight-mile areas of Detroit without a school. We no longer have the right to education. There is no transportation. It's not safe for kids to walk. I wouldn't let my kids walk to school," she said. "We have to continue the battle. There are a lot of good people fighting this battle in Detroit. People are on the front lines. They've become really worried about where we're headed."

Because the situation is so dire in hundreds of school districts across the country, students are standing up, raising their voices, organizing and finding inspiration from each other's actions. "I hope the girls in Detroit know that what they're doing is making a real difference and giving people agency," said Elisa Meza, a student at the University of Arizona and youth organizer with United Non-Discriminatory Individuals Demanding Our Studies (UNIDOS). "These movements are spreading across the country. We're all in this together."

On April 26, nine members of UNIDOS chained themselves to the Tucson School Board members' seats before a Unified School District meeting was scheduled to begin. The board was expected to introduce a resolution to turn ethnic studies courses into electives. The nonviolent demonstration, which received widespread support from the audience, forced the board to postpone its vote. Because the board ordered Tucson police to remain outside, no arrests were made.

Mayra Feliciano, a seventeen-year-old Rincon High School senior, took part in the action after receiving no response to letter-writing campaigns and boycotts. "We tried to communicate, but they failed to listen to us," she said. "They're finally listening." Like Baldwin, this was Feliciano's first action. "I was nervous. My heart was racing. I've never done anything like this before," she said. "I would see people fighting for what was right on TV. I thought they were brave, and there I was, sitting at home doing nothing. I became more involved and aware after taking an ethnic studies class. Now, I know what it takes to fight and make demands. I've become more organized. I see things differently now." Feliciano said UNIDOS won't back down until the resolution is withdrawn. "I'm not going to stop. This is just the beginning for me."

Here are a number of education actions that have taken place over the past few weeks:

- On Monday, more than a thousand California teachers, students, and their supporters kicked off a weeklong "State of Emergency" for public education, with rallies, teach-ins, and protests planned across the state. Over the past three years, education funding in California has lost a whopping $20 billion, forcing school districts to cut back on basic services and lay off more than forty thousand teachers, nurses, counselors, and support staff. Some schools no longer have any counselors.
- California Watch, a website run by the Center for Investigative Reporting, reports that State Treasurer Bill Lockyer recently suggested that budget cuts might shorten the school year by two months.[2] More than

sixty-five demonstrators, including several teachers, were arrested for staying inside the California State capitol in Sacramento after closing time to speak out against massive education cuts. Earlier in the day, hundreds of teachers converged on the capitol, chanting, "Tax, tax, tax, the rich; we can solve the deficit."

- About a hundred educators gathered at 5:30 a.m. in San Francisco and marched to the offices of the San Francisco Unified School District (SFUSD). "I think it's time to get mad as hell and say, 'Enough.' This is a disgrace, a national disgrace," said SFUSD superintendent Carlos Garcia to the early morning crowd. The district recently passed a resolution to issue layoff notices to more than three hundred teachers, administrators, aides, and civil service employees.

- Also on Monday, hundreds of citizens protested in front of the Washington, DC, American Federation for Children summit, which featured Wisconsin Governor Scott Walker and former DC schools chancellor Michelle Rhee as keynote speakers. Salon's Alex Pareene described the federation as a right-wing "education reform" organization founded and funded by religious-right activist multimillionaire Betsy DeVos (former Republican candidate for governor of Michigan and sister of Blackwater founder Erik Prince) and dedicated to electing state legislators who'll fund Christian schools with taxpayer money and crush public employees' unions—is having a party in Washington, D.C., today, and they have invited Republican governors who have been working to fix education forever by firing all the greedy teachers and letting profit-seeking private interests manage the schools more "efficiently."

- On Tuesday, more than three hundred Huntington Park High School students walked out of class to protest budget cuts and layoffs proposed by the Los Angeles Unified School District. KTLA reported that the district is considering a plan to require all faculty and staff to reapply for their jobs. If California fails to find a source of revenue, seven thousand Los Angeles district employees might lose their jobs.

- In Venice, California, about fifty Walgrove Avenue Elementary parents, teachers, and students wore red shirts while waving signs that read, "Education Can't Wait," and "Cuts Hurt Kids." "Three of our most dynamic teachers all got pink slips. I'm pissed!" said parent Francine Nellis in an interview with *VenicePatch*.

- California educators held "grade-ins" at malls and farmers' markets across the state to let the public know about all of the extra work they do after the last bell rings. "This is just for today," said Dale Murphy, a Reidy Creek Elementary teacher in Escondido, California, in an interview with the *North County Times*. Murphy brought a two-inch stack of papers to the Westfield North County mall, where she gathered with about 150 fellow teachers. "They stop paying us at three o'clock, but I don't leave school until five o'clock or six o'clock. I go home and feed my family, and then I'm working, grading papers and essays until ten o'clock every night."

- On April 30, more than a thousand teachers, education advocates, and their supporters rallied outside the University of Michigan commencement celebration to speak out against Republican Governor Rick Snyder's proposal to move money from the state's K–12 funds to give businesses $1.8 billion in tax cuts. "We're here for kids and we're here for our jobs and we're here for the state of Michigan," said Ann Arbor teacher Judith Dewoskin in an interview with the *Huffington Post*. "There's a sign here; it's beautiful; it says, 'The Reverse Robin Hood.' He's taking money away from the poor to give to the rich, which is really not a good thing to do in a state that is going down economically." In his commencement address, Governor Snyder told graduates that they need "a mission for the future. My mission is to make the world a better place and say I added value." A few dozen students turned their backs on Governor Snyder while he spoke.

- On April 26, twelve UC Berkeley students began a hunger strike to oppose the consolidation of ethnic studies with gender and women's studies and African American studies, resulting in staff reductions and the demotion of faculty to half-time. University officials say the consolidation would save five hundred thousand dollars in staff costs. "Even though you're physically hurting, you need to make sure your spirit is in good shape," said Zolia Lara-Cea, a third-year ethnic studies student, in an interview with *Berkeleyside*. "They're [the staff and faculty in the department] part of our family. An assault on them is an assault on our family." "We're still here, we're still fighting, and, basically, we're not going anywhere," said Lara-Cea in an interview with *New America Media*. As of Wednesday, seven people were still striking.

5

Teachers' Unions and Social Justice
Jesse Hagopian and John T. Green

*Now, when I say question the whole society, it means ultimately coming
to see that the problem of racism, the problem of exploitation, and the problem
of war are all tied together. These are the triple evils that
are interrelated.*
    —Dr. Martin Luther King Jr., "Where Do We Go from Here?"

*The two most dynamic movements that reshaped the nation during the past
three decades are the labor and civil rights movements. Our combined strength
is potentially enormous.*
    —Dr. Martin Luther King Jr., speech delivered on October 7, 1965,
    at the Illinois state AFL-CIO convention

If King is right that the problems of racism, exploitation, and war are interconnected, then movements against any one of them must fight all of them
in order to succeed. Moreover, if King is correct in his assessment of the potential power in the merging of civil rights and labor movements, then it is
clear that fights for social justice must become a central aim of unions.

Teachers' unions are critical today for those concerned about public
education, democratic rights for workers, and pushing back against Corporate America. They give us the right to exercise our most powerful weapon—
withholding our labor to demand justice. They protect academic freedom
and teacher creativity, which are particularly crucial in this era of scripted
curricula and standardized testing. And they give workers due process and
legal protection from being fired at the whim of capricious administrators
or axe-happy budget-slashers. Additionally—but just as important—unions
provide a key venue for organizing with parents without the fear of reprisal
by power-hungry administrators.

*Special thanks to Lee Sustar and Sharon Smith
for their editorial feedback on this chapter.* 141

The interests of teachers and the community coincide: smaller class size is not just about better working conditions for teachers, but also about the quality of education for our children. When teachers are better paid and more highly valued, as they are when represented by unions, the conditions then exist for a much higher quality of education. It is no accident, for example, that nine of the ten states with the highest average achievement scores on the last four rounds of testing conducted by the National Assessment of Educational Progress are those with the largest number of teachers covered by union contracts.[1]

The history of teacher unionism provides inspiring examples of struggles for social justice. At times, teachers' unions have led movements to tax the rich, demanding that the wealthy pay more to support public services. In Illinois, the movement to organize women teachers was an integral part of the struggle to win the right to vote. During the Great Depression, teachers' unions stood up to budget cuts. At the same time, particularly in New York, they organized against racism and fought for equal access to education and culturally relevant curriculum. The 1960s and '70s brought with them a wave of radical, often illegal, teacher strikes that won collective bargaining for teachers and hence a bigger say in the running of schools. In 2011, teachers' unions in Wisconsin were at the forefront of the sick-outs that started the weeks-long occupation of the capitol building. And teachers' unions are stepping up to participate in the Occupy Wall Street movement that demands that the richest 1 percent be forced to pay for the financial crisis that they created.

Teachers' unions have also suffered from some depressing low points. As we'll discuss below, in 1968 in a strike against African American community control of schools, the United Federation of Teachers in New York pushed back the possibility of cooperation between teachers' unions and organizers for social and racial justice for decades. Additionally, both historically and today, unions have at times been stuck in a model of organizing that has been unable to withstand the attacks. One crucial difference between the high points of struggle and the low points has been whether rank-and-file teachers—that is, teachers in the classroom—with a broader vision of social equality have organized to have a voice in the direction that their unions take. When there is a general spirit of "we are the union" as opposed to seeing the union as synonymous with its leadership, or as a service provider ensconced in some distant central office, unions have been better able to wage successful struggles.

While they may not be organizationally sufficient alone to transform our society to one based on economic democracy and the fulfillment of human needs, unions are certainly one necessary component of defending our living standards and beginning the fight for a bigger share of the pie for workers and the public.

This chapter takes up each of the following themes in turn. First, we extend the discussion from the previous chapter on the scale of neoliberal attacks on public education, but focus on teachers' unions specifically. Second, we assess the state of our unions today in terms of responding to these attacks. Third, we ground that assessment in a historical overview of high and low points in the development of our unions, and by discussing the contradictory role that unions play under capitalism. What our discussion intends to make clear is that unionism and social justice are inseparable: without a laser-like focus on fighting for social justice, our unions can't wage an effective struggle; but without the unions, educators working for social justice are hamstrung. Thus, social justice educators should help to transform their unions into effective weapons to fight for more resources for public services and to take on oppression in society.

The Neoliberal Attack and the Lies Behind It

The best evidence that unions are good for the public is the fervor with which they're being attacked by the business and political establishment bent on making the working class pay for the crisis. In January 2011, the *Economist* magazine made a full-throated call for an attack on teachers' unions to resolve the global economic crisis:

> Now that the sovereign-debt crisis is forcing governments to put their houses in order, the growing discrepancy between conditions in the public and private sectors has eroded much of the sympathy public-sector workers might once have enjoyed. . . . Public-sector unions combine support for higher spending with vigorous opposition to more accountability. Almost everywhere they have demonized competition, transparency and flexible pay. Teachers' unions have often acted as the Praetorian Guard in this fight.
>
> Unions have also made it almost impossible to sack incompetent workers. . . . Even people on the left are beginning to echo these complaints. Andrew Cuomo, the incoming Democratic governor of New York, is rattling his saber against public-sector unions despite the fact that they make up an important part of his base. Davis Guggenheim, an impeccably liberal film director whose credits include Al Gore's *An Inconvenient Truth*, subjected the teachers' unions to a merciless critique in *Waiting for*

Superman. . . . . But will governments have the courage to tackle the root causes of the problem (such as pensions) rather than dealing with secondary problems (such as wages)? And will they dare to tackle questions of power rather than just pay and perks? If they are to claim victory in the coming fight, they need not just to restore the public finances to health. They also need to breathe the spirit of innovation into Leviathan.[2]

Thus, in an act of political hocus-pocus, the investment banks and hedge fund managers disappear as the cause of the global economic crisis, and teachers' unions are revealed as Roman mercenaries preserving an empire marked by inept educators. The elites have ample reason to need a scapegoat: the year 2011 has been labeled the year of "municipal default" with some sixteen US cities, including Detroit, Los Angeles, New York City, San Francisco, and Washington, DC, threatened by bankruptcy if they cannot find substantial sources of new revenue or make deep spending cuts.[3] Forty-five states and the District of Columbia project budget shortfalls totaling $125 billion for fiscal year 2012.[4]

With state and city budgets in free fall due to evaporating tax revenue, the bull's-eye on the backs of teachers is not really about whether they develop effective learning objectives in their lessons. As education theorist and social commentator Henry A. Giroux writes, "Money-soaked foundations . . . pour millions into a massive public pedagogy campaign that paints America's system of public education, teacher unions and public school teachers in terms that are polarizing and demonizing. . . . Real problems affecting schools such as rising poverty, homelessness, vanishing public services for the disadvantaged, widespread unemployment, massive inequality in wealth and income, overcrowded classrooms and a bankrupt and iniquitous system of school financing disappear in the educational discourse of the super rich."[5]

The myth recounted by neoliberal education reformers has become so patently absurd that billionaires such as members of the Walton family, Bill Gates, and Eli Broad are positioned as heroic underdogs in the struggle for more equitable schools against the unions and the status quo. Politicians continuously lament the falling test scores of American students in relation to students internationally—particularly in Europe and Asia. Just as frequently, they portray teachers' unions as the primary obstacle to innovation. However, there is a glaring contradiction in this anti-union argument: the European nations that outperform the United States have much stronger teachers' unions and higher rates of unionization.[6] Neoliberal reformers also have no explanation for why southern "right-to-work" states, which have mostly managed to keep unions out of public schools, score lower on standardized tests. As Arizona State University's Education Policy Research Unit reported: "Several studies found math, economics and SAT scores in unionized schools improved more than in non-unionized schools. Increases in state unionization led to increases in state SAT, ACT and NAEP scores and improved graduation rates. One analysis attributed lower SAT and ACT scores in the South to weaker unionization there."[7] Moreover, numerous studies have revealed that charter schools, which are largely nonunion, rarely perform any better—and often perform quite worse—than their unionized public-school counterparts.[8]

If these attacks on teachers' and other public-sector unions are so intense today, it is because they follow a thirty-year assault on private-sector unions. While 11.9 percent of US workers are in a union, only 6.9 percent of private-sector workers are. This means that public-sector workers, 36.2 percent of whom are unionized, at once comprise the last bastion of organized labor—and the next target.[9] Within public employee unions, the 1.4-million-member American Federation of Teachers (AFT) and the 3.2-million-member National Education Association (NEA) represent the single biggest sector of unionized workers in the United States today.[10] From the perspective of the politicians, bankers, and captains of industry who direct the economy, busting teachers' unions is a key component to slashing salaries, benefits, and pensions in cash-strapped states.

The unprecedented attacks on teachers' unions are about a fundamental transformation of the American economy. Those holding America's purse strings are determined to transfer the burden of the Great Recession onto working people. In this era of austerity, even shamefully low teacher salaries are too high for a US government locked in an international competition to maintain its economic superiority, especially with the rising power of low-wage China. To complete the transition to a domestic economy based on the pauperization of the American workforce, any example of a section of the working class that has decent benefits and adequate pay must be broken—lest others get the idea that these basics of life are attainable by organized workers.

The question of whether teachers' unions will organize the scale of struggle necessary to defend public schools and their employees across the country is one that will come to define both the quality of public education and the very nature of employment in the United States. The following section, which assesses the state of the two main teachers' unions in the United States, underscores how far we have to go in rebuilding and reorienting our unions for that fight.

Struggle or Surrender? The Teachers' Unions Today

The irony is that far from being the impervious colossus portrayed in the media, teachers' unions—and the labor movement on the whole—have spent the last several decades in retreat, accommodating many of the demands made by business leaders and government. The "collaborative" strategy of top teachers' union leaders, detailed below, is marked by commitment to partnership with management; unwavering support for the Democratic Party despite that party's subservience to Corporate America; and ignoring the possibilities of rank-and-file initiative.

While both the NEA and AFT have adopted the defensive race-to-the-bottom approach of collaboration with management, it should be noted that the AFT and the NEA have important differences. For example, the keynote speaker for the NEA's 2010 national convention was Diane Ravitch, perhaps the most prominent opponent of corporate school reform. By contrast, the AFT's keynote speaker at its 2010 convention was Bill Gates, one of the most prominent proponents and financiers of neoliberal reforms. At the 2010 NEA convention, delegates passed a resolution rejecting Obama's Race to the Top initiative, while Randi Weingarten, president of the AFT, was equivocal: she didn't condemn Race to the Top, but rather said that it proves that "the federal government knows how to be a lever for change," at the same time giving a nod to some of the "concerns" that the AFT has.[11]

Their differences in organizational structure partially account for the different postures of the two unions. As *Education Week* explained, "If the NEA structure gives state affiliates the primary role in developing and overseeing policy among local unions, an inverse situation exists within the AFT, where the central leadership actively works to persuade locals to try out new ideas. . . . Ms. Weingarten exerts considerable influence over the union's policy landscape partly because many of its vice presidents and resolution-vetting committee members belong to the same internal political coalition she supports, the Progressive Caucus."[12]

But while the AFT organizes on a model that concentrates power in the national president and the NEA generally empowers state presidents, the differences between the two unions should not be overstated. Top officials in both unions have made it clear that rather than leading a determined struggle against privatization, their goal is to win a seat at the table to help shape the reforms. The outcomes of this relationship show that the unions have continued to lend their support to management-driven proposals, even when they have proven educationally bankrupt. As New York City teacher and member of the United Federation of Teachers (UFT, the local affiliate of the AFT) Peter Lamphere wrote: "Over the past year [2010], American Federation of Teachers (AFT) President Randi Weingarten has intervened in negotiations between local school districts and AFT locals across the US, pushing contracts that undermine—if not abandon—the traditional core of teacher collective bargaining agreements. In cities like Baltimore, Washington, DC, New Haven, Pittsburgh, and elsewhere, Weingarten has advocated deals that undermine tenure, impose unreliable evaluation systems based on student test scores and divide teachers with merit pay."[13]

Weingarten's unwavering pursuit of the partnership model of unionism even led her to get ahead of the neoliberal education reformers by spurring the UFT in New York to create and operate its own charter schools. Weingarten's reasoning was to prove to other charter operators that they could run their schools with a unionized staff. Unionizing charter school teachers is certainly an important goal. Yet, by becoming both the operator of the charter and the representation of its workers, the failed strategy of collaboration reached its zenith: Weingarten, now representing both labor and management at charter schools in New York City, is in fact in partnership with herself.[14] Teachers have complained that labor/management officials have arbitrarily fired teachers critical of the charter school, and the traditional public school teachers, who had to give up space to share the building with the new school, have lodged ongoing complaints.[15]

The need for member-driven unions was made evident again when NEA president Dennis Van Roekel undermined his union's resolution in opposition to Race to the Top, saying: "NEA supports the plan to limit Race to the Top to school districts. We commend the Administration's further refinement of this program, as long as it requires local collaboration, best practices that boost student learning, more flexibility for turnaround models without minimizing the need for results, and as long as it does not reduce the basic funding for children in poverty."[16]

The unions' unwavering loyalty to the Democratic Party has been another factor in their weakened ability to defend public education. The NEA made a combined $56.5 million in federal and state contributions during the 2007–08 election cycle, with the overwhelming majority flowing to Democrats.[17] These contributions poured into the party at the same time that Obama was stumping for the very corporate education reforms that later became his Race to the Top initiative. Imagine the clout that teachers might have had if the union had put the $56.5 million into strike funds for locals challenging contracts that included merit pay, charter schools, erosion of seniority rights, or lifting class size lids. Worse, when Democrats know they will receive millions of dollars from the teachers' unions while they advocate for policies that erode public education, they have little reason to pay attention to teachers' demands. Whether Democrats acknowledge teachers' issues or not, they can rest assured that union contributions will keep flowing.

While teachers' unions—and the labor movement in general—have long been in retreat, the struggle that erupted in Wisconsin in February 2011 against Governor Scott Walker's antiunion legislation could signal the beginnings of a new era for US labor. Unions that have long been surrendering to management's offensive were compelled to take action by the prospect that these new laws would destroy their organizations.[18] With state governments across the country proposing similar legislation against the bargaining rights of public sector workers, Wisconsin workers' struggle to preserve trade unions demonstrated an awakening of class solidarity and action, even though it ultimately suffered a legislative defeat. To be sure, progress on class solidarity and action has been halting. While entire unions entered into mass action to defend collective bargaining rights, many of Wisconsin's public-sector unions have since agreed to concessionary contracts, following the logic that concessions are the high price to pay for the salvaging the union at all.

But thousands of teachers have drawn important conclusions from their own direct participation in the rallies, sick-outs, and occupations in Madison and elsewhere, demonstrating that mass collective action holds promise for reanimating the entire labor movement. One teacher in the Madison Public Schools reflected on her experience of deciding to occupy the state capitol in opposition to Governor Walker's union-busting legislation: "Shutting down the state seems really scary to me . . . [And yet] when I'm in the Capitol, I love just walking around and talking to people from everywhere. The solidarity and camaraderie are amazing. You turn to your left, turn to your right, and you can chat with people who've come to support us from all over the state, and all over the world."[19] As part of Occupy Wall Street (and what is coming to be known as the "Occupy movement"), which began in September 2011, teachers all over the country have participated in protests and teach-ins at banks to highlight how banks got bailed out during the Great Recession rather than schools, even though banks precipitated the crisis through predatory lending practices.

The Struggle for the Spirit of Unionism

To understand where we are in the labor movement today, it's important to recognize the push and pull between various tendencies within the labor movement in general and within teachers' unions specifically. There have been many different philosophies about unions, their purpose, and how to win. However, they fit broadly into two categories.[20] These concepts are mostly borrowed from the private sector but are analogous to the public sector in ways that we'll demonstrate.

The first category is most familiar to unionists today. Its underlying principle is that of "partnership," sometimes called "collaboration." In this view, unions and management have common interests and should "work together" to meet those interests. In a recession, this means everyone should tighten their belts and "share the sacrifice." In the good times, we hope, the spoils will be shared. The old slogan from the 1950s and '60s sums up this approach to unionism: "What's good for General Motors is good for America." There are many specific models of unionism that fit in this category, such as "craft/professional unionism," "business unionism," and "service-model unionism." In the "service model," the union is viewed as an office of professionals that exists mainly to file grievances and represent its members in hearings and lawsuits. In this view, the union is equated with its leadership, and a great deal of importance is placed on functions like media messaging. Certainly, the approach of "labor-management cooperation" is also part of this camp. In this model of "collaboration," negotiations are key to success. There is a reliance on the troika of lawyers, lobbyists, and legislation to effect change. If politicians are doing something to harm the public interest or workers, they need to be "educated" about why this is against their interests or the interests of the nation as a whole. It assumes altruism or at least neutrality on the part of the state. Lois Weiner, a historian of teachers' unions, argues, "It may seem more practical to compromise, as did teacher unions when they first endorsed standardized testing as a fair, effective assessment tool and compensatory programs as providing much-needed funding to schools. In reality, these bargains undercut development of alliances with parents and citizens."[21]

The second, and counterposed, broad tendency in the labor movement is one of struggle. The underlying assumption is reflected in the slogan that built the labor movement, "An injury to one is an injury to all." This tendency assumes that the interests of the business and political establishment are actually opposed to the interests of workers and the public. For businesses, the harder and faster that corporations can force workers to work, and the less they pay them, the higher the former's profits will be. In the public sector, businesses attempt to use the state to help them transfer wealth upward. This is achieved through corporate welfare, privatization, regressive tax structures, and the use of the military to facilitate competitive business climates. Public-sector speedups—in our case, more students per teacher, or longer school days and years for the same pay—mirror those practiced on the assembly lines begun long ago. Far from being neutral, according to this view, the state serves the interests of the business elite.

"Class struggle unionism" is the idea that workers' essential power lies in their ability to withhold labor, and that this should be exercised to win positive change. For example, during the 1930s "industrial unionism" grew up as a specific alternative to "craft/professional unionism." It was based on the idea that all workers in a workplace, and in an industry, should organize together regardless of skill level. In the case of teachers' unions, for example, an "industrial" approach, which we would favor, would propose that all the workers in a school building, from teachers and paraprofessionals to custodians and health service workers, would be represented by the same union. Further, this approach to unionism assumes that there should be leaders in every workplace who organize with others, and that problems with management are best resolved, if possible, by collective action at the workplace instead of through the legalistic grievance process. Furthermore, industrial unionists attempt to organize industrywide job actions.

Also part of the "class struggle" tendency is "social movement unionism." Social movement unionism is based on the same principles of industrial unionism, but with an additional element. Unions should be leaders in the fight against oppression—racism, sexism, homophobia—as well as inequality in society more generally. The purpose is to fight against all divisions among workers and against injustices more broadly. Social equality, not just a narrow defense of one group of workers' rights, is the goal. According to Shermain Mannah and Jon Lewis in an essay entitled "South African Teachers and Social Movements Old and New," the term "social movement unionism" "was coined by labor analysts in the 1980s to describe similar movements—such as Solidarity in Poland, the Workers Party in Brazil, and COSATU in South Africa—where trade unionism had extended its influence beyond the workplace into the community and national political arena."[22]

The history of the labor movement is one of a constant battle to align unions with either the "collaboration" or, conversely, the "struggle" tendency. Below we'll discuss some examples. While this chapter won't provide an exhaustive history of teachers' unions, it relies on some of the best research on this topic, such as Marjorie Murphy's *Blackboard Unions: The AFT and the NEA, 1900–1980*, and the 2011 book by Clarence Taylor, *Reds at the Blackboard: Communism, Civil Rights, and the New York City Teachers Union*. And while this chapter focuses primarily on issues within the United States, there are many inspiring examples of teachers' unions fighting neoliberalism in other countries. The best collection of essays about those struggles to date is *The Global Assault on Teaching, Teachers, and their Unions*, edited by Mary Compton and Lois Weiner.

The Roots of the Teachers' Unions

The AFT was born out of struggle and conflict. At the turn of the twentieth century, elementary teachers in the United States were typically women possessing only a "normal school" education (that is, teacher training school). They labored in overcrowded classrooms and schools, were denigrated in public opinion, and were lorded over by male principals. The typical high school teacher, by contrast, was male and earned much more money. The AFT was far from ideal. Its founding president was a male high school teacher who endorsed the First World War and later left to become principal of a prestigious school. But the AFT *was* an explicit union of, by, and for teachers.

The NEA at the time was a "professional organization" run mainly by administrators and was totally male-dominated. Racism, as well, pervaded the NEA. Many state affiliates refused Black members, although African Americans could join the national association directly. Outrageously, the Louisiana state association remained segregated until 1974.[23]

The debate between the AFT and NEA over *how* to improve teacher salary clearly illustrates their differences. The NEA focused on improving pay for teachers as professionals, not as workers. In fact, the NEA's patronizing position held that pay needed to improve in order to recruit better teachers who could exemplify true professionalism. The AFT, by contrast, took an industrial approach to obtaining better pay through collective action.

Margaret Haley, Chicago's "Lady Labor Slugger," was the seminal figure in the birth of a class struggle approach to teacher unionism. As a tenacious feminist and labor leader, Haley ought to loom large in teachers' sense of history. That few teachers today know of her efforts to organize teachers is a striking example of the historical amnesia plaguing our movement.

William Harper, the first president of the University of Chicago, proposed a sweeping reorganization of Chicago's public schools in 1898. Modeled on New York City schools, the plan was shaped by elites across the nation who sought to reorganize public education to suit the needs of a newly emerging industrial society. Their main goals were to control children during the day while both parents worked, provide basic education to the next generation of workers, and acculturate them to the rigid schedules of factory life governed by ubiquitous whistles and bells.

But Harper's aims went well beyond technocratic efficiency. He sought to hire only teachers with college degrees, implement a new system of hiring and firing, and address the "feminization" of schools by establishing a sexist hierarchy—hiring more male teachers and raising their salaries above women's. Harper also proposed to lease schools, property tax free, to Chicago businesses for ninety-nine-year terms.[24]

Haley successfully organized teachers to resist, despite the electoral disenfranchisement of women. She reached out to women's clubs—suffragist-leaning social networks of "high society" women—sending speakers to win over the influential club members on the basis of female solidarity. Teachers organized their own afternoon teas at neighborhood schools, like the Hendricks School in one of Chicago's poorest neighborhoods, located next to the stockyards and meatpacking district immortalized in Upton Sinclair's *The Jungle*. This broad approach to struggle paid off: the Harper Bill to reorganize the schools failed in the Illinois state legislature.

This experience drew Haley to the Chicago Teachers Federation (CTF). Together with Catharine Goggin, Haley initiated the "Teacher's Tax Crusade" to examine the Cook County tax rolls and discovered some two million dollars in unpaid taxes. Haley and the CTF forced the local tax boards to collect the money and provide it to the school system. After three years of legal wrangling by outraged businesses, a court reduced the amount to six hundred thousand dollars. This still provided a substantial raise to Chicago's teachers, and news of the campaign spread across the nation. Haley, for her part, emphasized that teacher *agency* in the fight was more important than any monetary outcome.[25]

By 1902, Haley had led the CTF to formally join the Chicago Federation of Labor. Within a year, the teachers helped to overthrow the corrupt labor leadership in Chicago. Under the reform president, John Fitzpatrick, the AFL began to organize women workers all over the Second City: milliners, packinghouse workers, chorus girls, laundry workers, domestic servants, department store workers, garment workers, and more. For Haley, an officer in the Women's Suffrage Party of Illinois, organizing women workers was closely related to winning the right for women to vote. In fact, she was instrumental in winning this right in Illinois in 1913.

In 1916, the CTF hosted a groundbreaking, though modest, meeting of four local unions that formed the American Federation of Teachers. The AFT went on to challenge the NEA head-to-head to represent teachers and today claims more than a million members.[26]

The Depression and the Unions

The Great Depression proved to be no less a turning point for teachers than it was every other part of the working class. Throughout the Roaring Twenties school officials had initiated extensive, debt-financed construction projects in districts across the country. High debts and disappearing tax bases squeezed the schools. In Chicago, teachers went without pay throughout 1931. In the middle of the Dust Bowl, Arkansas closed the doors of three hundred schools after just sixty days of instruction. Alabama shut half its schools. The *Nation* magazine reported teachers panhandling on city corners after school.[27] The economic calamity was unlike any crisis teachers, or anyone, had ever experienced, as Marjorie Murphy described: "Those fortunate few teachers whose school districts did not force a pay cut, or close schools . . . still confronted daily the long-term effects of the depression. They observed the deterioration of school programs they had spent years investing their energies to improve. They had to direct their sights instead on poorly fed children whose families had been devastated by unemployment.

This incessant confrontation with the failures of capitalism had a radicalizing effect on the teachers."[28]

Contrary to the "savior" mythology surrounding his presidency, Franklin Roosevelt initially offered little to schools during the Depression. Even a personal appeal from Chicago's mayor Anton Cermak—who would end up taking an assassin's bullet intended for Roosevelt—failed to deliver federal support to a district that still sporadically missed paydays in 1933. The teachers could wait no longer; they finally rioted. Thousands of teachers marched in the downtown Loop business area, breaking windows, entering banks, and confronting bank president Charles Dawes, who responded by declaring, "I don't talk to troublemakers."[29]

Eventually, FDR released a multimillion-dollar loan to Chicago's schools, after the city's banks and businesses agreed to carry the tax loan for the teachers—contingent on their ability to determine the terms of the payout. The Roosevelt administration emphasized emergency relief as a temporary bridge during the crisis, not a new commitment to financing public education.

The impact of the Great Depression also exacerbated a long-standing, mostly unrecognized savagery in the nation's public schools: racial segregation. In the 1930s, a typical white school remained in session for seven months of the year. The average Black school, by contrast, was open just four months. This put the federal government in a politically tenuous position: provide temporary assistance across the board that left racial inequality intact or support every school *plus* additional support to bring up the resources for students of color to be on par with their white peers. Roosevelt's reluctance to aid schools was fueled not only by his fiscal conservatism, but also by his unwillingness to acknowledge racial inequality at the risk of upsetting southern Democrats.[30]

By the 1930s, the AFT, in contrast to the NEA, was mostly integrated. Segregated locals in the AFT were the exception, though they persisted. The AFT moved its conventions to nonsegregated cities and demanded respectful treatment by hotel staff toward all delegates. Some southern school districts passed rules forbidding membership in integrated unions, but the AFT pressed on. This established the union's reputation as a progressive, race-conscious organization—a reputation that played an important role in the many AFT victories in urban areas during the mad scramble over membership in the sixties and seventies.[31]

Puerto Rico's Teacher Rebellion[79]

Some 250 teachers and education activists gathered in Los Angeles in April 2008 at the eighth Trinational Conference to Defend Public Education. For three days, representatives from several cities in the United States, plus Canada, Mexico, and Puerto Rico, plotted a response to the creep of privatization into our schools.

In conversations, speeches, and workshops, teachers detailed the many facets of what neoliberal education policies look like in different locations—for example, the gutting of the public education system in New Orleans. There were also the faces of the struggle—teachers from British Colombia, Puerto Rico, and Oaxaca brought the stories of strikes that can help point the way forward for everyone.

During the conference, Gillian Russom and Sarah Knopp interviewed **Rafael Feliciano-Hernández***, president of the Teachers' Federation of Puerto Rico (FMPR). Teachers on the island struck earlier that year to try to win collective bargaining rights; oppose Law 45, which makes it illegal for teachers to strike; stop the transformation of Puerto Rican schools into charters; and stand up to reprisals against teachers who were organizing.*

How did you build up to the strike?

This wasn't the first time on strike for the Teachers' Federation. In 1993, we had a one-day strike against charter schools. It was a big defeat that led to the demoralization of militants. The corruption and antidemocratic practices inside the union became extreme.

But between 2003 and 2008, we have radically transformed a union that had been a conservative force in the Puerto Rican labor movement. The student rebellion contributed to the teacher rebellion. The students put up a banner, and their resistance was transmitted to the level of the teachers. In 2004, we disaffiliated from the American Federation of Teachers because their colonial relationship to us was impeding the development of our struggle.

From that point on, we had many short strikes around specific demands to improve education. They were all illegal. We had delegates' meetings of hundreds of teachers. The existence of political groups in the teachers' union facilitated the process. We had open debate in which everyone could expound their point of view, and this neutralized the agents of the state within the union.

We set the date of the strike for February 21. It was seen as a scandal that the teachers were talking about this. There were 1,300 representatives at our delegates' assembly meeting and we voted to strike by 1,200 to 15.

Some twenty thousand teachers supported the strike; eight thousand of them were on the picket line. During the strike, thousands of publications were produced, which created a great level of discussion. It was led from the bottom up. Leadership from the top kills the capacity to struggle.

How did teachers feel about the illegality of the strike?
It is important to say that the immense majority of teachers had never before participated in strikes or work stoppages. They had to overcome fears, threats, and pressure that management and its allies used to paralyze the strikers. This occurred in the context of the repressive Law 45, which prohibits strikes and criminalizes all actions that imply the interruption of labor in public agencies.

The state made it a conflict between the FMPR and the state. All the media were against us. They were joined by both the AFL-CIO and Change to Win, which didn't have links with the communities or specific struggles. The SEIU intervened with the Association of Teachers. Dennis Rivera and Roberto Pagán, among others, pressured the governor not to enter into agreements with the FMPR. This paralyzed the possibility of negotiation at the height of the struggle.

We didn't win our central demand, which was a collective bargaining agreement. We did win a raise, and the promise of a future raise, as well as an agreement that there will be no charter schools in Puerto Rico. We also developed a new layer of leaders and militants: eight thousand teachers who no longer just talk about struggle because they've done it. They speak from a class perspective. It's not just a matter of dollars and cents. The strike process is an emancipatory and decolonizing experience. We gained a lot: the union and the country are not the same.

Would we have been able to do all this without the political groups within the union, which made the connections with what's happening in the world, with the war, with the gap between rich and poor? I think not. The workers would have been too constricted by the bosses' vision of the world.

Do you think the strike was a victory?
When we ended the strike, I was so happy, because no repression and reprisals occurred. People were ecstatic. Other people asked me, "Why are you so happy? We didn't win collective bargaining." But for us, the strike was an act of liberation. A high percentage of the twenty-six thousand teachers fought actively. The only way to do this was to be democratic. We all decided to go out, and we all decided to go back.

The Teachers Union in New York City

The Teachers Union (TU) came to be the greatest challenge to top-down unionism. Birthed into a turbulent, radical atmosphere, the TU was originally led by members of the Socialist Party such as Henry Linville, who connected the fight for teacher pensions to the struggle against capitalism. Linville wrote: "Teachers are just as surely the employees of the interests in power as are the men who slave in factories."[32]

During the Depression, when New York City began to address its deficits by hiring substitute teachers at one-half of a regular teacher's pay, two responses emerged. The "old guard" of the New York TU, led by Linville, demanded that only properly credentialed teachers should be employed by the school district. The younger activists declared that all substitutes ought to be made permanent and given all the benefits of regular teachers. In this seemingly minor dispute we can see the core differences between exclusionary "craft" or "professional" unionism, which protects formally credentialed or educated workers at the expense of others, and "industrial" unionism, which includes all workers in a workplace irrespective of status, trade, or education.[33] In 1936–37, as the economy began its halting, shaky recovery from the Depression, the New York TU launched a campaign to adjust salaries back to their 1932 levels, increase pay for substitutes and junior clerks, equalize salaries for day-school and evening-school substitutes, and provide summer pay for substitutes.[34]

By 1935, more militant Communist Party (CP) members (and other activists whose orientation was on class struggle) gained in influence over the TU executive board.[35] In his 2011 history of the TU and its relationship to the CP, Clarence Taylor points out that while the CP was undoubtedly the strongest organized influence inside the TU, the union represented Communist and non-Communist teachers alike. At its height, in the era before collective bargaining and the closed shop, the TU was the largest of the unions representing New York teachers, collecting dues from and "representing" thousands of members. Taylor also demonstrated that TU leaders' claims about the internal democracy of their union were credible.[36]

The CP's Rank and File Caucus, a network of the most militant and activist-oriented teachers that had originally been organized to oppose the more conservative Linville-led TU leadership, had always reached out to parent and community groups, organized unemployed teachers, and demanded greater militancy from the union. In 1938, the Rank and File Caucus scored a major victory, convincing the New York City officials to build two new schools in Harlem, the first since 1900. Reflecting on this work years later, and after the impact of McCarthyism in ripping the organized left out of unions, one Harlem resident said: "Most of the teachers who they said were Communists and kicked out of the school system were much more dedicated to teaching black children the way out of the crucible of American life than the teachers we now have. When they left, Harlem became a worse place. They stayed after school with the children, and gave them extracurricular attention to bring them up to level. You didn't have these reading problems like you have today. These people were dedicated to their craft."[37]

Parent-teacher associations from all over the city stood up for the TU when it came under attack from the school board. Enid Tyler, a parent organizer, said that the board should focus on "cleaning up some other overt acts of prejudice in the schools rather than harassing" the teachers. According to Arthur Newman, a chairman of the Better Schools Committee in the Southeast Bronx, "The parents in our area want more schools and they want smaller class sizes and they want adequate health facilities. They want remedial teachers." Newman went on to describe the TU as one of the "sincerest and strongest allies on these issues."[38]

Influenced by CP politics, the TU became active on issues of international solidarity and social justice. Its newspaper published reports from teachers fighting in the International Brigades during the Spanish Civil War. The union developed antifascist curricula, fought against IQ testing and tracking, advocated for the hiring of more Black teachers, emphasized "whole child" education, and analyzed textbooks for racial bias while producing Black history supplements. As documented in *Reds at the Blackboard*, notes on the union's textbook campaign "included an analysis of pernicious images of Jews, immigrants, colonial subjects, and labor. Borrowing the methods and arguments of the NAACP, the TU issued a pamphlet, *The Children's Textbooks*, in April 1948 identifying several books used by the New York City schools that made children 'pray to anti-Semitism, Jim Crow and racism.'"[39] In addition, the TU led thousands of people in pickets against inadequate salaries in 1946 and 1947.[40]

Despite these remarkable actions, the TU faced a number of serious challenges. Public employees didn't yet have a right to collective bargaining, and the TU often claimed just two or three members on any given campus. Far more problematic for the TU was the Cold War hysteria that drove a wedge between teachers. New York City openly stockpiled two hundred thousand body tags to drive fear about nuclear war and the "red menace."

By 1948, the CIO required political conformity from all member unions.[41] A year later, the NEA issued a pro–Cold War statement, further isolating the New York radicals.

The challenges facing the TU did not just come from the outside, but also flowed from the internal contradictions in CP politics. The CP tethered itself to Stalin's brutal regime, which increasingly choked off the initiative and independence of local CPs in each country.[42] The 1939 announcement of the Hilter-Stalin Pact disoriented the CP's membership and arguably weakened TU members' resolve and clarity about the role of the party. This contributed to their inability to stand up to anti-Communist attempts to weed out the most outspoken teachers from the workforce. In other words, the TU's contributions to teachers' struggles in this period were made almost despite the CP's formal politics. In the end, though, those very politics contributed to the TU's final decline—just as teachers neared their goal of winning the right to represent all teachers in a collective bargaining agreement.

Minnie Gutride, a first-grade teacher on Staten Island, committed suicide after being interrogated by three members of the school board in 1948. They accused her of attending meetings of CP front groups in 1940 and 1941.[43] The constant harassment by school officials scared away nonparty members from joining the TU and left the TU fighting in court for twelve long years, rather than leading school- and community-based struggles like those described earlier. Many of the most experienced teacher organizers from the 1930s and 1940s, whether Communists or not, were removed from their positions. By 1950, under the Timone Resolution, the union had lost the right to represent teachers in collective bargaining and to deal directly with the school board. The TU had effectively been banned from New York public schools.[44] The tradition of confrontational struggle for academic freedom, racial justice, and economic justice for communities, teachers, and education workers had been crippled.

The Battle for Collective Bargaining and the Legacy of Shankerism

An era of political liberalization swept across the United States in the 1960s and 1970s. Pushed by teacher actions and facilitated by a postwar economic boom, states began to drop their legal statutes against public employee unionization and, in time, strikes. In 1960, just three teacher work stoppages occurred in the entire country. By 1968, some one hundred strikes took place, leading to 2,190,000 idle teaching days.[45] In the next few years, teachers' most important right—collective bargaining—was solidified.

The timid steps of teachers in 1960 began a process that sloughed off the conservative weight of McCarthyism. An influx of young teachers brought new attitudes toward unions and—despite rising wages—a sharpening disgust at bloated school bureaucracies. The successes of the civil rights movement and other social movements also influenced the outlook of educators. Because of the long post–World War II economic boom and the increasing number of children in schools due to the concurrent baby boom, teachers had leverage. Finally, as cracks appeared in the anti-labor facade of state governments, a tremendous competition emerged between the NEA and AFT to represent members on a scale previously unimaginable, in the hundreds of thousands.[46]

In the context of rising struggle among teachers, the NEA finally embraced the vocabulary and tactics of labor unions, including the right to strike. In Los Angeles, the NEA local of the California Teachers Association and the AFT's Los Angeles Federation of Teachers began to cooperate against the Board of Education in 1965. A joint conference established a temporary merger in which members retained their original affiliations, but coexisted inside United Teachers Los Angeles (UTLA). A successful strike in 1970 made the arrangement permanent, bridging a divide between the AFT and NEA for the first time since Margaret Haley's era.

In 1960, New York teachers struck—illegally—to protest arbitrary treatment by administrators, overcrowding, miserably low salaries, and sexist policies like mandatory unpaid maternity leave. While they didn't win many of their demands, this was the opening shot in the battle to win collective bargaining for teachers. In 1961, the UFT merged several organizations representing teachers and won the right to be a bargaining agent for teachers in the New York public schools. There has been a battle over public-sector workers' collective bargaining rights and right to strike ever since. In 1967, for example, New York implemented the Taylor Law, which both codified the right to collective bargaining *and* banned strikes, making them punishable with jail time.

Three years later, UTLA waged a twenty-day illegal strike to win a contract with the school board. Most of the gains were lost when the agreement was thrown out in court because public-sector workers had no collective bargaining rights.[47] However, the strike started the ball rolling and is usually celebrated as a victory for teachers in their efforts to organize. In 1975, unions won the Rodda Act, which granted teachers and public sector employees the right to strike[48] while regulating the conditions under which such a strike could take place very strictly.

The preeminent national teachers' union figure of this time was Albert Shanker, who has been called the "Father of Modern Teachers' Unions."[49] He led the UFT from 1964 to 1974, and then the AFT from 1974 to 1997. His politics came to symbolize to the public the politics of teacher unionism. He wrote 1,300 columns called "Where We Stand" for the *New York Times,* laying out the positions of the UFT.[50]

Shanker's legacy is at best a complicated one. On the one hand, he was a fierce defender of teachers' right to strike, and he spent time in jail in both 1967 and 1968 for leading strikes in New York City. His name became synonymous with a hard-nosed approach to winning collective bargaining rights for teachers. But he later became known as a "labor statesman" famous for keeping labor peace and making concessionary deals.

Shanker won additional renown for his insistence in 1972 that the UFT organize paraprofessionals, who were mostly young Black and Latina women, in the schools.[51] But in other instances, Shanker's racial politics were deeply problematic. While he believed in civil rights and marched with Dr. King, he also espoused a theory of "colorblindness." While this may seem at first blush to be an antiracist position, in the context of the racially charged New York of the late 1960s, it led Shanker and the UFT *away* from the struggle for racial justice. Two principles that Shanker held—that socioeconomic class *as opposed to race* was the real basis of oppression in this country, and that unions only exist to protect their workers in the narrow sense of bread-and-butter issues—led to disastrous results. Above all, these positions led Shanker and the UFT to oppose struggles for community control of schools in Black and Latino neighborhoods.[52]

The most famous example of the UFT's opposition to community control is the Ocean Hill–Brownsville conflict in 1968. Black parents demanded control over the hiring and firing of teachers in their neighborhood schools. Teachers complained of unsafe and run-down schools, and demanded, among many other things, greater control over removing students from their classrooms. Teachers could have tried to connect with parents by fighting for more democratic control of schools at the local level. They could have reengaged some of the strategies for taking racism in the school system head-on that the TU had used in the 1930s and '40s. Instead, Shanker allowed the UFT to be pitted against parents. Teachers struck to prevent parent input over the transfer of teachers in or out of their neighborhood schools. Chapter 2 explores this strike and its complicated legacy in greater detail. Suffice it to say that the strike created a lasting wound between teacher unionists and parents in New York City.

While Albert Shanker can be credited for leading the teachers' union movement in the era that secured collective bargaining rights, he has his share of responsibility for the continued misconception in this country that class interests and racial justice are counterposed.

In addition, Shanker embraced market-based incentives and charter schools early in the charter school movement as key planks in the school reform agenda.[53] To be clear, Shanker's support for charter schools was based largely on the role they were originally designed to play, that is, as sites of innovation. As charters were increasingly co-opted by the corporate forces that have come to define the "charter school movement" and morphed into what they are today (as described in the previous chapter), Shanker, to his credit, did express disagreement with the direction in which the charter movement was headed.[54]

Unions and Imperialism

Perhaps one of the most damaging elements of Shanker's legacy is one that he inherited and continued from many unionists before him—support for US imperialism. Shanker was a cold warrior who accepted the idea that labor organizations should support US foreign interventions. This legacy is clearest with respect to the war in Vietnam and the movement to end it. While unionists representing four million workers were taking part in Labor for Peace conferences and supporting the antiwar movement,[55] Shanker in fact supported the war effort.

In his support for US imperialism and war, though, Shanker was not alone among union leaders. Even one of the proudest examples cited above of a union that fought for social justice, the TU, fervently supported the war efforts of the United States during World War II—although this had more to do with the influence of CP members' adherence to dictates from Moscow than patriotic or principled support for US imperialism among teachers. Thus, throughout World War II, the TU persuaded people to stand up to racism on the basis that it would help the United States to win the war. The full integration of Blacks into society would not only create a better fighting force for the United States but also undermine Hitler's propaganda that this was a hypocritical and racist country. In March 1942, the union published a pamphlet called *Schools for Victory*, and in 1945 said that among its most important accomplishments for the year was "the fullest use of schools for the [prosecution] of the war."[56] One teacher-activist accused of being a Communist bragged that he had contributed to convincing hundreds of his students to enlist in the war effort.

The legacy of support for wars continues today. Even though some 226 union locals have passed resolutions against war since 2001,[57] the AFT supported the wars in Iraq and Afghanistan from 2001 until 2006. As Stephen Zunes argued in *Truthout:*

> Had the hundreds of billions of dollars used by the federal government to pay for the Iraq war through 2006—the period during which the AFT supported the costly occupation and counterinsurgency operations—instead gone to education, none of the massive teacher layoffs and other draconian cutbacks to education would have been necessary. Indeed, funding for education (as well as health care, housing, public transportation, environmental protections and other human needs) could have been dramatically increased, or the federal deficit—currently being used as the excuse for cutbacks in such programs—could have been dramatically reduced. As a result, the AFT is faced with the politically difficult task of arguing for the federal government to borrow additional money to support public school teachers in the states, money Washington would have available were it not for the war the AFT supported.[58]

Teachers, the Working Class, and Unions: A Marxist Perspective

Given the checkered record of teachers' unions, it's no wonder that people question their effectiveness for fighting back. In fact, many of the most dedicated and talented social justice educators have long since voted with their feet, deciding that their unions were too much a "part of the problem" to be a venue for social change or improvements in the workplace. And yet, the central argument in this chapter is that militant unions are indispensable. So, to make sense of the history we've just presented, and of the contradictions we've raised about teachers' unions, we address two issues in this section. First, we argue that teachers are members of the broader working class in society. Second, we describe the role that unions play generally in capitalist society.

Teachers play an integral social role in industrial capitalism. Indeed, public school teachers stand out as the largest unionized workforce in America.[59]

The question of teachers' place in society—whether as professionals or workers, middle class or working class—is increasingly important as they see their pay slashed, their workloads increase, and their control of the workplace decision-making process slipping away. There has been a longstanding assumption that teachers somehow stand above other workers—a stance often promoted by our own unions.

Even labor's allies, such as left-wing economist Michael Zweig, don't believe that teachers are members of the working class. In his book *Working Class Majority*, he argues:

> The fact that middle class professionals are increasingly exposed to capitalist power does not, however, immediately put them into the working class. . . . Public school teaching is another profession caught in the middle. . . . School teachers, fighting for authority, are caught between pressures. . . . [The] unions have insisted that teachers should play a central role in guiding curriculum reforms and other changes in school operations. In doing so, the unions are trying to preserve the professional status of their members, to distinguish the work life of the teacher from the experience of the cafeteria worker or janitor.[60]

Zweig understands class as the interrelationship between status, authority, and consciousness. Following this logic, because teachers' unions fight for more authority over the workplace (for example, writing curriculum, collaboratively running schools, and so on) and because many teachers believe themselves to be professionals and not blue-collar workers, they cannot be classified as working class. But many blue-collar Americans also consider themselves to be "middle class" or living the "American dream" (although, after thirty-five years of a one-sided class war against the working class, these beliefs are shifting). A person's belief that she is in the middle class doesn't put her there any more than a person's religious convictions make the afterlife any less or more a reality.

From a Marxist perspective, by contrast, teachers are indeed firmly rooted in the working class. Like other public-sector workers, teachers do not work directly for private companies, yet their jobs exist to satisfy the functioning of the capitalist system as a whole.

Three main criteria define "working class" in Marxist terms. The first criterion is that working-class people are those who create surplus value for capital. In other words, they produce a good or service that generates far more money than they are paid, and the extra wealth from their labor goes to the employers' profit. Some have objected to applying this definition to teachers: profits are not directly made from the work teachers perform, so they can't be accurately characterized as workers. Yet, by taking care of young people while their parents are at work, teachers play an indirect—but critical—role in the creation of profits. Moreover, by educating the next generation of workers, teachers play an essential role in enhancing the productivity of the workforce, thus increasing the labor power and the potential for capitalist extraction of surplus value. As Marxist economist Chris Harman noted: "Enterprises under modern capitalism require labor power with at least minimal levels of literacy and numeracy. The teachers who provide this have to be considered as part of the collective worker, ultimately working for the complex of nationally based capitals that the state services. Apologists for capitalism recognize this inadvertently when they refer to the provision of education as 'adding to social capital' and demand 'value added' in schools."[61]

The second criterion defines class in terms of the power relationships that exist in a given workplace. Working-class people can live only by selling their labor; they have little control over the real decisions about how to structure their workplaces. Any teacher who has attempted to raise objections to oversized classes and workload, who has been told by his or her principal he or she is not "highly qualified" under No Child Left Behind, or who has had to follow a scripted or paced curriculum will find this definition of the working class quite familiar.

Finally, the working class is a "collective" class—in other words, workers have to cooperate to get their jobs done. While most teachers spend their days isolated from their coworkers in a separate classroom, even the most mundane aspects of our jobs require a tremendous amount of cooperation and collaboration—between and among us and our students, but also among teachers, staff, and community members. Our bosses see us this way as well—as a "workforce" that has to be controlled. Moreover, politicians don't care about the welfare of teachers as individuals. Therefore, teachers (as workers) can only improve their lives by uniting together to protest against the status quo and the power of the elites and to propose alternatives.[62]

As a collective, we need the protections that unions afford. We need to better our working conditions—and therefore students' education—by organizing together against the politicians who would like to cut out our voices totally, devalue our work, and spend as little money on education as they can get away with.

The Role of Unions in the Class Struggle

All this points toward the basic theory, in Marxist terms, of the role of unions under capitalism as self-defense organizations for the working class. Unions are the vehicles that enable workers to organize as a "collective" class. Without them, individual workers have no choice but to compete with each other when negotiating with their bosses. Since capitalism exploits every opportunity to keep workers divided, whether by race, gender, skill, or pay scale, unions offer the opportunity for collective struggle against the employers, thereby reducing competition between workers. In 1845, Marx's lifelong collaborator Friedrich Engels argued that "what gives these Unions and the strikes arising from them their real importance is this, that they are the first attempt of the workers to abolish competition. They imply the recognition of the fact that the supremacy of the bourgeoisie is based wholly upon the competition of the workers among themselves; i.e., upon their want of cohesion."[63]

The strength of unions lies in their ability to represent all the workers in a given workplace, industry, or school district, thereby strengthening workers' bargaining position. But unions are also vehicles for struggle, allowing workers to experience their collective class power. Participating in unions and fighting around immediate demands, like smaller class sizes, how teachers are evaluated, or defending collective bargaining itself, can lead to important gains at work. Equally important, such participation is a crucial factor that facilitates working people viewing the bigger picture about the character of the whole system.

Writing at the height of the Chartist[64] movement in England, Karl Marx documented the leaps and bounds of the early labor movement:

> If the first aim of resistance was merely the maintenance of wages, combinations [unions], at first isolated, constitute themselves into groups, as the capitalists in their turn unite for the purpose of repression, and in face of always united capital, the maintenance of the association becomes more necessary to them than that of wages. This is so true that English economists are amazed to see the workers sacrifice a good part of their wages in favor of association, which, in the eyes of those economists are established solely in favor of wages. In this struggle—a veritable civil war—all the elements necessary for a coming battle unite and develop. Once it has reached this point association takes on a political character.[65]

In other words, every struggle for better wages has the potential to advance the struggle against the capitalist system itself. For this reason, Engels argued that unions, especially as they employ their main weapon, the strike, are "schools of war" that train workers in class struggle as a step forward toward their own self-emancipation.[66]

This is the essential reason why social justice advocates should participate in union struggles. Unions can be a starting point for many other struggles. They are a beginning, not an end, and they raise questions about equality—even if unions by themselves cannot win radical economic and social equality.

Marx and Engels experienced firsthand both the enormous potential for unions to advance the class struggle at certain points and also their ability to hold back the struggle at other crucial junctures. During periods of retreat and setbacks, their frustration was often directed at union officials. As Marx argued in 1878, "the leadership of the working class of England has wholly passed into the hands of corrupted union officials and the professional agitators."[67]

At the most basic level, unions function to negotiate the terms of exploitation under capitalism, and union officials act as the negotiators for their members. The officials' class position is thus contradictory. Full-time union officials are not workers themselves, and the contracts they negotiate on behalf of their members do not affect their own salaries and working conditions. If the contract agrees to layoffs, union leaders still keep their jobs. If wages are slashed or speedups imposed, union officials will maintain the same salaries and working conditions as before.

At any given time, the union leadership is caught in a delicate balancing act. Accommodating too few of the membership's demands will see them turned out of a job and potentially back under the pressures of the classroom (if they started out as teachers), or just out of a job. Pushing too hard against the local school board or federal lawmakers creates a conflict that threatens to upset the apple cart. In a word, the role of a union official is to act as a *mediator* between workers and their bosses. She is sandwiched between the two major classes in society: workers and employers.[68]

Teachers' unions are no exception, even if their bosses are government officials rather than private employers. Teachers' unions, much like the rest of the labor movement today, have evolved into bloated bureaucracies, thereby creating their own conservative union officialdom. Union leaders often choose and mentor their successors. This perpetuates a continuity of policy. Executive directors, who often wield greater influence over the union than elected presidents, can remain in their positions for years or even decades. Union staffers often provide the most continuity in terms of operating unions on a "business as usual" basis.

Moreover, the union leadership is abundantly privileged over the workers they represent. A stunning case in point is AFT president Randi Weingarten herself, who earned just under $429,000 in salary in 2010, according to US Department of Labor records. This figure is almost ten times greater than the median teacher salary in the United States, and thirteen times greater than the average starting salary.[69] This privilege betrays an objective interest the bureaucracy has in maintaining the status quo—whether by ducking necessary fights with the employers or by subverting internal democracy through control of union staff and resources.[70]

An active membership that challenges the decisions and strategies of the bureaucracy is threatening to union leaderships. This explains officialdom's reliance on lawyers, lobbyists, and electing (usually Democratic) legislators to forward the union's agenda, as opposed to job actions. Leaders hold members at arm's length while they cultivate comfortable relationships with political elites.

But by definition, as mediators between workers and capitalists, union officials are subject to pressure from both above *and* below. Rank-and-file union members can demand less compromising positions in the struggle for better pay and conditions. They can also demand that unions embrace those movements that prioritize the needs of the entire working class (for example, universal health care) rather than accept narrow compromises (for example, increased employer contributions to teachers' medical insurance costs). While several large unions have formal positions of support for universal single-payer health care, only a few, like National Nurses United, actively and vocally campaign around this issue and devote resources to advancing this demand. Ideally, union power would be harnessed to demands for social justice in order to strengthen those movements. For the past decades, though, in practice they mostly have not.

Indeed, despite the structural pressures put on bureaucrats, and despite the important continuities that run throughout various labor-leader administrations, it *does* matter who the elected union officials are. Some union leaders may be more open to class-struggle unionism. Others will create more democratic space for rank-and-file union organizing. Certainly, it made a real difference that the leadership of the Wisconsin Education Association Council (WEAC) and its president, Mary Bell, decided to stand behind the Madison teachers in their sick-out from February 16 to 21, 2011, and telephoned all ninety-eight thousand Wisconsin teachers to argue for them to leave work.

But the example of the union struggles in Wisconsin also shows that union leaders can be timid about carrying a struggle to its logical conclusion. When the section of Republican governor Scott Walker's bill that stripped public sector unions of most collective bargaining rights passed, the leadership of Madison Teachers Incorporated, the same union that had backed a two-day sick-out, also pushed for a quick contract that agreed to many of the concessions that Walker was looking for, such as increased employee contributions to health and pension benefits and a pay freeze.[71] Whereas WEAC president Mary Bell had played a positive role in encouraging teachers to come to the Capitol on the first few days of the struggle, by Monday, February 21, she told teachers to go back to work.[72]

Connecting the immediate struggles of today to greater struggles against the inhumane market system itself will be a process. Increasing numbers of teachers have become aware of the contradiction between bailouts for the very investment banks that catalyzed the collapse of the global economy and the cuts in public school budgets as they develop a more holistic critique. Some are developing a broader analysis of the current crisis that moves beyond frustration with a particular policy or politician in order to begin to question the very functioning of the current economic system. In places where our unions have started to fight back, no matter how haltingly, such as Wisconsin, Michigan, New York City, California, and elsewhere, participating in rallies, sick-outs, and occupations has been a crucial school of struggle for thousands of teachers. If this questioning is to become a full-blown critique and a guide to action, it will require the development of a critical mass of social justice educator–activists that can participate in and shape the coming struggles.

The Hope of Today: Rank-and-File Pressure and Social Movement Unionism

Building union democracy and rank-and-file involvement is crucial to achieving the objective of fighting for equality in broader ways, with parents and students, around demands that affect our whole communities. Above, we have looked at the role that bureaucracies can play in making unions more conservative. We as classroom teachers cannot cede the ground to this conservative leadership. The more that teachers facing the everyday pressures of the classroom are involved in their unions, the more unions will be forced to fight back. The stronger their alliances with parents and community at the school-site level, the more likely unions will be to take up broader issues of equality, such as immigrant rights and universal health care.

There are many current examples of this dynamic. In Los Angeles, UTLA school-site activist teachers and parents organized a massive effort to win greater public control of neighborhood schools and to save these schools from charter takeovers when the school board passed a "Public School Choice Motion" in 2009. The City of Los Angeles had just spent $16 billion on new school construction in the largest public works program in the entire country. The school board then voted to open up the new schools (as well as some existing "failing" schools) to outside bids from charter operators. Teachers, parents, and administrators came together to write plans for the new and existing schools that easily defeated the charter plans in each and every case where the public got an "advisory" vote (although those votes sometimes weren't honored by the school board). In the first year of public school choice, only four schools out of thirty-six were awarded to charters. But in spring 2011, the school board voted to get rid of the public advisory vote in the school "choice" process. This is because in every case when there was a vote, the public sided with teachers and public schools as opposed to charters.

In 2008, the Puerto Rican Teachers' Union (FMPR by its Spanish acronym) was able to lead a successful island-wide strike in March 2008 (for more on the strike, see page 155). Twenty-six thousand teachers participated, and FMPR leader Rafael Feliciano-Hernández credits the victory of the teachers to two things: first, the democratic participation of all the membership, and second, the solidarity built up with whole communities of people across the island.

The scale of the attacks, and the inability of most union leaderships to lead sufficient opposition, has meant that in recent years, member-initiated rank-and-file caucuses have sprung up in teachers' union locals across the country. For example, Educators for a Democratic Union (EDU) working inside United Educators of San Francisco have set as their goal "building a union that fights for a better world. We think that includes more direct democracy, protecting the right to public education, and social justice."[73]

In many cases, rank and filers intent on reforming our unions have run for union office. EDU ran an unsuccessful bid for office in San Francisco, but reformers have been elected union leaders in other cities. In Los Angeles, Progressive Educators for Action (PEAC) and a broader organization, United Action (UA), were able to elect a reform slate to the leadership of UTLA in 2005.

In Chicago, one hundred schools were slated for closing under Arne Duncan's Renaissance 2010 plan. When the Chicago Federation of Teachers didn't step up to the plate to lead a fight, teachers in the Caucus of Rank-and-File Educators (CORE) organized teachers and communities across sixteen schools to resist closures. They organized hundreds of parents to picket and protest at Chicago Board of Education meetings. As a result, teachers from this slate were elected to leadership positions in the Chicago Teachers Union (CTU) in spring 2010.[74] This group, with Karen Lewis elected as president, has campaigned to run the union in a different, more participatory way. Mass participation in union decisions is a necessary precondition for the kind of resolve it will take to win when unions have to strike against austerity measures. For this reason, the CTU and Karen Lewis personally have come under intense attack by Democratic Chicago mayor Rahm Emanuel. Emanuel spearheaded this attack by trying to add ninety minutes to the Chicago public school day while only increasing teacher pay by 2 percent.

In addition to CORE's 2010 election victory in Chicago just mentioned, Bob Peterson, the editor of the social justice educators' magazine *Rethinking Schools* and a longtime teacher and fighter for social justice in public schools, won an election for president of the Milwaukee Teachers' Education Association after the mass protests of 2011.

In each of the examples cited above, there have been both opportunities and major obstacles for union reformers in office. Opportunities include the possibility of retooling the structures of the union to ready them for battle. The Puerto Rican teachers wielded this power and electrified the entire island by giving teachers a taste of their collective power. The obstacles, though, are many. The FMPR became the target of the colonial government, which refused to recognize it as the collective bargaining agent of teachers after the strike and forced a decertification campaign. In Chicago, the CTU has not been able to face down a statewide legislative attack designed to limit the collective bargaining power of Illinois teachers. In Los Angeles, the reform leadership of UTLA has faced layoffs of almost a thousand teachers in 2009, fourteen hundred teachers in 2011, and pay cuts in 2010 and 2011. While UTLA planned a one-day illegal strike against layoffs in 2009, the union backed down after a temporary restraining order by a judge threatened to fine the union as much forty million dollars and strip individual teachers of their credentials.

These defeats cannot be explained for the most part by shortcomings of reform leaderships, though. In each case, what it would have taken to stem the tide of the attacks would have been mass mobilizations by a majority of union members, even when these mobilizations were illegal. This simply underscores the point that rank-and-file involvement and mobilization is not the same thing as rank-and-file reformers taking control of union leaderships.

Rank-and-file involvement means that teachers need to use their unions as a weapon for justice at every school, in ways large and small. Unions will only be able to turn the tide to the extent that members at every single school are willing to mobilize. From organizing to allow teachers adequate access to the copy machine and stopping malicious, arbitrary treatment from overbearing administrators to ensuring the participation of all teachers at a school in a job action, it's important for teachers at a school to stay united and to organize collective solutions to our problems. No matter what union contracts say or how many pages long they are, they will be violated at the workplace unless they are enforced through on-the-ground collective action and organizing.

Rank-and-file teacher-activists also have to politicize our union meetings by putting forward resolutions against the war in Afghanistan, against the Race to the Top initiative, for immigrant rights, in solidarity with other districts facing layoffs, and in favor of same-sex marriage. Unions are supposed to represent all members, from conservative to progressive, so some people object to resolutions that don't represent all workers and may not even represent most. But raising resolutions creates space for discussing why our unions will be stronger if they stand in solidarity with other groups fighting for justice. A Marxist view of consciousness is that people's opinions aren't static and shouldn't be taken as a given. Even conservatives may be won to a position of supporting equal rights for immigrants or legalization if they can be convinced that it will benefit them. Our government's policy of labeling some labor as "illegal" puts downward pressure on everyone's wages and weakens the union movement overall.

At the same time, too narrow a focus on passing resolutions can sometimes serve to give a union the veneer of social justice, even when very little is done to achieve the ideals to which they nominally agree. "It is," according to Lois Weiner, "the mobilization of members in defense of social justice issues—rather than only the passage of resolutions—that is the hallmark of a union that has adopted the strategy that I recommend [social movement unionism.]"[75] Thus, progressive educators must draw up lesson plans to reinvent our unions on the very models of social justice we often teach about, such as Martin Luther King Jr.'s Poor People's Campaign or the huge boycotts and protests for immigrant rights starting in 2006.

As teachers organize rank-and-file caucuses, they should be aware that "social movement unionism" or "social justice unionism," two terms that are used interchangeably by most, are not ideologically homogenous. There are tensions within these tendencies. To give one example: we put a premium on community engagement. Does this mean that teachers should strike only *after* we have built up "sufficient" community support? This can often be a formula for passivity, because in reality, *action* and support build on each other simultaneously.

As another example of a tension within social justice unionism, most would agree that it's important to strategize about "teacher professionalism" as a part of taking responsibility for the quality of schools.[76] But this is where the sharp debates begin. On one of the central issues of the day, teacher evaluation and seniority, social justice/social movement unionists are trying to chart new territory and don't always agree with each other. Context has a lot to do with the source of these disagreements: a public school teacher looking for a fair evaluation without being given the resources to succeed in a given school system is a little bit like a Black man trying to get a fair trial in Alabama in the 1930s. At the same time, we do need to find better ways of improving the quality of teaching—but in the spirit of helping each other to improve our practices, not for reasons of evaluation or sanction.

In addition, social justice/social movement unionists are grappling with and debating the key next steps for unions to take in order to move forward in the face of a political and economic elite bent on crushing public-sector unions. Sam Gindin, the former research director for the Canadian Auto Workers, has argued for the sort of radical shift in strategy that could make unions a viable social force. He writes:

> In the 1930s—the last time the working class went through comparable economic chaos—workers radically and creatively adjusted their strategy by developing sectoral-based unions. A comparable strategic adjustment for unions today would lie in transforming the confrontation from one between workers and the individual employer, to one between public sector workers and the province by consolidating bargaining strength and moving into a position to strike together. . . . If jobs go, wages are secondary, but if public sector workers lead a fight to protect and extend

services, this not only addresses jobs but builds community support for taking on future wage improvements. The strategic shift for public sector unions might be posed as follows: the government, by removing wages and benefit improvements from negotiations, is trying to dramatically narrow collective bargaining. What if the unions responded by *expanding* collective bargaining? What if public sector unions refused to settle collective agreements unless the settlements address the level, quality, and administration of the services being provided?[77]

It's almost universally accepted inside unions that we are, and must be, on the defensive right now. Gindin proposes that the only way to win is by going on the offensive, and trying to win an expansion of collective bargaining rights by uniting all public-sector unions together and taking public sector-wide job action. Going on the offensive, while it will feel risky to many, is the only way of defending the rights that come along with union membership: the right to due process, the right to strike, higher wages, academic freedom, and the right to negotiate issues of the quality of education—from class sizes to shared decision-making councils.

The interplay between unions and other social forces is much more common outside the United States. In Europe, unions are more amenable to working with the global justice movement, for example. But the impact of workers' power and social movements, when linked, was highlighted most powerfully in the February 2011 uprising in Egypt that toppled Hosni Mubarak's thirty-year dictatorship. Unionists—including teachers—played a critical role in organizing opposition to the Mubarak regime for years prior to the revolution. Moreover, the massive strike wave that swept Egypt in the final days of the regime played a critical role in providing the economic muscle to finally topple the dictatorship. When teachers and other public-sector workers were struggling for their right to collectively bargain in Wisconsin, Kamal Abbas, an organizer in the Egyptian revolution and general coordinator of the Center for Trade Unions and Workers' Services in Egypt, sent some good advice. In a message of solidarity that was broadcast to the tens of thousands of protesters who occupied the Capitol Building, he said,

> I am speaking to you from a place very close to Tahrir Square in Cairo, "Liberation Square," which was the heart of the Revolution in Egypt. This is the place where many of our youth paid with their lives and blood in the struggle for our just rights. From this place, I want you to know that we stand with you as you stood with us. I want you to know that no power can challenge the will of the people when they believe in their rights. When

they raise their voices loud and clear and struggle against exploitation. No one believed that our revolution could succeed against the strongest dictatorship in the region. But in 18 days the revolution achieved the victory of the people. When the working class of Egypt joined the revolution on 9 and 10 February, the dictatorship was doomed and the victory of the people became inevitable. We want you to know that we stand on your side. Stand firm and don't waiver. Don't give up on your rights. Victory always belongs to the people who stand firm and demand their just rights.[78]

The contributors to this book hope that we will see the same process mature in the relationship between organized labor, the Occupy Wall Street movement, other social justice movements, and unorganized workers.

You can't fix schools without fixing the society in which they exist. That is because a student whose home is foreclosed on will not be able to do the economics homework. A student whose loved one has been killed in a war in the Middle East will have difficulty connecting with the science teacher's attempt to bring alive the learning of human bodily systems. A student whose parents have been deported will have difficulty crossing the barrier of the parent signature needed for a field trip to the civil rights museum. A student whose family lacks affordable health insurance may find herself chronically absent from health class. A student with parents who have been laid off may see his dream of going to college deferred for lack of funds. A student forced to carry an unwanted pregnancy to term because of the lack of access to an abortion provider may find her studies of the women's suffrage movement abruptly terminated. A student of color who has been warehoused in a prison will miss the lesson on Martin Luther King Jr.'s "Letter from a Birmingham Jail."

As have our Egyptian sisters and brothers, it is time we demand our rights. The same power of working people to protest, strike, and create change exists in the United States. There is a vast potential for teachers who are facing mass layoffs around the United States to organize a struggle that unites broader social forces to demand an end to the practice of spending more to bomb children in the Middle East than to educate them at home. For this to succeed, educators will need to remake their unions based on principles of social justice that connect the fight for education with the broader labor movement and social movements striving to confront the intertwined evils of war, racism, and exploitation.

FOCUS ON

The Madison Protests

Dan Trocolli and Sarah Knopp

The teachers who led the occupation of Wisconsin's Capitol in February 2011 captured the spirit of educators who are fed up with being blamed for society's problems. The sick-outs by Madison teachers that started on February 16 soon spread statewide, and teachers from across the country went to Madison to show their solidarity by joining a series of enormous demonstrations that spilled over into March.

On March 12, 2011, some one hundred and fifty thousand people convened at the Capitol Building in Madison. Just two days prior, the Wisconsin Senate had used legislative shenanigans to get Governor Walker's union-busting bill passed. The momentum from a month of rallies and occupation, combined with this maneuver by state Republicans, imposed huge questions on those demonstrating. Are the rallies enough? If not, what will it take? As labor journalist Lee Sustar put it: "The question was posed point-blank: Would the massive March 12 rally . . . be a springboard for labor action that would stop the bill, such as a general strike? Or would it remain the electoral rally that union leaders wanted?"[1]

In hindsight, the answer to that question has been made clear. The AFL-CIO state union leadership successfully steered the resistance from the Madison spring into an electoral effort to recall Republican state legislators who voted for the anti-union bill. Of six Republican state senators up for recall, only two were successfully unseated.[2] Additionally, the unions have since agreed to major concessionary contracts. On March 13—just one day after the massive rally in Madison—members of the union that had taken the lead, Madison Teachers Incorporated, ratified a contract with major concessions. These included a pay freeze, an increase in teachers' contributions for pensions and health insurance, and a longer school day. The contract was rushed through to ratification, as were contracts in other Wisconsin districts. The intent was to get the contracts through before Governor Walker's anti-union law would take effect. Namely, automatic deduction of union dues was still in place—something that Governor Walker's bill would end. But these contracts include almost every economic cut that Walker has demanded at the state level.

Despite this setback, the teachers' struggle in Wisconsin remains an inspiration to social justice educators across the United States. Below are excerpts from interviews conducted by Dan Trocolli, a teacher in Seattle, Washington, and a founding member of Social Equality Educators. In addition, we have included an excerpt from a report about the March 12 rally, "Needed: A National Teachers' Movement," by Sarah Knopp.[3] While participating in the rallies, Dan and Sarah spoke with various teachers, students, and other unionists. Taken together, the excerpts from these interviews provide powerful insights about what is at stake in the neoliberal attack on Wisconsin's teachers and schools. They also show the potential for a different set of strategies of resistance.

Rick, a First-Grade Teacher from Madison

What's the significance of what is happening here in Wisconsin?
This bill will mean a $430 pay cut for me and my family. I will have to get a second job, and that means less time in the classroom preparing. A lot of my students' families have been out here with me, and that means a lot. This bill is coming from fringe people with a lot of corporate backing, people that we can't afford to keep up with. This [protest] is the way we can show our voice. Unfortunately they, Walker and [the] corporations, are not listening to it.

What do you think about the sick-outs as a tactic?
It's necessary. Look at what it's started. We need to stand up to make our voice heard. We can't be silent. My wife is pregnant and we are going to have a daughter in three weeks. It's important for us to stand up so that she can do that. We can't say to her "you have to stand up" and not stand up ourselves.

What do you think about education reform?
It's hard. It takes so long to become a good teacher. There's only so much you can learn in school. You have to devote yourself to study. Merit pay, you know it takes more than just me to educate the children in my classroom. It takes the special education assistants that are in my room constantly helping. [It takes] the school psychologist that comes in and talks to the girl that's having a hard day, or the school social worker. It takes more than just me to come in and make my kids successful. I feel pretty confident in the growth that I've seen in my students . . . but I don't think [merit pay] is fair. I think that what needs to happen is that we need to take the funding for education out of the hands of the politicians. I'm sick and tired of people getting elected based on railing against education. It needs to stop. Democrat, Republican, same thing, they all do it.

Carlene, a Middle-School Teacher from Madison

What's at stake in this fight?
It's really difficult to name it all. For working people, this is a clear attempt at union busting. People are kidding themselves if they think it's going to stop with public employees. If they are successful with us, the rest is just a domino effect. There are some really sweeping changes to Medicare, which

we call Badgercare, in the bill. There are about three-quarters of a million people on Badgercare in the state of Wisconsin, and about two-thirds of those are children. They would lose access to health care. Then there are provisions that would allow the governor to sell off public assets such as power plants. There are about thirty-seven statewide, and it's no accident that the Koch brothers in the last month opened their first lobbying office in the state here in the capital. It's their industry and they are the second biggest contributor to Walker's campaign. They've made no secret as to where they stand on workers' rights, wages, and the environment.

What is the impact around the country of the fight that's been happening here?
Honestly, I've been inside the capitol building so much that I don't really know. Well, you're here. I hear that it's something that is being watched around the world. People are charging food to their credit cards and having it delivered here from all over Europe, the Middle East, and all over the country. It really is big. You feel the gravity of what we're doing here when you look at the sign that announces all the places that food has been donated from.

What do you think about the statewide sick-outs of teachers?
Well, I'm a teacher. I participated in that. I was here till three o'clock in the morning the first night of the Joint-Finance Committee meeting. So I was *sick* the next day [*she tears up*]. The part that's really sad about this is we really are sick about all this. It's sick here, the heart. This is a struggle that affects us all, and we'd be kidding ourselves if we think it's just about teachers and public employees just milking the system. That's a bunch of bull! I go to work at six thirty in the morning and I'm lucky if I get back home by six thirty at night. I take work home every night and every weekend. I educate myself, I have a master's degree that I paid for. The state didn't pay for my master's degree. I want to be the best teacher possible. I take my job very seriously. I affect the future. My students are my number one priority. And to call me a bottom-feeder is so insulting, it makes me sick.

Hallie, a Special-Education Teacher from Madison

What do you think about the teachers' sick-out as a tactic and its impact?
I think it was huge. I was here all four days; it was scary for teachers. You

know, we're an urban school district and a lot of kids come to school and it's the only meal they get during the day. So it was heartfelt, it was not easy for teachers to leave. It was not a day off—we took it without pay. But when I saw the senators hanging out the windows, and the YouTube clips from when they were in assembly and as we were in the sit-in outside the doors when the senators were trying to run out of state, I realize they never would have felt we have their back, had we not had thirty-five thousand people outside the day before and if the teachers didn't call in sick and [get] lots of people to wake up when they were home with their kids for four days, it did start something. It is sad that some of those kids had to miss some things, but this is their future. I mean, really, four days is nothing compared with what they are going to lose with, say, not being able to have a job in health care again.

Excerpt from

"Needed: A National Teachers' Movement"
by Sarah Knopp

After I gave solidarity greetings from Los Angeles at the mic [inside the State Capitol Building], Kristine, who's now a graduate student and teaching assistant at the University of Wisconsin, approached me to talk about what she'd learned since leaving K–12 teaching. Coincidentally, she had been a teacher in Los Angeles, too.

> I wish it was easier to stay in teaching. I feel like some of the best ones leave. Because as teachers, we feel like we want to take on everything, but we can't. Those of us who want to actually do the job the way that it's supposed to be done realize that we're working under impossible circumstances.
>
> I know teachers feel afraid about striking, but if we don't, we have to realize the long-term effect. Even in the short term, the benefit of us striking is for the kids. If we don't, people like Scott Walker are going to destroy their futures.

Meanwhile, students from all over the city were staging walkouts and gathering at the Capitol. A group of students from Middleton High School had gathered at the Capitol, and I asked them why they cared enough to be out here. "We love our teachers," they said.

"Really?" I asked. "Like all of them?"

"Ninety percent of them are nice," Nicolaus told me. "We're learning English, so we need extra help. Ninety percent give us attention and don't act racist."

Ann Marchant from Stevens Point, Wisconsin, was obviously the kind of teacher they were talking about. She teaches English as a second language (ESL), but they have so few ESL teachers in Stevens Point, despite a large student population, that she moves from school to school and teaches all grades, K–12.

"The big difference I've seen," she said, "is in the community of the school. We have been marching in front of the school together every day for four weeks. I feel like I live in a community now instead of a bubble. I had always felt safe, I'm an ESL teacher, I'm in demand, I'm going to have a job, security, retirement. Now . . . I feel more connected to the union."

Ann reminded me of the situation of my cousin, who teaches middle-school ESL in suburban Chicago. Her new superintendent told all the ESL teachers to fill out applications to transfer to general education. This was a move on his part to segregate all ESL students in the whole district into one school. "I guess we pulled our own Wisconsin," she told me, because they all refused to sign the papers.

Later that day, about two thousand students from all over Madison gathered on Library Mall. Some organizers from Wisconsin Students Solidarity were speaking from the elevated platform—with a bullhorn, 1960s-style. I was glad to see that they were using statistics to back up their arguments, something I feel like I've been repeating in my classroom like a broken record every day for the past eleven years.

"When they cut $390 million from education," the organizer explained, "that means the total elimination of alternative education. It means the elimination of AP [advanced placement] programs. It means the elimination of alcohol [abuse] prevention and intervention programs."

"Who the hell thought that was a good idea?" asked the kid next to me. Eleanor, from Madison East High School, was circulating in the crowd getting others to sign a petition, so I asked her why she was so passionate about standing up for public workers' rights, given that schools often seem below standard. "I think that as students, we know that it's not teachers' fault," she said. "They aren't given the funds they need to succeed. And no one knows better than students that teaching is a really hard job. We need more money, but there's no way to get it."

Lynn Miyagawa, from Orchard Ridge Elementary, was crying at the end of the day. "I'm emotional because I'm surprised. I really didn't think that this would pass," she said of Walker's union-busting bill. Miyagawa said that she had also felt proud when the fourteen Democratic state senators commended the crowd for standing up and leading. I decided to ask her about something uplifting, like the impact that this has had on her teaching.

"When you teach third grade like I do," she said, "fairness is a big concept. So what this struggle has done is to make the concept of fairness really multidimensional for them. It's also making the concept of democracy very multidimensional for them."

Teachers' Struggle in Oaxaca, Mexico

Jessie Muldoon

In the United States, our teachers' unions too often separate social justice from the economic and workplace issues in specific contract struggles. And the political action that we do see in our unions all too often looks like unconditional support for Democratic policies and candidates. But this is not the only model.

Teachers in Oaxaca, Mexico, have taken the lead repeatedly over the last few years in demonstrating what sort of struggle is possible. Oaxaca is in southern Mexico, one of the poorest states—with one of the largest indigenous populations—in the country. Teachers in Oaxaca barely make a living wage and are generally responsible for providing their own classroom resources. As Alejandra Favela describes, the seventy thousand mostly indigenous teachers of Oaxaca have a long history of organizing, including fights to win and maintain control of their union, Section 22 of the National Education Workers Union (SNTE in its Spanish initials).[1]

Their strike in spring 2011 exemplifies the best of social justice unionism. The teachers struck to protest an attempt by Felipe Calderón's government to make 50 percent of a teacher's evaluation based on his or her students' score on national standardized tests, and also to force the state to pay for electricity and computers for their students to use at school.[2] In part, this fight was also about rebuilding union democracy—the president of the national teachers' union, Elba Ester García, had already signed off on the new evaluation scheme. Still, rank-and-file teachers in Oaxaca struck to challenge the policy.[3]

This strike is both a product of an international neoliberal attack on teachers and their unions and the continuation of a long tradition of struggle in Oaxaca. As Mary Compton and Lois Weiner point out in *The Global Assault on Teaching, Teachers, and Their Unions: Stories for Resistance*, the World Bank issued a report in 1999 that prescribed privatization, charter schools, standardized testing and accountability for measuring teacher performance, and ultimately removing the institutional "blocks" of teachers' unions as an international model of school "reform."[4]

Oaxacan teachers are setting the example for how to stand up to this broad agenda. And they've had lots of experience in doing so. In 2006, another strike by Oaxacan teachers intersected with anger, worsening economic conditions, and government repression and transformed an almost routine teachers' strike into a powerful social movement. The Oaxacan teachers' union had initiated the strike centered on the basics: an increase in wages and money for classroom infrastructure, such as permanent roofs. At the start of the strike, it was not obvious what its trajectory would be. One new element that spurred the struggle was the actions of Oaxaca's governor at the time, Ulises Ruiz. He refused to negotiate with the union. This simple refusal helped transform the struggle into a broader movement for social change, specifically demanding the removal of Ruiz as governor.

Broadening the demands also broadened the struggle, as people joined the strike and turned a labor dispute into a social movement. Strikers and activists occupied the *zócalo* (town square) and convened their new governing formation, APPO, the Popular Assembly of the Peoples of Oaxaca—which was more than a union. While Section 22 comprised a large part of APPO, students, farmers, health care workers, indigenous activists, and members of other community and nongovernmental organizations were active in the assembly. Moreover, women played a particular role in leading this movement.[5] The formation and makeup of APPO reflected the development of the struggle from a union battle to a social movement. APPO's slogan sums up the dynamic: "The movement has no leaders; it is from the grass roots." The level of spontaneous self-organization was impressive indeed. Any movement faces massive challenges, though, like the challenge of police repression, and perhaps even more difficult, the challenge of time. Whether or not a movement needs leadership to withstand these tests is a hotly debated topic among social justice activists.

APPO was met with what many believe to be harsh and disproportionate repression. This grassroots upsurge posed enough of a threat to the state that Governor Ruiz sent riot police into Oaxaca's *zócalo* to uproot the strikers and supporters. Armed with batons, these forces beat teachers while tear gas grenades were fired from above. However, this assault backfired. Rather than beating the teachers into submission, it sparked such outrage that the movement's ranks swelled. As John Gibler reported from Oaxaca:

> The failed attempt to violently uproot the teachers—coming only five weeks after police brutality in San Salvador Atenco erupted in a national scandal—backfired dramatically: it led disenchanted local residents to hit the streets and

thicken the teachers' civil disobedience encampments. On June 16, teachers and locals organized a massive march to demand Ruiz Ortiz's immediate resignation. With one day's notice, they put half a million people on the streets in a metropolitan area of one million inhabitants.

"As of June 14, our movement ceased to be a teachers' movement, and became a social movement, a movement of the people," Juan de Dios Garcia Santiago, a Section 22 union representative, told me outside of the blockaded entrance to the state attorney general's office.[6]

The repression against the teachers generalized the opposition, and rather than squashing it, strengthened it. At issue was no longer simply working conditions and pay for Oaxaca's teachers but also basic questions of equity and power. Oaxaca was becoming ungovernable as demands for Ruiz to step down grew.

Ultimately, this battle lasted more than six months. In the short term, the union did win modest wage gains and increases in funding. More important, according to one Section 22 delegate, the movement that emerged in 2006 "left something good—because the people of Oaxaca—despite everything—the people were united."[7] However, while the spirit of APPO still exists in Oaxaca, and the feeling that "we are all APPO" is still a popular one in the collective memory, APPO no longer exists in the same way as an organization. Its spontaneity may have been inspiring, but its lack of long-term, battle-tested, democratically elected leadership may explain why it has not been able to maintain organizational continuity.

But the Oaxacan struggle of 2006 demonstrated that a labor struggle does not have to limit itself to only the perceived needs of its own members. Teachers' demands for salary increases are demands for stable work and a stable life. Demands for improved working conditions are demands for improved learning conditions for students. The rebellion in Oaxaca demonstrates that there is not an iron wall between a union's demands and social justice demands. This is a crucial lesson for today's teacher-activists around the world.

These examples in Oaxaca may feel a world away—after all, the *zócalo* where the APPO convened in 2006 lies some thousand miles south of the main stretch of the US-Mexico border. However, the long history of migration between Oaxaca and the United States means that the legacy of these struggles is closer than we might think. A 2007 study documented an indigenous Oaxacan population in California of between a hundred thousand and a hundred and fifty thousand people.[8] In San Diego schools alone, more than three thousand Oaxacan students attend a migrant education program administered jointly by the United States and Mexico.[9] In other words, the possibility exists that some of our own students' parents participated in—and learned critical lessons from—these struggles. By collaborating with Oaxacan parents and incorporating the stories and experiences of our Oaxacan students into daily classroom work, we stand to learn a great deal from them about social justice unionism and the rich history of social struggles in indigenous Mexico.

6

Pedagogy and Revolution:
Reading Freire in Context
Adrienne Johnstone and Elizabeth Terzakis

Like the demands for bilingual education that emerged from the Chicano Power movement and the insistence on equal access to educational resources that came out of the civil rights movement, Paulo Freire's prescriptions for critical pedagogy were informed by a broader battle for social justice. They were also, importantly, a product of his commitment not just to social reform but also to socialist revolution. Freire was a Marxist, and his conviction that the shortcomings of the educational system were inextricably tied to the inequality and injustices of the capitalist system is everywhere evident in *Pedagogy of the Oppressed*.

Unfortunately, and as has been noted in previous chapters, the gains of the movements of the sixties and seventies have been eroded, if not completely reversed, by forty years of neoliberal ideology and policy and a lack of coordinated grassroots struggle. This is as true in the realms of criminal justice and welfare as it is in education. But the degree to which a lack of experience of struggle has allowed the neoliberal dictate of "individual responsibility" to pervade society is particularly apparent in the way that Freire's ideas have been stripped of both their historical context and their revolutionary theory. In the absence of collective struggle and without the underpinnings of Marxism, it is easy to see *Pedagogy of the Oppressed* as a set of principles and best practices for individual teachers—guidelines for a "revolution in one classroom."

This chapter aims to resituate and reclaim *Pedagogy of the Oppressed* as a specifically Marxist revolutionary text that requires educators to look beyond the classroom to achieve liberatory education. Such a rereading and representation of Freire is particularly important now, as the revolution-in-one-classroom understanding of *Pedagogy* is consistent with the neoliberal idea that the current crisis state of public education is caused by incompetent teachers and the corrupt unions that protect them.[1] As social justice educators, we cannot afford to be pitted against each other, nor can we ignore our unions or allow them to be disbanded; we must use them to build the kind of collective action that makes truly liberatory pedagogy possible.

Roots

Paulo Freire was born in Recife, Brazil, in 1921. He worked briefly as a lawyer but soon turned to education, specifically to developing literacy programs for the Brazilian peasantry, which was widely disenfranchised due to a literacy requirement. When the reform government of João Goulart was ousted by a CIA-supported military coup in 1964, Freire, considered an "international subversive" trying to turn Brazil into a "Bolshevik country," was immediately arrested and imprisoned for seventy days. Before he could be imprisoned again, or worse, he began a sixteen-year self-imposed exile.

During exile, he worked with the revolutionary nationalist leadership of Guinea-Bisseau and the World Council of Churches in Geneva, taught at Harvard, and built educational reform projects around the world. He returned to Brazil in 1980 and joined the Workers' Party, or PT (according to its initials in Portuguese), as a founding member along with, among others, former Brazilian president Luiz Inácio Lula da Silva.[2] After the military dictatorship ended in 1984, the PT gained strength throughout Brazil. In 1989, the party's candidate won the mayoral race in São Paulo, and Freire was appointed secretary of education, a position from which he resigned in 1991. He is probably the best-known theorist of critical pedagogy in the world.

In *Pedagogy of the Oppressed*, his most widely read work, Freire presents a theory of education and social change, arguing that education is inseparable from the struggle for what he called the "ontological vocation of humanity"—the completion of ourselves as human beings. When the book was published in 1970, Freire believed that a complete transformation of society would be necessary in order for this vocation to be realized. Capitalism— which is not organized to provide for, let alone encourage and develop, the overwhelming majority of the planet's people—prevents humanization. Consequently, it must be replaced by a system that allows for, as Marx put it, "an association in which the free development of each is the condition for the free development of all."[3]

Your Money and Your Life:
Banking versus Problem-Posing Education

Pedagogy of the Oppressed includes an analysis of education under capitalism and a critique of what Freire describes as the "banking" concept of education. In banking education, teachers deposit knowledge in the empty vaults of students' minds. The curriculum is either in the hands and mind of the teacher alone or determined at a distance from the classroom by administrators or school boards or some other organ of the state. Once the information has been deposited in the students' brains, the only thing left to do is to ascertain how well they have memorized it, which is easily done through standardized tests, since what is important for the students to know has already been determined and is easily measurable. The banking concept forces on students an almost-total passivity and can easily render the teacher equally passive. Freire and Ira Shor speak at length in *A Pedagogy for Liberation* about how banking education works to produce glassy-eyed, checked-out students and droning, deadly boring instructors.[4]

Underpinning Freire's characterization of schools is a Marxist understanding of the state—the structure of laws, institutions, armed bodies, and prisons—that orders our society. According to Marx, the state is not a neutral body evenhandedly mediating the relationship among the various social classes. Rather, it is a structure that is set up for the sole purpose of protecting and serving the interests of the ruling class.[5] Chapter 1 describes in some detail the Marxist understanding of the dynamic relationship between the economic base and the political, social, and ideological superstructure that characterizes any class society, capitalism included. Freire's concept of banking education is generally consistent with this idea. Under capitalism—and Freire is quite clear about this—schools exist to socialize the next generation of workers in the values and interests of capital, and those of us committed to the liberation of ourselves and our students should never expect an initiative coming from the state to tend in any other direction.

Because they are structured to serve the interests of the ruling class, schools tend to hide or mystify conflict, injustice, inequality, poverty, suffering, and struggle. For example, in the 1970s, US society was characterized as a "melting pot," but nothing was said about the genocide of Native Americans or the sending of Native American children to schools in which their language and religious beliefs were denigrated and forbidden. More recently, US society has been described as a "mixed salad," but, for the most part, nothing is said about the struggles—like the Chicano Power movement—that have been necessary to keep the salad a salad and not gazpacho (that is, puréed and homogenized).

This mystification, perversely, occurs alongside a hyper-valuation of science and technology. Scientifically corroborated facts are not only measurably knowable but also more valuable to capitalism than critical thinking, which allows us to shatter the opaqueness of the dominant ideology and see the world for what it is—to point out, for instance, that science is historical: that it changes, too. The promotion of critical thinking is one of the key benefits of Freire's counter to banking education—the problem-posing, dialogical method of education.

In problem-posing education, as the name suggests, the world is presented not as a fact but as a problem, a living entity in a constant state of becoming. Because it is unfinished, it cannot simply be known; it must be interpreted. One of the jobs of the teacher is to figure out how to present the students' world to them as something to be solved. Dialogical education—also as the name suggests—consists of a dialogue or series of dialogues between teacher and students, students and the world, students with each other, teacher and the world, and so on. Unlike banking education, dialogical education does not assume that the teacher has all the funds and that the students' accounts are empty. Instead, it is taken for granted that the teacher will need to learn from the students in order to be able to teach them anything useful. Students cannot be passive; they must contribute and interpret. Rather than presuming a wide gap between students and teachers, Freire introduces the concepts of "teacher-students" and "student-teachers." On the table between the teacher-student and the student-teachers is an object of study drawn directly from their world. The object of study mediates their dialogue; *both* learn from it and from each other.

How does this work? Teacher-students direct their student-teachers in the generation of what Freire calls *themes*: that is, the teacher-student presents to the student-teachers an opportunity to talk about the concerns that are on their minds. From these themes the teacher-student chooses those that are *generative*: that is, those that will tend to expose the contradictions lurking beneath the mists of the dominant understanding of the world. Then the teacher-student performs an act of what Freire calls *codification* through which he or she objectifies—turns into an object of study—the theme raised. Finally, together, the teacher-student and student-teachers perform an act of *decodification*—they interpret the significance of the object of study and relate their conclusions back to the original theme.

What would this look like in practice? Say you are teaching a composition class at a community college, and you want to focus the class on the issue of public education. Despite the dominant ideology on the subject, you think that our government does not value education at all. But you don't go in and start pontificating bombastically or droning on and on about banking education and ideological state apparatuses and the historicity of science—not because students cannot grasp these concepts, but because starting from that kind of academic language will alienate them and shut the discussion down. So, instead, you ask your students to write a paragraph about how they got to school that day. You already know that transportation is a big issue for them: recent cuts to an already-unreliable bus service, cars that break down, and relying on rides from friends who get sick a lot make it an ongoing problem. After the students are finished writing, you can either have them share their paragraphs with each other or you can read them yourself and choose examples from which to work. You then use these examples, or perhaps a picture of people waiting for the bus or a repair estimate from a mechanic, to "codify" the theme—to represent it to the students as an object of study. You and your students look at the object and discuss it, interpreting the faces of the people at the bus stop or the high numbers on the repair estimate in whatever way you will. This discussion leads you into relevant reading assignments, which lead into further discussion, and so on.

Note that while Freire wants liberatory teachers to respect and value the knowledge and languages of our students, he also makes quite clear the need for the teacher-student to direct the class, to have clear and well-thought-out goals, based on clear politics: "Even though you are being open to a new thing, you must from the beginning of your action have your dream, have it with some clarity. . . . You lose the objective of your dream when you become spontaneous. It happens to teachers and militants who lose touch with their politics."[6]

Just as Freire's critique of banking education meshes well with Marx's conception of the state and dominant ideology, a problem-posing, dialogical education is consistent with Marx's dictate that socialist revolution must be an act of self-emancipation on the part of the working class. In order to be capable of emancipating ourselves, working-class people must be able to think critically about the world and see behind and beneath the myths of dominant ideology. We must be active and not passive. And we must see that values that currently seem natural and immutable—like the value of a particular kind of science or a particular kind of English—are actually historically specific and serve the needs of a particular ruling class.

The Shape of the Struggle: Limit-Situations and Limit-Acts

Liberatory education reveals the class nature of society and all the oppression it creates. Through the codification and decodification of themes, the positions of the individual and of classes and social groups in the larger society come to the fore. Students who no longer identify with the ruling class learn to "read" and "see" the world in a new way. We learn that the world is not "closed," that struggle is possible and necessary to confront inequality and to fundamentally change the world. Freire uses the concepts of *limit-situations*, *untested feasibilities*, and *limit-acts* to explain the ways in which we confront social reality.

Some examples of generative themes, those themes that expose the contradictions at work in the world, are presented in figure 6.1 below. These generative themes compose a *thematic universe* in which we live. This thematic universe is historically variable and is not the same for every location. It can be represented as a series of concentric circles, with the themes becoming broader as you move out from the student. Following from the previously mentioned example, the innermost ring is "transportation to school," and inside it are all the opposing forces that interact with what should be a simple process: good days when the car works or the bus comes on time; bad days when the car is broken down and you can't afford to fix it, or it's pouring rain and the bus is late and crowded. Within each ring are forces that coexist and contradict, push and pull on each other. The forces at work in these themes are not always apparent, but are often hidden or covered by dominant, ruling-class ideas.

Broader themes in this thematic universe—represented by circles moving outward from the center—could include "the cost of higher education,"

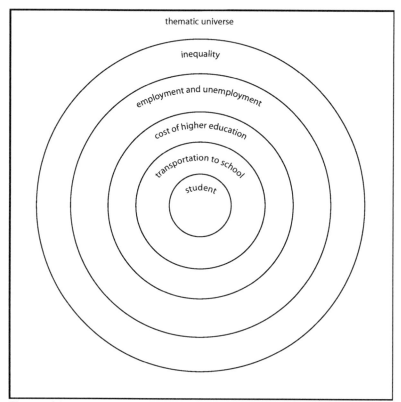

Figure 6.1

"employment and unemployment," or "inequality." These themes may be harder or easier to uncover depending on how strong "commonsense" notions are in the consciousness of a student. That is, we are taught that we are individually responsible for getting ourselves to school, that we are to blame if it doesn't happen, and that we are paid for the value of the work we do in the world. Following this logic—which supports the status quo—if we can't afford or access a reliable mode of transportation, it is somehow our fault as individuals living in a meritocracy.

Within the theme of transportation to school there are *limit-situations.* A limit-situation is a condition that appears, at first, to be unchangeable. For example, a limit-situation for many students is that the cost of owning a car—gas, insurance, and maintenance—is high, but public transportation is incredibly limited and increasingly unavailable. This situation may appear fair, or just "the way it is." But with a little imagination things could be really different: free and plentiful public transportation and smaller schools that are closer to home come immediately to mind. We could think of more, but let's start by examining the possibility of free and plentiful public transportation. This is an example of what Freire calls an *untested feasibility*—it is a demand that the working class could make, but would clearly have to struggle for. An untested feasibility is a perception of a potential reality. Untested feasibilities require *limit-acts*. These are challenges to the limit-situation—a protest at the meeting to cut bus routes or a strike to demand the hiring of more bus drivers. Any action that flows out of a full understanding of the limit-situation and pushes toward the untested feasibility is a limit-act.

These interrelated concepts are components of *praxis* and *conscientization*. Freire defines conscientization as "a way of reading how society works. It is the way to understand better the problem of interests, the question of power . . . a deeper reading of reality."[7] This is consistent with two central and fairly well-known ideas of Marxism—first, that philosophy exists in order to change the world, not merely to understand or be aware of it,[8] and second, that "the history of all hitherto existing society is the history of class struggle."[9] Conscientization implies recognizing both limit-situations and untested feasibilities and engaging in limit-acts. That is, conscientization is not merely becoming conscious of the world, what Freire called *emergence*, but choosing to act—what Freire termed *intervention*.[10] Liberation, therefore, is a real, material act in the world and is not limited to "freeing your mind." It can only be achieved by challenging ruling ideology and engaging in real, on-the-ground class struggle. *Praxis* is a word that captures the unity of recognizing limit-situations and acting to change them. Freire defines praxis as "the action and reflection of men and women upon their world in order to transform it."[11] It is the Marxist idea of the relationship between theory and practice. While we can only present these ideas in a linear, written fashion, Freire's theory is deeply dialectical and should not be understood as a series of stages through which a learner moves (see figure 6.2 below). Freire states, "Let me emphasize that my defense of the praxis implies no dichotomy by which this praxis could be divided into a prior stage of reflection and a subsequent stage of action. Action and reflection occur simultaneously."[12]

This interplay of praxis and conscientization may appear immediately relevant to college and high-school teachers. After all, these students are young adults, coming into their own in the world. But what about teachers

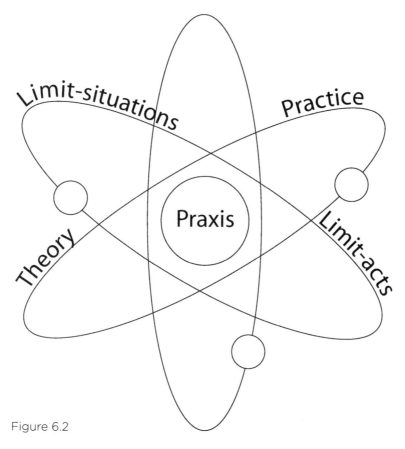

Figure 6.2

who work with young students in elementary schools? Can our students participate in a true dialogic education with us? There are several limiting factors in developing any pedagogy of the oppressed with young children. As noted above, the primary function of schools under capitalism is to socialize the next generation of workers in the values and interests of capitalism. This explains why, throughout history, schools experience repeated pressure from the top to adopt common national curriculum standards and to increase the standardization and regulation of what goes on in schools. This doesn't leave much room for most teachers to create a learning environment that is built from the learner's world outward. It definitely excludes almost any possibility of seeing the world outside the school walls as an essential component of a real education.

There is also a commonsense notion that children are just easily swayed because of their young and mushy brains, that they cannot dialogue with adults and develop their own ideas, that they are too young to intervene in the outside world. This idea helps prop up the public education system and the nuclear family, both of which primarily serve the needs of capitalism. It is beyond the scope of this chapter to provide a Marxist analysis of the family, but it is worth noting here that we are thoroughly saturated with the belief that children are the property of their families and as such are mostly expected to stay in a critically dormant state until their eighteenth birthdays. They may be taught about people who questioned the world, but they should not do so themselves. If they do question, they definitely shouldn't try to *do* anything about it. They should learn critical thinking, but apply it only to word problems and literary analysis, not to the world they live in. Any engagement of young children with the world outside of them is regarded as highly suspect and a likely product of some nefarious adult manipulation.[13] This is a situation that will not *fundamentally* change under capitalism.

However, children can, and *should*, examine themes present in their lives and explore untested feasibilities and the potential of limit-acts. They can study the limit-acts of others throughout history. But until we begin to change society to allow children to fully interact with their world and their environment, children will not be able to develop conscientization or a real praxis. There are exceptions to this in history: boy soldiers in the US Civil War who came to understand the war as a fight to end slavery; African American children participating in the Montgomery bus boycott; the teenage workers striking the Lawrence, Massachusetts, mills in 1912. You will notice that these examples of children coming to conscientization and developing their own praxis are educational experiences and activism to change the world that flowed directly out of movements and did not start in the classroom.

The pedagogy of the oppressed comprises much more than a set of teaching strategies, and is consciously in the service of oppressed people and the working class (which, by the way, includes most educators). It cannot be realized on a general level under capitalism and furthermore must be considered as part and parcel of revolutionary struggle itself. We certainly don't expect to see any school district proclaiming implementation of a pedagogy of the oppressed anytime soon. The capitalist class, of necessity, has ideological hegemony in the public education system. Freire was clear about this: "If the implementation of a liberating education requires political power and the oppressed have none, how then is it possible to carry out the pedagogy of the oppressed prior to the revolution? . . . One aspect of the reply is to be found in the distinction between *systematic education*, which can only be changed by political power, and *educational projects*, which should be carried out *with* the oppressed in the process of organizing them."[14] Freire recognized that, under capitalism, a pedagogy of the oppressed will be carried out by a minority of teachers and most likely outside of schools, in social movements and labor unions.

The Forest and the Trees: Organizing for Revolution and Critical Pedagogy

Despite Freire's firm grounding in Marxist thought, it is possible to strip away the political context of his writings and simply see his prescriptions as a set of classroom techniques. Taking a narrow view on Freire's theory might also lead one to believe that the ability to engage in progressive "educational projects" is the best we can hope for—the idea that the most we can do is effect change in our own classrooms and empower students, one at a time, primarily in terms of how we teach them. But to represent Freire in this way is to misrepresent him. In much of his writing, Freire emphasizes the importance of organizing outside the classroom. In *Pedagogy of the City*, the book of interviews conducted after Freire had led the Municipal Bureau of Education in São Paulo for two years, Freire insists that being a progressive educator "means to motivate the mobilization and organization not only of your own professional class but of workers in general as a fundamental condition for the democratic struggle leading up to the necessary and urgent transformation of Brazilian society."[15] In *A Pedagogy for Liberation*, he is equally explicit: "Precisely because education is *not* the lever for the transformation of society, we are in danger of despair and cynicism if we limit our struggle to the classroom."[16]

In 1987, when *A Pedagogy for Liberation* was published, Freire was dismissive of the idea of individual liberation and critical of the term "empowerment" more generally, noting that while dialogical education may "develop in students a certain level of independence . . . this level of autonomy is not enough to transform them for making the necessary political and radical transformation of Brazilian society."[17] That is, he thought that to talk about empowerment through teaching is to oversimplify an incredibly difficult

ELEMENTARY STUDENTS CONFRONT DEPORTATIONS: TEACHING BEYOND CLASSROOM WALLS

In 2008, two colleagues and I conducted a nine-week, inquiry-based project in our three fourth- and fifth-grade classrooms at a San Francisco public school. It was a year in which Immigration and Customs Enforcement (ICE) was sharply stepping up raids around the country. In three terrifying weeks in San Francisco, 436 people were arrested by ICE agents[49] and, in the predominantly immigrant neighborhood where I teach, students had seen ICE vans and knew of friends and neighbors whose homes had been raided.

We began with a trip to the El Balazo taqueria, which had been the site of a high-profile raid in May, and a visit from an El Balazo worker who was fighting deportation. Starting with the question of why raids are happening and how we can respond as a community, we explored a number of generative themes that flow from this question: employment, family, historicity of immigration policy, law, morality, and civil disobedience. We examined the limit-acts of others who had experienced crisis in their communities—the attempted murder charges against the Jena Six, the ordinary men and women surviving the aftermath of Hurricane Katrina, and the struggle of Elvira Arellano, who took sanctuary in a Chicago church to prevent deportation and family separation. Through this examination, a two-way dialogue between student and teacher emerged in which I, as a white, US-born descendant of nineteenth-century immigrants, heard and confronted the commonsense notion that the United States is a white nation in which people of color are "foreign." It is a notion to which both student-teacher and teachers-students had to respond, as nightly news reports counterposed descendants of Native American and Spanish people crossing borders ("foreigners") with guntoting white Minutemen ("defending" their America).

Throughout the project students asked themselves a question originally put forward by their teachers: is there anything that we, as children, can do in this situation? This led to further examination of the limit-acts of other children their age—child laborers past and present, children in the civil rights movement. This developed our understanding of our capability to respond to this situation, one that was clearly much larger than us and beyond our ability to fundamentally change from our location and time in history.

> Students developed a series of educational materials that they used for leafleting in the community. The materials explained the immediate situation facing the El Balazo families. But they also expressed a general opposition to raids and deportations based on a very concrete desire for family unity and the basic human right to adequate employment. Their understanding of the situation exposed the contradiction at the heart of the rhetoric used to justify the raids themselves. The United States wants to maintain its mythical "land of opportunity" image while simultaneously denying people the ability to work to provide for themselves and their families.
>
> Students wrote a petition to the governor that demanded an end to raids. They encouraged adults to sign this petition during leaflet distribution, although they admittedly did not expect the governor to respond to this tactic. They acknowledged that they were unable to collect anything near the thousands of signatures the supporters of the Jena Six had collected, and that there had been no huge protest for this group of workers. Lastly, students decided to collect money for the families of the El Balazo workers. This last decision was made in response to requests for donations from the workers themselves and the members of the El Balazo Defense Campaign. We raised money and bought, wrapped, and delivered gifts. At the close of the project we received photos from the El Balazo Defense Campaign Christmas party and students saw the presents they chose in the hands of children whose families looked very much like their own. This project became a point of reference for much of the rest of the year—a basis for asking the question: "Does it have to be this way?"
>
> —Adrienne Johnstone

task, much of which will happen outside the classroom. Freire and Shor also point out that social movements are necessary for social transformation and make transformative teaching more relevant and possible.[18] A total transformation of the economic system and the removal of one ruling class and its temporary replacement by another until all classes are made obsolete will require a very big movement, involving all sectors of society—in other words, it will have to go far beyond the classroom. That Freire had in mind something like what Marx described as the "dictatorship of the proletariat" is implied throughout *Pedagogy of the Oppressed*, but stated most explicitly in a footnote on page 139 of the book: "Once a popular revolution has come to power, the fact that the new power has the ethical duty to repress any attempt to restore the old oppressive power by no means signifies that the revolution is contradicting its dialogical character. Dialogue between the former oppressors and the oppressed as antagonistic classes was not possible before the revolution; it continues to be impossible afterward."

Although Freire is clear about his desired ends and suggested means, when you look at the body of his work, there are points at which he opens himself up to the "revolution in one classroom" interpretation. In *A Pedagogy for Liberation*, for example, he emphasizes more than once his "respect" for teachers who wish only to work in the classroom.[19] Given the lion's share of what he argues, this seems coy at best: go ahead and just work in the classroom even though it will lead to your despair and make revolution impossible. I respect that, but it won't be what I'm doing.

The idea that he espoused a "revolution in one classroom" strategy could also be inferred from Freire's conflation of teachers and revolutionary leaders in *Pedagogy of the Oppressed*. At first, he places them side by side—"the truly humanist educator and the authentic revolutionary"[20]—and then at one point in chapter 3 he drops "teachers" entirely and refers to revolutionary leaders exclusively, as he does through most of chapter 4, suggesting that the roles of teachers and revolutionary leaders are substantially the same. Up to a point, the analogy is accurate and useful. Teaching and revolutionary organizing *are* similar in many ways. Like teachers, revolutionaries have to meet the people with whom they wish to organize where they are. Those of us who are revolutionaries do this by grounding ourselves in Marxist theory and a study of the world around us, which includes listening and posing questions to the people with whom we are organizing, engaging in dialogue and critical thought with them, and coming to an understanding of the world and how it might be changed for the better.

However, seeing the roles of teachers and revolutionaries as interchangeable in all moments and situations can lead us away from effective political practice. As Freire points out in *A Pedagogy for Liberation*, in the classroom, teacher and students are never equal; the teacher has more training, more experience with critical thinking, and the authority of his or her position, which it is both impossible and foolish to hide. As a consequence, the teacher must often withhold his or her opinions at times so that the students have room to think rather than just absorb and repeat.[21] This is partially because students are already trained in the banking mode of education—they are accustomed to being told what to think by teachers, and will often resist *both* being told what to think *and* being asked to think for themselves.[22]

In his conflation of teachers and revolutionary leaders, Freire seems to posit the same unequal relationship between "revolutionary leaders" and "the people" as he does between teachers and students. Referring to revolutionary leaders, he writes: "Usually this leadership group is made up of men and women who in one way or another have belonged to the social strata of the dominators. At a certain point in their existential experience, under certain historical conditions, these leaders renounce the class to which they belong and join the oppressed in an act of true solidarity (or so one would hope). Whether or not this adherence results from a scientific analysis of society, it represents (when authentic) an act of love and true commitment."[23] Throughout the book, he implies that both teachers and revolutionary leaders are necessarily coming to the oppressed class—the peasants or the working class in Freire's case, the working class in ours—from a middle-class or even ruling-class background, and that their identification with the oppressed is voluntary—a moral duty.

This is problematic for several reasons. First, although Freire insists on the right to directiveness on the part of teachers, he seems to disallow it on the part of revolutionary leaders. In *A Pedagogy for Liberation*, he argues, "I have to convince students of my dreams but not conquer them for my plans. Even if the students have the right to bad dreams, I have the right to say their dreams are bad, reactionary or capitalist or authoritarian."[24] However, perhaps because they are portrayed as coming from *outside* the ranks of the oppressed, revolutionary leaders are not allowed this same sharing of convictions: "[Revolutionary leaders should not] forget that their fundamental objective is to fight alongside the people for the recovery of the people's stolen humanity, not to 'win the people over' to their side. Such a phrase does not belong in the vocabulary of revolutionary leaders, but in that of the oppressor." He even seems to imply the passivity of the oppressed: "After all, the task of the humanists is surely not that of putting their slogans against the slogans of the oppressors, with the oppressed as testing ground, 'housing' the slogans of first one group and then the other."[25]

Considering the fact that working-class people resist oppression—*despite* the constant, daily, lifelong barrage of dominant ideology in mainstream education and media telling them that they are worthless and stupid, telling them that there is no alternative to the current social order, telling them that humans are, by nature, greedy and competitive, and so on—the idea that teachers or revolutionary leaders could easily inject their ideas in students or the "people" by speaking or even arguing rather than dialoguing seems far-fetched. Like students, working-class people are resistant to being told what to think. That's why the ruling class works so hard at achieving cultural hege-mony, why it blankets us in mystification, and why reactionaries like Glenn Beck get so much airtime. To deny revolutionaries the right to "win people over to their side" is to make impossible the kind of organization necessary to take on capitalism.

In addition to undermining effective organizing, assuming that revolu-tionary leaders are always or even mostly ruling- or middle-class traitors doesn't allow for the prospect of leadership coming from within the working class. This idea runs counter to both Marx's theory of working-class self-emancipation[26] and much of working-class history, but it is consistent with popular conceptions of the politics of Che Guevara, who is frequently and positively quoted in *Pedagogy of the Oppressed*. Guevara was certainly an im-portant revolutionary figure who considered himself a Marxist. While his po-litical ideas and actions were complex, few of them were consistent with Marxism. This inconsistency is clearest around the question of working-class self-emancipation. Marxists use the historical materialist method to understand the objective position of the working class in relation to production under capitalism. This method is based on their position that working people have the potential to put an end to capitalism as a system, to emancipate themselves from the exploitation and oppression on which capitalism relies, and to create a new society based on democratic control of the economy and society. Gue-vara's vision for revolutionary change, by contrast, assigned only a passive role to the working majority in society. Instead, he cast revolutionary change as above all a question of ideas and moral duty. For Guevara, revolutionaries were to organize themselves into small, committed, armed groups and bring change from the outside. He wrote: "The peasant must always be helped technically, economically, morally and culturally. The [revolutionary] guerrilla fighter will be a sort of guiding angel who has fallen into the zone, helping the poor always and bothering the rich as little as possible in the first phases of the war."[27] This model prescribes revolutionary change as made by revolutionary guerrilla fight-ers on behalf of workers and peasants, not by the latter themselves. The elitism at the heart of this model is both clear and diametrically opposed to the theory of revolutionary change that guides Marxism.

This model, however, is consistent with the experience of the Cuban Revolution. To be sure, that revolution overthrew a brutal dictator, thus serving up defeat to the US imperialism that had propped up the Batista regime. Moreover, no matter how passive the majority of workers and peasants were in the making of that revolution, at first they supported it broadly. And the revolution initially delivered significant material and social gains to the masses of Cuba. (The next chapter, for example, looks at the impact of the revolution on literacy.) Nevertheless, it was a revolution carried out by a self-selected "vanguard" of armed guerrillas on behalf of the majority of working and peasant Cubans. A full discussion of Guevara's politics and the history and legacy of the Cuban Revolution would take us beyond the scope of this chapter. The point here, however, is that we can see that Freire's vision of teacher-students—driven by moral imperative, necessarily coming to the working and peasant classes from the outside, and so forth—overlap in important and problematic ways with Guevara's.

It is also worth noting that the idea that teachers come to working-class students from somewhere on high does not characterize the class position of most teachers here in the United States. As detailed in chapter 5 of this book, most teachers are working class not by inclination, but in terms of our position in relation to production. We may be better educated and in some cases better paid, and the AFT may call itself "a union of professionals," but we are still dependent on our labor to live. If we take our labor and go home, we will not make rent; and our better pay is the product of our struggle and the struggle of those before us, not our exploitation of someone else. So, in arguing for the necessity, say, of working-class solidarity in the face of administrative divide-and-conquer maneuverings, we are not coming from the outside and imposing our middle-class ideas on working-class people. We are acting in our own interests. Our interests and those of our students—who in public school are also largely working class—are the same, both in and out of the classroom.

The Impact of Struggle—and Its Absence

While Freire's conflation of teachers and revolutionaries could certainly lead some educators to the idea that one's political activity may be confined to one's teaching methods, another explanation is that they either have never been won to the idea of social revolution or have abandoned it as a goal. Freire himself, because of his experience and the historic decline of the left, backs away from social revolution as a goal in later writings. In *Pedagogy of the Oppressed*, however, his commitment to social revolution is still fresh.

In later works, Freire's concept of *utopian pedagogy* becomes a more central feature of his writing while revolution recedes from view. Because *Pedagogy of the Oppressed* was, and continues to be, a self-consciously revolutionary document, the concept of utopia has no place in it. *Pedagogy of the Oppressed* is filled with the hopeful optimism of the left of the seventies, a left that was confident that imperialist chains would continue to be thrown aside, that revolutionary guerrilla movements were on the rise, and that Mao's China represented some progressive step forward for the oppressed of the world.

The Merriam-Webster dictionary defines *utopia* as "an imaginary and indefinitely remote place; a place of ideal perfection." Despite Freire's assertion that utopia is neither idealism nor mere optimism but "a historical commitment,"[28] the word itself is imbued with a sense of the unattainable. We cannot simply remake this word, re-create its definition, and attempt to sidestep its political content.[29] Freirean theorists Henry Giroux and Peter McLaren have defined Freirean utopia as "dynamic, harmonious, creative, reflexive and dialogical."[30] But what Freire's utopia primarily communicates is a sense of eternal striving. This is not because Freire's dialecticism won't allow him to put an end point on history, but because for Freire, and the left more broadly, the goal has changed from revolution to striving for the best possible conditions under capitalism.

In Freire's *Pedagogy of the City* (1992), he writes, "My utopian dream has to do with a society that is less unjust, less cruel, more democratic, less discriminatory, less racist, less sexist."[31] This is a goal of any revolutionary, to be sure. But another goal, without which there will be no true human liberation, is the *elimination* of the capitalist system that reproduces injustice, racism, sexism, and discrimination on a daily basis, to divide and weaken the working class. Only then will we be able to discover and create a true education in which all the racist, sexist, homophobic ideas that pollute our world can be systematically confronted and eliminated.

This shift in Freire's thinking can be understood as both a product of his political ideas and of the overall decline of left-wing politics in the 1980s. Freire accepted the popular Guevarist conception of revolution and with it a belief in the voluntarist role of the party and the inherent, revolutionary spontaneity of "the people." According to this belief, the will of the revolutionary leadership could galvanize the people and ignite the revolutionary process regardless of the state of working-class organization. From this conception of revolution—which is idealist, not materialist—it is understandable that the world of the 1960s and 1970s appeared to be on the brink of revolution. Nationalist guerrilla movements in Latin America, Africa, and Asia had toppled governments. The student uprising of 1968 in France prominently raised the question of revolution. But despite this, and despite a wave of militant working-class strikes that helped bring an end to the Brazilian dictatorship in 1984, the global left, and revolutionary politics more broadly, entered into a long decline in the 1980s.

Not only Freire, but the left that he instructed and inspired, moved away from revolutionary goals and toward a bitter accommodation with capitalism. In the 1980s, revolutionary politics linked to radical action appeared to be a plan that had been tried and failed. The nationalist revolutions in Africa did not develop into global socialism; guerrilla movements did not grow and win; and China proved to be no people's paradise, but rather hyper-exploitative state capitalism and the world's cheapest labor market. The collapse of the Soviet Union seemed to close the book on the possibility of another kind of world.[32] Particularly in the face of a vast global transfer of wealth from bottom to top and a sharp decline in the number of strikes to resist falling living standards in industrialized nations, many on the left seemed to accept the slogan often attributed to Margaret Thatcher that "there is no alternative" to capitalism.

Many in the classroom today came to teaching in a period of reaction against the widespread radical left ideas of the sixties and early seventies. Radical educators confronted the assault on so-called "politically correct" speech and behavior, an assault that was essentially a cover for belittling left-wing critiques of culture and politics. Affirmative action was rolled back, and segregation in schools reasserted itself with a vengeance. All this unfolded in the context of an increasingly standardized and deskilled teaching climate. Both the AFT and the NEA have proved ill-equipped to stave off attacks on educators and unwilling to lead on broader questions of social justice and oppression. This has left the current generation of radical teachers in the United States with neither the experience nor a collective memory of working-class struggle, providing fertile ground for the blossoming of postmodern ideas that reject the centrality of class in general and of the working class in particular. College courses examining the myriad intersecting oppressions are plentiful. But they lack any sense that this state of affairs could be challenged beyond ideology. The poisonous notion that education is neutral was replaced with the equally poisonous idea that "discourse" and "micropolitics" are the limits of educative practice.[33] Thankfully, Paulo Freire did not go as far as the majority of postmodern theorists of the 1980s and 1990s. He did not reject the "totalizing" notion that global capitalism was the root cause of continued suffering and oppression. But he did make a sort of peace with "progressive postmodernism."[34]

In 1993, Freire wrote, "Instead of decreeing a new History, without social classes, ideology, struggle, utopia, dreams—which day-to-day living throughout the world bruisingly negates—what we need to do is reinsert into the center of our preoccupations and efforts that very human being who acts, thinks, speaks, dreams, loves, hates, creates and recreates, knows and ignores, affirms and denies, constructs and destroys, and who has both inherited and acquired traits. In this way, we restore the profound significance of radicalism."[35] This is a far more individualized notion of radicalism than the one Freire presented in *Pedagogy of the Oppressed*, which consistently placed both teacher and student as subjects in a history that they could potentially transform—and be transformed by—through collective action and organization. There is little significance in individual radicalism unless it is aimed at finding and uniting with others who can go beyond individual acts to organize resistance and struggle.

Freire made this peace with progressive postmodernism a couple years after retiring from his position as municipal secretary of education in São Paulo. While there, he instituted a radical reorganization of curriculum design and implementation. He launched projects throughout the city that allowed teachers to immerse themselves in the communities in which they taught and develop curriculum out of this experience. He advocated for increased wages and better working conditions for teachers. Unfortunately, these projects were short-lived.[36] Since change cannot simply be delivered from on high, we could not expect it to have been any other way. Freire wrote:

> Voluntarism is idealistic, because it is based precisely on the naïve notion that practice and its efficacy depend only on the will and courage of the subject . . . voluntarism and impulsiveness are principal obstacles in progressive educational practice. . . . I cannot consider myself progressive if I understand the school space as something neutral, with limited or no relation to class struggle. . . . An understanding of the level of class conflict in any given society is indispensable as a way of demarcating the spaces,

the content areas of education, what is historically possible, and the limits of political-educative practice.[37]

Given his clarity on where social change comes from, Freire's attempt to find common ground with postmodernism and to zero in on individual subjectivity must be seen as a retreat, and can perhaps be partially credited to the difficulties he experienced in attempting to reform one of the largest school systems in the world in the absence of broader class struggle.

Rescuing Freire

Today there is an entire body of work, a near-industry in fact, built on critique and analysis of Freire that we can't possibly hope to assess adequately here. We will make a few points that we believe to be representative of the kind of misreading of Freire that dominates among postsecondary schools of education and education reformers. We agree with Peter McLaren's claim that "contemporary critical pedagogy needs to rescue Freire's work from the reformists who wish to limit his legacy to its contribution to consciousness-raising."[38]

Such a rescue mission would necessarily include repopularizing Freire's favorable treatment of class struggle, union organizing, and working-class dignity. While Freire believed that "dialogue cannot exist . . . in the absence of a profound love for the world and for people,"[39] love for students cannot become a substitute for the organization and struggle that will be required to improve our teaching conditions. Freire would strenuously disagree with Peter Roberts, who wrote that "without the profound love many teachers have for their vocation, they would not be able to put up with such 'shameful' wages, under-resourcing, and poor working conditions."[40] In fact, Freire did not exhort teachers to tap into their love for their students to "put up with" poor working conditions. He said that teachers cannot teach well *because of* low salaries and lack of respect and that we have to fight against this every step of the way.[41]

Unfortunately, some teachers not only model but directly teach a strictly individualistic, middle-class, consciousness-raising perspective on social improvement to their students. Pedro Noguera writes of using problem-posing education to get young men of color at Rikers Island prison to "recognize their own capacity to free themselves."[42] Though he did talk to them about the prison industry and how policing is set up to keep Black and Latino men like themselves behind bars, simply stating the truth should not be mistaken for critical pedagogy. A critical pedagogical approach would have been to examine some untested feasibilities like an end to the death penalty, abolition of prisons, increased funding for drug rehabilitation, demands for jobs programs in the inner cities, anything that would attack the root causes of incarceration and racist injustice in this country. Instead, Noguera hoped just a few of these men would "reject the idea that using violence to get what you want was legitimate or that taking advantage of the weak and vulnerable was justifiable."[43]

Even more troubling is how Noguera critiques Freire's dichotomous concepts of oppressor and oppressed, revealing that he does not share Freire's understanding of the oppression that flows from the capitalist class down onto the necks of the very young men he was trying to reach. According to Noguera, "the terms Freire used—oppressed and oppressor, liberation and emancipation—are increasingly outdated and anachronistic in contemporary usage. Is a low-level drug dealer or pimp a member of the oppressed or oppressor class? . . . What about Bill Gates or Warren Buffett? . . . Both men are also among the largest philanthropists in the world . . . neither falls easily into the types of categories that Freire relied upon as he made the case for a pedagogy of the oppressed."[44] There is no doubt in which category Bill Gates and Warren Buffet belong. They are oppressors. Freire's terms are neither outdated nor anachronistic. They are casualties of the left's decline. In this period of global economic crisis, of money for charter schools and war, of bailouts for banks while school districts go broke, we must revive this vocabulary as activists in movements and in our unions, and as liberatory teachers in our classrooms.

The refusal to recognize class differences and the power dynamics they engender is not a modernization or elaboration but rather an *obfuscation* of Freire's ideas. Greg Ruggiero, as quoted by Peter McLaren, characterizes Freire's conception of revolution as emphasizing "communication and dialogue over authority and force. . . . This is the revolution that Paulo Freire wrote of in *Pedagogy of the Oppressed*, a revolution that seeks not only to liberate the oppressed, but the oppressors as well."[45] In *Pedagogy of the Oppressed*, far from "seeking" the liberation of the oppressors, Freire simply notes that, as a by-product of the liberation of the oppressed, the oppressors will be freed from their inability to truly complete themselves as human beings, which their oppressive role prevents. According to Freire, oppressors may or may not appreciate this happy coincidence, and the footnote on page 139, quoted above, makes clear his attitude toward those who don't.

Despite its contradictions and because of the ways it has been used and misused, *Pedagogy of the Oppressed* is a groundbreaking work that should be read closely and in the context of the many discussions and interviews that comprise Freire's later theoretical work. Because it refuses to ignore the links between education and social transformation, while not mistaking education as the path to revolutionary change, much of what Freire argues in *Pedagogy of the Oppressed* deserves to be defended and revived against the postmodern, post-Soviet-Union-collapse critics who are convinced that Lenin led to Stalin, that Marxism and Freire are overly "totalizing," and that the time for mass political parties has passed. Adherents of Freire who ignore the revolutionary content of his thought and limit questions of pedagogy to the school building must also be challenged.

Furthermore, authors who have done much to counter misreadings of Freire but who also hold to anti-party, Lenin-led-to-Stalin dogma undermine the building of desperately needed left-wing organizations by insisting that revolutionary parties are inherently evil and that the best we can fight for is a kinder, gentler capitalism. Stanley Aronowitz, who writes otherwise excellent books on labor and education, is hostile to revolutionary politics in general and to socialists in the tradition of Lenin and Trotsky in particular. Ironically, he seems not to realize that he identifies the need for exactly the kind of political organization that both Trotsky and Lenin built when he writes, "It is evident that the crucial educational issue is how to address the political hegemonies, how to bring the practical and theoretical consciousness of the most 'advanced' political actors together. In short, beyond the 'masses,' how to overcome the power of common sense among those who are charged with political leadership within the great social movements."[46] The answer to the issue Aronowitz posed is the concept of the vanguard party as articulated by Lenin—not a body that stands above and dictates to the revolutionary movement, but one in which the most organized sections of the movement cohere and attempt to lead ever-larger layers of revolutionaries. Yet Lenin and Leninism are heaped with scorn.

While it is possible to adhere to Freire and reject Leninism, to do so is neither necessary nor beneficial. If Freire were alive today, we would argue with him that the voluntarist approach to politics espoused in *Pedagogy of the Oppressed*—on the one hand, "the people" are always right and can't be argued with directly, and on the other, well-meaning and morally committed middle-class activists must incite change from the outside—is not only contradictory but also will never produce the scale of change required for a truly liberated society. To achieve the kind of social transformation consistently called for by Freire, explicitly revolutionary organization of the working class is necessary.

As important as it is to contextualize and clarify Freire's ideas and recoup them for a revolutionary movement, it is also vital that we recognize that any attempt to put them into practice will require a long-term fight led from the bottom up that involves far broader layers of students and workers than we see in the streets today. Freire wrote that only "when the revolutionary cry is in power, then revolutionary education will take on another dimension: what was before an education to contest and challenge becomes a systematized education, recreating, helping the reinvention of society."[47]

Without a revolutionary movement—which in its turn requires revolutionary organization—we will be limited to winning fleeting reforms that, while important, do not even approach the realization of the ontological vocation of humanity as Freire imagined it. To engage in building a revolutionary movement is to bring back the best in Freire. He wrote in *Politics and Education* that true progressive educators "force the State to comply with its responsibilities. They can never leave the State in peace . . . they can never permit the dominant classes to sleep in peace."[48] It is time for us to wake them up.

Keeanga-Yamahtta Taylor

FOCUS ON

The Freedom Schools

1964 was a turning point in the southern civil rights movement. For the previous three years, the movement had been marked by strategies such as civil disobedience, mass street protests, and filling local southern jails with activists to demonstrate a political resiliency and refusal to comply with white supremacy across the region. But despite years of protest, struggle, confrontation with law enforcement, and growing support for the movement nationally, the state of Mississippi still embodied the intransigency of southern racism and Jim Crow. Marked by savage rural poverty contained by the naked racism and terrorism of organized white racists, Mississippi was targeted by student civil rights activists for a campaign they hoped could break the political will and power of the white elite in the state. The Student Non-Violent Coordinating Committee (SNCC, pronounced "snick"), whose members were known as the "shock troops" of the movement for their relentless willingness to endure violence and terrorism against the movement, believed that if they could break white supremacy in Mississippi, it would weaken the will of other elected officials across the South.

Freedom Summer was to be a campaign of voter registration and political education among the Black rural poor across Mississippi, with the aim of having new Black voters challenge white political power across the South. In many counties across the state, African Americans were the majority of the population but were ruled over by white elected officials who used economic coercion, political intimidation, bombings, rape, and lynching to keep the Black population "in its place." In order to highlight the conditions that existed in Mississippi, SNCC organizers decided to recruit white students from elite universities in the North to come south to help register Blacks to vote. The idea was that if white activists were attacked or killed, the federal government would act to defend civil rights workers. Up to this point, the experience in SNCC had been that when Black civil rights activists were killed, no one in the federal government cared. Civil rights workers in Mississippi were frequent targets of violence and murder while the federal government claimed its hands were tied when it came to protecting the activists.

This was the tumultuous context within which SNCC's Freedom Schools were organized. The Freedom Schools of Mississippi were part of the strategy of Freedom Summer. According to Charles Cobb, who came up with the idea of organizing a network of independent schools across Mississippi, the many college students being recruited to come south to register Blacks to vote could also be put to work in teaching. The Freedom Schools targeted high school and college-aged Black Mississippi youth for both academic and political education. The point of "freedom education" was to counter the cycle of fear and domination born from a climate in which Black youth were viewed as either labor in waiting or laborers in deed. Freedom Schools were not only intended to replace the woefully inadequate public education provided by the state of Mississippi but also to create educated citizens and recruit new activists into the movement.

Public education in Mississippi was indeed woeful, spending $81 per white student on average compared to $21 per Black student. One local white school board went so far as to mandate that "neither foreign languages nor civics shall be taught in Negro schools. Nor shall American history from 1860 to 1875 be taught."[1] According to Cobb, the little education that did exist was used to stifle independent thought, self-determination, and creativity. In order to counter this, SNCC would have to rebuild its "own institutions to replace the old, unjust, decadent ones which make up the existing power structure."[2]

SNCC activists in Mississippi were not the first to come up with the idea of Freedom Schools for Black youth. In fact, the concept was born out of northern struggles against racism and school segregation in New York City, Chicago, and Boston. For example, in the fall of 1963, tens of thousands of Black parents on the South Side of Chicago kept their children out of school to boycott and protest overcrowding in predominantly Black schools. The problem was so bad that students were forced to attend school in shifts while schools attended by white students on the north side of the city had half-filled classrooms. While students were out of school, parents organized education so that the children would not miss any instruction.[3]

The Mississippi Freedom Schools were organized with the same idea in mind, but with a much more explicit political agenda meant to inculcate a sense of pride based on the history of Black struggle against white racism. The curriculum of the Freedom Schools came out of a convention in New York City in 1964 that gathered Black activists, scholars, teachers, and leftists who believed that although standard academics like mathematics and science mattered, an understanding of the "power structure" and its impact on the lives of Black people in Mississippi was of equal importance. Pedagogically, the cultivators of the Freedom Schools did not want to replicate what they believed to be a hierarchical approach to public education, but rather to encourage questioning, intellectual curiosity and a sense of collaboration between students and teachers.

Former New York City schoolteacher Noel Day was primarily responsible for creating the curriculum. He drew many of his teaching concepts from a very disappointing experience as a teacher in public schools. During one of his first years as a teacher he was assigned to a class of illiterate ninth-graders. He taught them to read by encouraging them to bring the materials they were interested in reading to class. By the end of the year, the students were reading at fourth- and fifth-grade levels. But when Day went to proudly announce this to his principal, he was upbraided for not following prescribed teaching methods. He said of the experience, "I felt the school culture brutalized the children and brutalized the teachers and required us to be brutal. . . . We teachers were basically in the business of behavioral control. You were basically serving as a prison guard."[4]

Activists had a radically different notion of education for Mississippi Freedom Schools. Classes were organized both by age and by student interests. A typical day at the Freedom School in Ruleville looked like this:

9:00 a.m.–9:15 a.m.	Civil rights songs
9:30 a.m.–10:30 a.m.	Core classes: Negro history and citizenship curriculum
10:30 a.m.–11:30 a.m.	Choice of dance, drama, art, auto mechanics, guitar and folk singing, or sports
12:00 p.m.–2:00 p.m.	School closed
2:00 p.m.–4:00 p.m.	Classes in French, religion, crafts, music, playwriting, journalism
4:00 p.m.	Seminar on nonviolence[5]

Instead of lecturing to students about the history of racism in the South or imposing on them a specific political agenda, Freedom School teachers based lessons and discussions on students' own experiences, using those experiences to help define key questions to guide learning. For example, Stokely Carmichael, teaching in a Freedom School in Greenwood, used language in one lesson to organize a discussion on racial oppression. On the left side of the blackboard, he wrote four sentences in the African American variety of English used in the region. On the right side, he wrote the same sentences in standard English. Historian Robert Weisbrot documents the discussion that followed:

> **STOKELY:** Will society reject you if you don't speak like on the right side of the board? Gladys said society would reject you.
>
> **GLADYS:** You might as well face it, man! What we gotta do is go out and become middle class. If you can't speak good English, you don't have a car, a job, or anything.
>
> **STOKELY:** If society rejects you because you don't speak good English, should you learn to speak good English?
>
> **CLASS:** No!
>
> **ALMA:** I'm tired of doing what society say. . . . People ought just to accept each other. . . . If I change for society, I wouldn't be free anyway. . . . If the majority speaks on the left, then a minority must rule society? Why do we have to change to be accepted by the minority group?
>
> **STOKELY:** Let's think about two questions for next time: What is society? Who makes the rules for society?[6]

While few, if any, teachers in Freedom Schools had been formally trained, they used the same practices they had learned as antiracist activists, such as role-playing, music and poetry, and open-ended discussions, as the basis for their teaching.[7] In the Freedom Schools as in other social movements, curricular shifts were a product of the needs of the struggle, not the product of a brilliant lesson plan that sprang forth from someone's mind.

Whatever their innovations in curriculum or teaching practice, the Freedom Schools had a deeper purpose. According to one volunteer, they were intended to "start young Mississippians thinking about how they could change the society in which they lived. . . . We tried to draw these students out and for the first time in their lives to express themselves—in writing, in speaking. We encouraged them to have discussions and in Freedom School . . . how we taught was just to ask questions. We didn't have a political doctrine or ideology that we were trying to impose on the students, but simply ask them why or what is the problem. Then, how are you going to solve it?"[8]

The schools were a wild success. While SNCC activists had planned for twenty schools with one thousand students across the state, more than forty schools were set up, attended by more than two thousand students. Despite this success, the schools did not really exist beyond Freedom Summer. The two main reasons for this had to do with SNCC's politics. First, SNCC rejected what they described as "institutionalized" leadership. Their entire program was aimed at developing a local leadership that could exist after the "outsiders" were gone. There were efforts to train Black students to carry on with the schools after the core SNCC organizers had moved on to the next campaign. But without a plan for how these schools would continue to be funded, including the salaries of those teaching in the schools, the Freedom Schools were not sustainable.

Second, SNCC's organizing devolved in some ways. In December 1963, when the idea of Freedom Schools as a component of Freedom Summer first developed, SNCC was still imbued with an egalitarian ideology of multiracialism in response to rigid racism and segregation of the South. Moreover, many of the activists still had what they would later come to describe as "illusions" in the possibility of "American democracy" working for African Americans in Mississippi. Not surprisingly, they were disappointed—especially by the racist maneuvering of the Democratic Party to keep the fairly elected Black delegates of the Mississippi Freedom Democratic Party out of their convention. But rather than drawing the conclusion that the problem lay with the system and its institutions and defenders, many SNCC activists concluded that the problem was that white people could not be trusted. Within a year, SNCC voted to expel its white members and abandoned efforts to work within the electoral system. The shift in SNCC was driven by disillusionment with the idea that the "power structure" could be transformed by electoral means, an idea that I agree with. But the Freedom School project was, unfortunately, conceived of mainly as a strategy to help Blacks gain power at the ballot box. And so when SNCC took a more revolutionary turn and voting as a primary strategy for winning electoral change was abandoned, the crumbling of the Freedom Schools was an unfortunate and unnecessary consequence.

7

Literacy and Revolution
Megan Behrent

*All Russia was learning to read, and reading—politics, economics, history—
because the people wanted to know. . . . In every city, in most towns, along
the Front, each political faction had its newspaper—sometimes several.
Hundreds of thousands of pamphlets were distributed by thousands of
organisations, and poured into the armies, the villages, the factories, the
streets. The thirst for education, so long thwarted, burst with the Revolution
into a frenzy of expression. From Smolny Institute alone, the first six months,
went out every day tons, car-loads, train-loads of literature, saturating the
land. Russia absorbed reading matter like hot sand drinks water, insatiable.
And it was not fables, falsified history, diluted religion, and the cheap fiction
that corrupts—but social and economic theories, philosophy, the works of
Tolstoy, Gogol, and Gorky.*

> —John Reed, *Ten Days That Shook the World*[1]

*Always and everywhere, it must be said once more, people are reading. They
are reading books, both foreign and domestic. They are reading newspapers,
pamphlets, magazines. They are reading while they stand in line, sit on buses,
wait for a train. It is a phenomenon for almost any North American, or
possibly for any foreigner, to see. It is this—this seemingly obsessive wish to
read, to write, to learn, to know, and then to read and write some more—it is
this, above all, that I had come to Cuba to attempt to understand.*

> —Jonathan Kozol on the Cuban Revolution in
> *Children of the Revolution*[2]

At its core our educational system reflects the class divisions that lie at the
heart of a capitalist system. Not surprisingly, it therefore also reflects the
dominant ideological biases of capitalism—competition instead of collaboration, individualism rather than collective learning and action, and the
idea that humans are motivated by rewards and punishments, without

which they would have no possible reason to do anything at all. All the basic assumptions underlying education and pedagogy under capitalism distort learning and make schooling a profoundly alienating experience.

In schools today, education is standardized, sterilized, and stripped down. Achievement on a high-stakes test takes the place of meaningful learning, and by design, meaningful teaching. In this upside-down world, each subject is taught separately with a list of specific skills to be taught as unrelated exercises in futility. As such, each unit bears no relation to the one before and knowledge is fragmented and abstract. Most fundamentally, learning or knowing is separated from doing or creating in a way that is intrinsically unnatural. As Linda Darling-Hammond remarks, "If we taught babies to talk as most skills are taught in school, they would memorize lists of sounds in a predetermined order and practice them alone in a closet."[3]

Despite all evidence to the contrary, we are told that competition and the logic of the free market are the keys to improving education. For students, this means more standardized tests; for teachers, merit pay and evaluations based on "value added" to students' test scores; for parents, competing to get their students into limited spots in the most desirable schools.

The fundamental flaw in this logic is ignored. Countless studies have proven that, in fact, competition encourages "surface-level thinking" and makes students dislike school and show less interest in a given subject. In fact, research tells us that "people of different abilities tend to learn more effectively when they are cooperating with each other rather than trying to defeat one another."[4] As Alfie Kohn argues, "If competition were a consumer product rather than an ideology, it would have been banned a long time ago."[5]

As a result, for the vast majority of people who do not have the privilege of being born into the ruling class, education is a profoundly alienating experience that serves to maintain inequalities, is oppressive rather than empowering, and functions to crush the real potential that humans have for creative, intellectual, and productive labor.

The experience and research of radical educators instead begin with fundamentally different ideas about learning and pedagogy which are (not coincidentally) based on a fundamentally different view of society. Educators and theorists such as Paulo Freire, Myles Horton (of the Highlander Folk School), the Russian psychologist Lev Vygotsky, and Jonathan Kozol are a few of the giants on whose shoulders we stand when we begin to talk about a truly liberatory pedagogy. But these radical thinkers and pedagogues did not come up with their ideas in the classrooms of teacher education programs on their own. Rather, it was the experience of struggle, their connection to social movements, and the radical and revolutionary climates in which their ideas came into being that provided the impetus and material conditions for the birth of radical pedagogy—a pedagogy that goes hand in hand with an understanding of the need for radical restructuring of society.

Radical educators begin with the basic idea that learning is natural, and that children have a natural curiosity to understand and explore their worlds. In fact, as Deborah Meier argues, "A passion for learning isn't something you have to inspire kids with, it's something you have to keep from extinguishing."[6] Among both children and adults, radical pedagogy begins with the premise that people learn best when learning is meaningful, providing them with a direct ability to use it for liberatory purposes. We learn best when we develop critical thinking skills through collaboration and collective discussion or action, rather than memorizing bits of random information. We learn best when we are empowered to make choices over what we learn and how we learn it.

Their Literacy and Ours

This is a far cry from the rhetoric and policies that guide education in the world today. Literacy, long one of the key goals of any educational system, is reduced to a "skill" that is stripped of meaning or critical thinking. "Education," as President Obama remarked, is an economic issue, if not "the economic issue of our times." He continued: "It's an economic issue when eight in ten new jobs will require workforce training or a higher education by the end of this decade. It's an economic issue when countries that out-educate us today are going to out-compete us tomorrow."[7]

Education's sole purpose here is to "out-compete" the rest of the world—hardly the best motivation for children struggling to learn to read. In this regard, Obama's comments reflect what Harvey Graff, an eminent scholar in the field of literacy studies, calls the "literacy myth," which has been a cornerstone of the institutionalization of learning for several centuries. As Graff argues, "The rise of literacy and its dissemination to the popular classes is associated with the triumph of light over darkness, of liberalism, democracy, and of universal unbridled progress. . . . Primary schooling and literacy are necessary, it is so often repeated, for economic and social development, establishment and maintenance of democratic institutions, individual advancement, and so on. All this, regardless of its veracity, has come to constitute a 'literacy myth.'"[8]

Under the guise of this myth, literacy becomes a means of economic advancement and assimilation into dominant ideology. Should literacy fail to provide such a path out of darkness, it is undoubtedly the fault of the student himself or herself. To enforce this vision of literacy, Graff argues, schools must train people in the behaviors necessary to be a good worker because "literacy alone . . . was feared as potentially subversive."[9] Thus, Graff continues,

> the purpose of literacy was to integrate society through binding men and women in it and instilling in them the principles of correct behavior. The importance of print and of the ability to read was grasped by those most interested in social order and progress. They saw, on the one hand, that more and more people were becoming literate, and thus potentially able to use their literacy without restraint. On the other hand, there were the illiterate, especially among the young. Both elements constituted a threat, a barrier to the spread of values considered essential to social order and economic progress. The result, of course, was the determination to seize upon print and literacy as socializing agents, to provide them in environments specifically and carefully structured for their dissemination, and to teach the moral code and the approved uses of literacy. Literacy was now necessary for moral control and control was required for literacy; progress would be advanced through the behavior of properly schooled persons.[10]

As Graff makes clear, literacy has always been "political" despite all attempts to sanitize it and isolate pedagogy and classroom practices from the world students live in. The literacy myth as we know it is premised on the political ideology of capitalism. Literacy can serve, thus, to *contain* rather than to *liberate*. It is a skill to be commodified rather than the basis for understanding and transforming one's world. It is no wonder, then, that most literacy campaigns of this ilk fail. As Raul Ferrer, a leader of the Cuban literacy campaign, explains: "It is because their starting point is anti-human. . . . They do not dare to speak of land reform, to speak about the sick and the starving . . . nor about the ones who make those people sick and poor. . . . The North American corporations and the banks . . . they do not dare to put these words into the hands of the poor people. And because they do not dare, therefore they fail—*and they will always fail until they do!*"[11]

By contrast, a cursory historical overview of twentieth-century literacy campaigns makes it clear that successful campaigns have been inextricably linked with political attempts to understand the world and change it. As education researchers Robert Arnove and Harvey Graff argue in *National Literacy Campaigns and Movements*, the most successful literacy campaigns of the last century were "usually associated with revolutionary upheavals,"[12] in which "literacy is almost never itself an isolated or absolute goal. It is rather one part of a larger process *and* a vehicle for that process."[13] It is not surprising that two such literacy campaigns in Cuba and Nicaragua were among the most successful of the century, owing little to ideologies of competition, deregulation, and the free market. Rather, they were imbued with the revolutionary impulse from which they were born. As Ferrer argues: "A man . . . in order to feel that he can be the owner of the word . . . must sense that he can also be the owner of REAL THINGS. I mean the owner of his own existence, of his toil, of the fruit of his own work. In order to sense that it can be within his power to possess the *word*, he must believe that he can thereby gain the power to transform the *world* . . . to shape the world . . . to make it a more noble and more humane place to be. . . . There is no way to do this which is not political."[14]

Ferrer is certainly not alone in this belief. Indeed, even the United Nations' own statement on literacy from the 1975 Declaration of Persepolis echoes much of the sentiment, despite that body's decidedly nonrevolutionary nature, stating: "Literacy . . . [is] not just a process of learning the skills of reading, writing, and arithmetic, but a contribution to the liberation of man and to his full development. Thus conceived, literacy creates the conditions for the acquisition of a critical consciousness of the contradictions of society in which man lives and of its aims; it also stimulates initiative and his participation in the creation of projects capable of acting upon the world, of transforming it, and of defining the aims of an authentic human development."[15] Sadly, this vision of literacy is fundamentally at odds with the way literacy is often conceived of today, stripped of critical thinking, divorced from real meaning or potentially radical possibilities, reduced to a basic skill to be evaluated on a standardized test.

Ultimately, while we can learn from innovations in radical pedagogy, real education reform—including meaningful literacy—can occur only if it is based on revolutionary struggles that fundamentally change social conditions and people's relationship to the world and to each other. It is when literacy is part of a political struggle that it is most successful, as students and teachers are no longer passive participants but political actors engaged in collective struggle to remake the world in their own interest.

The 1961 Cuban Literacy Campaign

It is perhaps one of the most astounding feats of the Cuban Revolution that within a few years it had all but eradicated illiteracy through a mass literacy campaign. Indeed, as Jonathan Kozol notes, within two years of the revolution, "Cuba's triumph in the eradication of illiteracy already exceeded anything that has to this day been achieved by any other nation in the world."[16]

In 1959, on the eve of the Cuban Revolution, only half of Cuba's children were enrolled in school and "among peasant families less than half the adults had ever had any education."[17] According to the 1953 census, 23.6 percent of the Cuban population was illiterate. This figure equaled 1,032,849 adults, the vast majority of whom lived in rural areas.[18]

The 1961 literacy campaign thoroughly transformed Cuba. In the battle against illiteracy, 250,000 "literacy workers" were recruited and mobilized. More than 100,000 of these were young people who volunteered to move to the countryside to teach people to read in rural areas. Of the student volunteers, 40 percent were between the ages of ten and fourteen, and an additional 47.5 percent were between fifteen and nineteen. Many of the *brigadistas* (student volunteers) had not been in school themselves prior to 1959.[19] During the course of the campaign, literacy workers taught more than 707,212 people.[20] Within eight months, the illiteracy rate in Cuba was down to 3.9 percent.[21] This initial mass literacy campaign was followed by the dramatic expansion of education at all levels. "By 1976, over three million three hundred thousand Cubans—workers, farmers, adults, kids—were enrolled in formal education at some level: one out of three in a population of nine million five hundred thousand people. No other government in the Latin world comes even close."[22]

The battle against illiteracy was seen as "intimately connected to the revolutionary transformation of society and the economy."[23] Both *alfabetizadores* (adult volunteers) and *brigadistas* (school-age volunteers) were recruited with the appeal that "the Revolution needed" them as education became a national collective effort under the slogan: "Those who know, teach. Those who don't, learn."[24] As Rene Mujica, who became a student volunteer at twelve years old, explains, "I felt that I had to do something for my country, even though I was very young, I felt that I had the responsibility and that I could do it."[25] This mass outpouring of energy, creativity, and dedication from students who participated in the literacy campaign is a powerful rebuke to any notion of teenagers as apathetic or reluctant learners who need extrinsic motivation to do anything. Given the chance to actively participate in transforming their world, an entire generation of young people jumped at the opportunity, learning and teaching in an unprecedented collective educational experiment.

To prepare volunteers for the literacy campaign, teachers were trained in pedagogical techniques based on Freire and given orientations to rural areas. A primer was created that explicitly put politics at its center. Entitled *Venceremos*, it included fifteen lessons on topics such as "The Cooperative Farm under the Agrarian Reform," "The Land," "A Healthy People in a Free Cuba," "The Revolution Wins All the Battles," "Cuba Is Not Alone," "The Year of Education," and "Poetry and the Alphabet."[26] The first lesson, for example, was on "La Organización de los Estados Americanos (OEA)" (the Organization of American States). As Leiner explains, it "was chosen to introduce the primer and to begin the reading program by teaching the vowels. Thus, the instructional usefulness of the OEA letters was coupled with the political significance of the lesson's content—Cuba had been expelled from the OEA just before the campaign. Similarly, the second lesson focused on INRA (National Institute of Agrarian Reform), an agency which, in 1961, very much affected the lives of Cubans, particularly the peasants.[27] As educator and Ministry of Education official Alberto Prieto explains, "We decided that in addition to the appropriate didactic method adult illiterates required a book whose contents would reflect the reality, offer information on the revolutionary changes, and awaken in people the desire to know more by reading. The *Venceremos* primer was based on this premise in which the content and method were in harmony."[28]

Each lesson began with a photograph, to spark discussion between teacher and student. The political discussion served as an entry point to engage the student prior to analyzing the phrases and key words syllable by syllable.[29] Jonathan Kozol recounts his discussion with one woman who learned to read during the campaign. Cristina had worked as a domestic servant for an abusive couple who fired her when she told them she was going to learn to read and write. Without money and separated from her family, she went to her first class in tears, "determined that I *had* to learn to read and learn to write."[30] Of the primer, she recalls, "When we read *Venceremos*, it was very real to me. We learned our own position through the lessons and the pictures."[31]

The pedagogy of the Cuban literacy campaign was consciously modeled on Paulo Freire's research, borrowing his notion of "generative words" and likewise placing a heavy emphasis on the "dialogical relationship between

the teacher and 'the one who chooses to be taught.'"[32] Teachers were exhorted
to "avoid giving orders!" and to "avoid the authoritarian tone. Never forget
that the work of learning how to read and write is realized and achieved in
common."[33] The young literacy workers lived with families, worked in fields
with them, and engaged in lessons with them after the workday was over. As
such, the "teachers" also learned from the "students" about rural life, the
land, and history. As one *brigadista* remembers, "Sometimes the students,
the peasants themselves, though they couldn't read, had lived more, so it was
they who would explain things to us. The OEA [OAS] for example. I had
some idea of what it was, but the peasants, they knew. They had knowledge—I'd call it historical knowledge—related to the history of Cuba—what
they had lived through and what they'd heard spoken of."[34]

Cuba's literacy campaign differed from Freire's methodology by beginning with a much more explicit political message directed by the teacher and
the primer itself. Despite the emphasis on collaborative learning between
teacher and student, few of the students and teachers actively participated
in creating the curricula or debating pedagogy. The training process for teachers itself was somewhat rigid and, at times, tended toward dogmatism rather
than critical thinking. For example, the training manual for teachers that accompanied the curricula included chapters like "Fidel Is Our Leader," which
veered dangerously close to the banking model that Freire so adamantly opposed. This was, at least in part, a product of Cuba's embattled status after
the revolution, in which the stakes were high and political education was
deemed paramount. If this perhaps lent itself to doctrinaire distortions at
times, it was justified on the basis that "in a state of revolution, as Freire himself has said, certain things cannot be left to chance."[35] Ultimately, despite
its success, Cuba's literacy campaign reflected the contradictory nature of the
revolution itself, which enjoyed mass support, but was nonetheless led by a
self-selected group of at most two thousand guerrillas. The Cuban revolutionary Che Guevara described this process as follows: "The mass carries out
with matchless enthusiasm and discipline the tasks set by the government,
whether in the field of the economy, culture, defense, sports, etc. The initiative generally comes from Fidel, or from the revolutionary leadership, and is
explained to the people, who make it their own."[36] In this model, as in the
literacy campaign itself, the mass enthusiasm and revolutionary zeal of the
people were harnessed for a populist and nationalist revolution, which, despite its appeal, failed to institute any genuine workers' democracy. As Paul

D'Amato argues, "the revolution was wildly popular for its land, educational and economic reforms, but the Cuban masses neither carried out the revolution nor created the state that emerged from it. For Fidel, the mass organizations created after the seizure of power were sounding boards and conduits for his policies rather than organs of mass struggle and self-organization."[37]

The top-down nature of the Cuban Revolution imposed severe limitations on the revolutionary transformation of education, despite the initial success of the national literacy campaign. The militaristic language used to describe and promote the literacy campaign was, in this regard, perhaps not accidental, but instead a reflection of the nature of the revolution itself. Furthermore, because the campaign depended on a mass volunteer teaching force, it was inherently unsustainable, dependent on voluntarism instead of the transformation of schools themselves into democratic institutions run by teachers, students, and parents collectively. While it unleashed an immense amount of creativity and enthusiasm, the most innovative and radical aspects of the pedagogy developed in the literacy campaign proved increasingly inconsistent with the goals of a repressive, bureaucratic, one-party state.

The immense promise of the Cuban Revolution was ultimately limited as the level of investment in education proved unsustainable—as was the enthusiasm and spirit of freedom and experimentation that characterized schools in the early years. The contradictory nature of Cuba's revolution (that is, instigated by a small, self-selected group of leaders and lacking genuine workers' democracy), coupled with its isolation internationally, made the early gains of the revolution difficult to sustain. This fact is highlighted by the shortage of teachers that plagues Cuba's schools, despite an ongoing commitment to education that shines in comparison to countries with far greater resources. Revolutionary zeal alone cannot sustain a long-term transformation of Cuba's educational system—a fact that becomes more glaring as teachers in Cuba have begun to be replaced by televised classes and privately paid tutoring has been on the rise, both disturbing trends that point to the limits of Cuba's educational revolution.[38]

Nonetheless, Cuba's mass experiment in literacy transformed, at least for a time, both students and teachers as they became actors in history rather than passive participants. Reflecting on his conversations with children in schools during his extended visit to Cuba, Kozol observes, "Whenever children can comfortably speak, as Leonara did, about 'my obligation in'—not 'to'—the revolution; when Carlos can say, 'If it is true . . . , it is a fact for which I feel great shame. I will find out'; when Sandra can say, of women's secondary role in history, that 'it won't be that way for long,' it seems to me a tragic and debilitating aspect of the public school as we have known it for one hundred years has been substantially transcended."[39] Kozol's words point to the enduring legacy of Cuba's mass experiment with education, which not only eradicated illiteracy in one of the poorer countries of the hemisphere but mobilized an entire generation of students to see themselves as actors in history, transforming literacy with a political power and purpose that was truly revolutionary.

Literacy and Radical Pedagogy

The most successful literacy campaigns of the twentieth century have been those based on radical pedagogy, which rejects the institutionalized mode of schooling that we all know. The work and ideas of Paulo Freire are perhaps the most influential, although the central methods and principles that guide his pedagogy have been shared by other radical pedagogues both before his time and since. In part, this is because Freire's theories themselves stem from a political framework that is shared by many other important innovators in pedagogy and literacy. It is no coincidence that for many radical educators, reading Marx was a crucial turning point in their own education and has had a lasting impact on the type of pedagogy they profess.

Through his engagement in and research on literacy campaigns in Brazil, Paulo Freire discovered that "any adult can begin to read in a matter of 40 hours if the first words he deciphers are charged with political meaning."[40] Indeed, this experience has echoed throughout the world. Instead of the "banking" model in which students are seen as empty containers to be filled up by authoritarian, all-knowing teachers, Freire begins with the idea that people already know a lot about their world, that they learn through their own experiences, and that the teacher's job is to facilitate its expression. Drawing on Marxism to inform his *Pedagogy of the Oppressed*, Freire's pedagogy understands literacy as a political process.

Myles Horton of the Highlander Folk School in Tennessee—a school where both Rosa Parks and Martin Luther King Jr. participated in workshops prior to the Montgomery boycott—describes how the "Citizenship Schools" of the 1960s used similar ideas. Literacy in the Jim Crow South was inherently political, used by the segregationists as a barrier to prevent African Americans from exercising their right to vote. In the mid-1950s, activists at the Highlander School decided to create literacy programs whose primary purpose was to help disenfranchised African Americans to get the right to vote. Led by Esau Jenkins and Septima Clark, the first Citizenship School opened on Johns Island, South Carolina, in 1957.[41]

For many who came to the Citizenship Schools, formal education had proved to be a humiliating and alienating ordeal. In other unsuccessful literacy programs, adults were placed in classrooms where their grandchildren went to school, and sat at children's desks where they were laughed at and called "granddaddy longlegs." The new Citizenship Schools' first job, therefore, was to find an educational setting outside of school and create a program whose basis was first to "respect people."[42] The first school Horton helped to organize held classes in a beauty parlor. The classes were taught by Bernice Robinson, a beautician with no formal teacher education, but who had attended workshops at the Highlander Institute and was respected in the community. She began her classes by reading from posters of the Universal Declaration of Human Rights. This became the students' introduction to literacy as they first discussed the meaning of rights, democracy, and citizenship. Later, Bernice had the adults in the class tell her their life stories, which she wrote down as they narrated them. These texts became the "primers" through which they learned how to read. Not surprisingly, this method proved far more successful than traditional schools with their tiny desks and Dick and Jane primers. As Horton says, "It wasn't a literacy class. It was a community organization. . . . They were talking about using their citizenship to do something, and they named it a Citizenship School, not a literacy school. That helped with the motivation."[43] By the end of the class, more than 80 percent passed the "examination"—in other words, they were able to go down to the courthouse and register to vote.[44]

Within two years, the Citizenship School program had grown by hundreds. In fact, by 1961, it had grown so big that the Highlander Institute decided to turn the program over to the Southern Christian Leadership Conference, which had greater resources to devote to the program. Summarizing some of the lessons of the schools, Horton explains that "people learn faster and with more enjoyment when they are involved in a successful struggle for justice that has reached social movement proportions, one that is getting attention and support outside the movement, and it's socially big enough to go far beyond the individuals involved. It's a much bigger experience than anything you've had before as an individual."[45]

Despite very different contexts, the experience of radical educators in El Salvador in the midst of civil war echoed these conclusions. During the Salvadoran war from 1980–92, the Farabundo Martí National Liberation Front (FMLN) worked with communities in which they held sway to conduct popular education.[46] Despite the hardship of learning in the midst of war and poverty, often in refugee camps or prisons, there were some important successes. In one refugee camp in Honduras, for example, "85 percent of the refugees were illiterate when they arrived; when they returned home in 1989 and 1990, 85 percent knew how to read and only 15 percent were illiterate. At the end, about two-thirds of the camp's population was enrolled in school."[47] As with the Citizenship Schools, teachers in El Salvador found that people learn best when literacy is imbued with political and social meaning, when it goes hand in hand with political struggle, and when learning happens in an environment that encourages respect, collaboration, and cooperative learning.

The same philosophy is at work in other successful literacy campaigns of the twentieth century. The Nicaraguan Revolution, for example, transformed a country in which illiteracy rates hovered around 50 percent (60–90 percent in rural areas) through an intensive literacy campaign. Within six months of the revolution, the campaign had reduced illiteracy to 15 percent of the population—an accomplishment that would be remarkable anywhere, but was truly astounding in a country recovering from a civil war with devastating economic and human tolls.[48] Literacy in this context was more than simply about words, but rather a mutual process of learning and understanding the world. As one farmer explained to the parents of the young literacy worker who helped teach him how to read: "Do you know I'm not ignorant anymore? I know how to read now. Not perfectly, you understand, but I know how. And do you know, your son isn't ignorant anymore either. Now he knows how we live, what we eat, how we work, and he knows the life of the mountains. Your son, ma'am, has learned to read from our book."[49] The words of this farmer give a sense of the real empowerment that literacy can bring when it is politically meaningful, relevant, and genuinely liberatory.

Education *should* be a process through which a person explores the world and his or her own potential, and becomes liberated. In these examples and countless others, teaching and learning is literally liberatory when directly connected to social upheaval. Permeated with political importance by concrete struggles, literacy is no longer an isolated skill but a way to understand the world and transform it. At its core, this kind of radical pedagogy begins with the principles that:

1. People learn best when words are charged with political meaning and relate to the issues and struggles they are actively engaged in for social justice.
2. The most successful pedagogy is one that involves active participation in collective and cooperative learning and emphasizes development of critical and political consciousness to understand the world, one's material conditions and social relations, and how to change them.
3. Literacy is not an individual or competitive process, but rather a collective one in which teacher and student learn from each other equally. In a discussion with Myles Horton, Freire argues that the success of the teachers trained at the Highlander Folk School is based on the understanding that "the educators here have been educators but have accepted to be educated too. That is, they understood, even though they did not read Marx, what Marx meant when he said that 'the educator himself must be educated.'"[50]
4. Literacy and education do not exist in a vacuum. Literacy is most empowering when it goes beyond words, to become a tool for self-emancipation and for the radical restructuring of society as a whole.

Literacy and Social Change: The Student Revolt of May 1968

Perhaps one of the most inspiring examples of a student-led struggle to transform education was the revolt of students in France in May 1968 when students occupied universities and *lycées* (high schools), creating democratic committees with teachers and other staff to run schools. The events of May 1968 began with small numbers of students at Nanterre, a university in a *banlieue* of Paris that in many ways was a testament to the immensely alienating nature of education under capitalism. As a "modern" university dedicated to progress and technology, the overcrowded campus was located near the living quarters of many of the poorest workers, among them many immigrants who labored for low wages in France's factories—a not-so-subtle reminder of the squalor and misery that was the reality of much of working-class life in postwar France.[51]

Radicalized by the wars in Algeria and Vietnam, a small group of leftist students began to organize on campus for goals as diverse as the right to visit the dorms of members of the opposite sex after hours and ending the war in Vietnam and police repression. Greeted with immense repression and violence from the police and the state, the student movement soon expanded far beyond Nanterre as students and workers joined forces to bring the state to its knees. A general strike was called for May 13, which galvanized workers and students to organize demonstrations, strikes, sit-ins, and occupations of factories and schools. The Sorbonne, as an occupied university, became the cultural center of the student movement. However, it was the solidarity of workers who occupied factories around the country that gave the movement its strength. As Matt Perry writes of the events:

> As in other revolutionary upsurges, during May 1968 it was as though the banks of the Seine burst under the weight of ideas expressed in leaflets, pamphlets, graffiti, posters, newspapers and speech, inundating the entire country. A great diversity of opinions cascaded through the streets, momentarily overwhelming the conformity of the mainstream press and the official stranglehold on public broadcasting. Reading these documents provides a compelling sense that the events shook French society, questioned its every institution and transformed the horizons of countless numbers of participants: that this was the beginnings of a revolutionary process prematurely concluded.[52]

A notice posted on May 13 gives expression to this revolutionary fervor as students rejected both the politics and pedagogy of the old university. With the headline "13 of May = The Return to School," a leaflet satirically proclaimed the success of all students on their required examinations (many of which were suspended for the duration of the strike). The notice congratulates all students for passing the tests of:

> spirit of initiative
> developing a political conscience
> revolutionary discipline
> solidarity
> protests and barricades[53]

The leaflet continued by noting that classes were set to begin once more and invited all students to participate in a program of:

> Critical University
> Critique of society

Student-worker alliances
Autonomy of the University[54]

Many historical accounts of the student revolt in 1968 in Paris focus primarily on institutions of higher education, but the activism of *lycéens*, or high school students, is an often-overlooked, crucial contribution to the movement as a whole. Like their counterparts at university, they were radicalized by the wars in Algeria and Vietnam and angered by a rigid educational system that was hostile to student initiative and independent thought. As the Action Committee's Commission on Examination explained: "We are preoccupied with curricula, we cram, we bluff, and learn more for the sake of the exam than to form our personalities. We are judged on bookish knowledge hastily stocked and that one quickly forgets as soon as the exam is finished. The exam privileges competition, emulation for social success, and reinforces individualistic mental habits."[55]

In response to the *evenements de Mai*, *lycéens* organized Comités d'Action Lycéens (High School Students' Committees of Action, CAL according to its initials in French) and mobilized to democratize their schools and support the demands of university students and workers throughout Paris. At the height of struggle "all 60 Paris lycées . . . were occupied by their pupils, 20 [all] day and night, as well as numbers of technical (working-class) schools, and 400 schools outside Paris."[56] High school students participated en masse in all the major strikes and demonstrations and were, sadly, not exempt from the repressive state violence that met protesters. One high school student, Gilles Tautin, who joined the May 13 protest to demonstrate his solidarity with the Renault workers, was murdered by the police. His death served as a chilling reminder of the brutality of the state. But it was also a stunning example of the bravery of students who fought for a world in which, to paraphrase one slogan, to be realistic was to demand the impossible.[57]

On May 19, after teachers decided to strike again, students occupied the schools, embarking on an experiment in democratic education that has rarely been replicated. Student and teacher delegates organized committees to discuss all aspects of education and school organization. Traditional "classes" were abolished, as students were grouped based on knowledge, not exams or grade. Schoolwork was divided between more "basic" lessons in the morning and "free and collective" learning in the afternoon, which, despite being more "recreational," was nonetheless meant to "establish continuity with the work of the morning which it will contribute to illustrate and nourish."[58]

While there were many skeptics, the seriousness of the occupiers had a profound resonance on many observers. As one participant explains: "They imagined that the *lycéens* would take advantage of the occasion to run wild and even damage places. But why should they damage *their* materials, smash up *their* classrooms, sabotage *their* own work? It is on this point that the *lycée* occupations run parallel to the factory occupations. In both cases, the work tools were respected because they felt so much more responsible on discovering that they could function by the activity of the rank and file alone, without the interference of administrative hierarchies or the bosses."[59]

At one school, Henry IV, a historic lycée in the fifth *arrondissement* of Paris, they launched the following experimental schedule:

> Starting at 9 a.m. "each group organized its work as it wanted, studying one subject in the morning and deciding how to make the time-table (introductions, practical exercises, small groups, etc.). From 12 to 12:30 the pupils of each class: 1) decided the aim of the operation and wrote down conclusions which would help them when they returned to the matter; 2) prepared the next day's work deciding who would introduce a subject, what books to bring, etc.
>
> In the afternoon there were political discussions (in the widest sense of the term) and cultural activities: theatrical works, the reading of passages, films till 4. Then a general meeting, then sports."[60]

The student committees and occupations thoroughly transformed the repressive and hierarchical structure of schools. By working with teachers, *lycéens* transformed the relationship between student and teacher from one of unequal power to one of collaboration. This was reflected in one of the more practical yet radical and political demands of the movement to eradicate the raised platform upon which the teacher's desk was placed in most French classrooms. As the CAL Bordeaux explained, "In order to render the role of the teacher more human it is desired that the platform upon which he sits be abolished. It was seen during the lycée occupation that the participation of the pupils was much more effective when the pupils found the teacher no longer on his pedestal but among them, the respect for the teacher not depend[ent] on the difference in height of the teachers' and pupils' desks. We also suggest that desks be differently arranged in the form of a horseshoe.[61] In the same vein, another CAL argued for the principle of the three-day week for teachers "to give them time to work on enlivening their lessons."[62]

While the student movement fell short of many of its goals, it won lasting reforms at both the university and high school levels. New universities were created and all universities were given greater autonomy, as they were to be governed cooperatively with students playing a leading role in these decision-making bodies.[63] In high schools, students won the right to smoke—a dubious right from the perspective of modern health standards, but, nonetheless, a reflection of the assertion of students' rights. More importantly, they won the right to elect peer representatives at the councils that evaluated students, the right to criticize teachers in these councils (or through leaflets), and the right to discuss politics in the school and distribute political materials.[64] What this meant in many schools was that "the staff had to radically revise their attitude and for the first time regard pupils as human beings."[65]

Although the events of May 1968 fell short of a revolution, they gave a glimpse of what the world of students organizing to transform both education and society at large looked like and that the corporate education "deformers" would love for us to forget. As Raul Ferrer, the architect of the Cuban literacy campaign, said in words that resonate in the United States today: "Ever since the student upheavals in Paris during May of 1968 hundreds of people have been traveling the world in an attempt to isolate the crisis of our pupils from the moral struggles of our times. It is a gross diversion. We deny that there is 'a crisis in the schools.' . . . It is not a crisis in the classroom. It is a crisis in the social order.[66]

Education, Literacy, and Revolution: The Russian Revolution

There is no greater school than a revolution. It is therefore not surprising that some of the most innovative, radical, and successful literacy campaigns are those that are born out of revolutions—when, on a mass scale, people fight for a better society. In revolutionary periods, ideas matter as never before, and literacy needs no motivation as it becomes a truly liberatory endeavor. Thus, from the trenches of the US Civil War and the Russian front to the battle lines of El Salvador, there are innumerable stories of soldiers teaching each other to read newspapers in the midst of war and famine. One of the most inspiring examples of the revolutionary transformation of literacy and education is the Russian Revolution of 1917.

The Russian Revolution was a watershed historical moment. That workers and peasants were able to overthrow tsarism and create a new society based on workers' power was an inspiration to millions of oppressed and exploited people around the world. At the time of the revolution, the vast majority of Russians were peasants toiling under the yoke of big landowners and eking out a meager existence. More than 60 percent of the population was illiterate.[67] At the same time, however, Russia was home to some of the largest and most advanced factories in the world, with a highly concentrated working class. By October 1917, the Bolshevik Party had won the support of the majority of workers and established political rule based on a system of soviets, or councils, of workers, peasants, and soldiers.

The revolution itself, occurring in two major stages in February and October, took place in conditions of extreme scarcity. In addition to the long-standing privation of Russia's peasants, the First World War caused further food shortages and disease. No sooner had the revolution succeeded than the young Soviet government was forced to fight on two military fronts: a civil war against the old powers just overthrown, and a battle against some dozen countries that sent their troops to defeat the revolution. As the Bolsheviks had long argued, the longevity and success of the Russian revolution depended in large part on the spread of revolution to advanced capitalist countries, in particular to Germany. Despite five years of revolutionary upheaval in Germany, the revolution there failed. The young revolutionary society was thus left isolated and under attack.

Despite these conditions, however, the Russian Revolution led not only to a radical transformation of school itself but also of the way people conceived of learning and the relationship between cognition and language. Indeed, the early years of the Russian Revolution offer stunning examples of what education looked like in a society in which working-class people democratically made decisions and organized society in their own interest. In the immediate aftermath of the revolution, education was massively overhauled with a tenfold increase in the expenditure on popular education.[68] Free and universal access to education was mandated for all children from the ages of three to sixteen years old, and the number of schools at least doubled within the first two years of the revolution.[69] Co-education was immediately implemented as a means of combating sex discrimination, and for the first time schools were created for students with learning and other disabilities.[70]

Developing mass literacy was seen as crucial to the success of the revolution. Lenin argued: "As long as there is such a thing in the country as illiteracy it is hard to talk about political education."[71] As a result, and despite the grim conditions, literacy campaigns were launched nationally among toddlers, soldiers, adolescents, workers, and peasants. The same was true of universal education. The Bolsheviks understood that the guarantee of free, public education was essential both to the education of a new generation of workers who would be prepared to run society in their own interests and as a means of freeing women from the drudgery of housework. Thus, there were attempts to provide universal crèches and preschools.

None of these initiatives was easy to accomplish given the economic conditions surrounding the young revolution. Victor Serge, a journalist and anarchist who later joined the Russian Communist Party, describes the staggering odds facing educators and miserable conditions that existed in the wake of the civil war: "Hungry children in rags would gather in winter-time around a small stove planted in the middle of the classroom, whose furniture often went for fuel to give some tiny relief from the freezing cold; they had one pencil between four of them and their schoolmistress was hungry."[72] One historian describes the level of scarcity: "In 1920 Narkompros [the People's Commissariat for Education] received the following six-month allotment: one pencil per sixty pupils; one pen per twenty-two pupils; one notebook for every two pupils. . . . One village found a supply of wrappers for caramel candies and expropriated them for writing paper for the local school."[73] The situation was so dire that "in 1921, the literacy Cheka prepared a brochure for short-term literacy courses including a chapter entitled 'How to get by without paper, pencils, or pens.'"[74] Nonetheless, as Serge explains, "in spite of this grotesque misery, a prodigious impulse was given to public education. Such a thirst for knowledge sprang up all over the country that new schools, adult courses, universities and Workers' Faculties were formed everywhere."[75]

Historian Lisa Kirschenbaum describes the incredible gap between the conditions imposed by famine and what kindergartens were able to accomplish. On the one hand, these schools had to provide food each day for students and teachers in the midst of a famine simply to prevent starvation. And yet, as Kirschenbaum writes, "even with these constraints, local administrations managed to set up some institutions. In 1918, Moscow *guberniia* [province] led the way with twenty-three kindergartens, eight day cares (*ochagi*) and thirteen summer playgrounds. A year later it boasted a total of 279 institutions. . . . Petrograd had no preschool department in 1918, but a year later it reported 106 institutions in the city and 180 in the *guberniia* outside the city. Other areas reported slower, but still remarkable, increases."[76]

Within these preschools, teachers experimented with radical pedagogy, particularly the notion of "free upbringing," as "teachers insisted that freedom in the classroom was part and parcel of the Revolution's transformation of social life."[77] Kirschenbaum elaborates: "By allowing, as one teacher expressed it, the 'free development of [children's] inherent capabilities and developing independence, creative initiative, and social feeling,' *svobodnoe vospitanie* [free upbringing] played a 'very important role in the construction of a new life.'"[78]

A central aspect of expanding literacy in revolutionary Russia was deciding in which language, or languages, literacy should be developed. Before the revolution, tsarist colonialism had forged a multinational empire in which ethnic Russians comprised only 43 percent of the population. A central political question for the Bolsheviks—the majority of whom were Russian—was how to combat the legacy of Russian chauvinism while also winning non-Russian nationalities to the project of the revolution. A full discussion of this history is beyond the scope of this chapter.[79] But it is important to underscore how progressive Bolshevik politics were with respect to native language education.

Already in October 1918, the general policy was established to provide for native language education in any school where twenty-five or more pupils in each age group spoke the same language. Implementing the policy depended on a number of factors. For example, within Russia proper, where some national minorities such as Ukrainians and Byelorussians were already assimilated, few native-language programs were set up. Within Ukraine itself, however, the extent of native-language education was reflected in the rapid demand for Ukrainian language teachers and Ukrainian-language textbooks in the years following the revolution.

Nativizing language and literacy education for populations in the Caucasus and Central Asian regions of the old empire was a more complicated task. In part, the difficulty stemmed from efforts under tsarism to use differences in dialect to divide native peoples in these regions. In addition, in some cases the languages most widely spoken had not yet developed a writing system. Thus, part of nativizing education meant deciding which language should be used in school, and which system (for example, Cyrillic, Roman, or Arabic script, or something different altogether) should be used to write it. Despite these practical challenges, native language education became the rule rather than the exception. Again, a key indication is the number of languages in which textbooks were published, which grew from twenty-five in 1924 to thirty-four in 1925 to forty-four in 1927. As British socialist Dave Crouch summarizes: "By 1927 native language education for national minorities outside their own republic or region was widespread, while in their own republic it was almost total."[80]

At the same time universities were opened up to workers as preliminary exams were abolished to allow them to attend lectures. The lectures themselves were free, art was made public, and the number of libraries was dramatically increased. There was an incredible hunger for learning in a society in which people were making democratic decisions about their lives and their society. One writer describes: "One course, for example, is attended by a thousand men in spite of the appalling cold of the lecture rooms. The hands of the science professors . . . are frostbitten from touching the icy metal of their instruments during demonstrations."[81]

A whole new educational system was created in which traditional education was thrown out and new, innovative techniques were implemented that emphasized self-activity, collectivism, and choice, and that drew on students' prior experience, knowledge, and interaction with the real world. Anna-Louise Strong, an American journalist who traveled extensively in Russia after the revolution, wrote about her experiences and recounts a conversation with one teacher:

> "We call it the Work School," said a teacher to me. "We base all study on the child's play and his relation to productive work. We begin with the life around him. How do the people in the village get their living? What do they produce? What tools do they use to produce it? Do they eat it all or exchange some of it? For what do they exchange it? What are horses and their use to man? What are pigs and what makes them fat? What are families and how do they support each other, and what is a village that organizes and cares for the families?"
>
> "This is interesting nature study and sociology," I replied, "but how do you teach mathematics?" He looked at me in surprise.
>
> "By real problems about real situations," he answered. "Can we use a textbook in which a lord has ten thousand rubles and puts five thousand out at interest and the children are asked what his profit is? The old mathematics is full of problems the children never see now, of situations and money values which no longer exist, of transactions which we do not wish to encourage. Also it was always purely formal, divorced from existence.

We have simple problems in addition, to find out how many cows there are in the village, by adding the number in each family. Simple problems of division of food, to know how much the village can export. Problems of proportion,—if our village has three hundred families and the next has one thousand, how many red soldiers must each give to the army, how many delegates is each entitled to in the township soviet? The older children work out the food-tax for their families; that really begins to interest the parents in our schools."[82]

Within schools, student governments were set up—even at the elementary school level—in which elected student representatives worked with teachers and other school workers to run the schools.[83] In so doing, schools became places where students learned "collective action" and began to put the principles of the revolution in practice. As Strong described: "We have our self-governed school community, in which teachers, children and janitors all have equal voice. It decides everything, what shall be done with the school funds, what shall be planted in the school garden, what shall be taught. If the children decide against some necessary subject, it is the teacher's job to show them through their play and life together that the subject is needed."[84]

She continues by describing a school for orphans and homeless children where basic needs such as food, clothing, and hygiene had to be met before any real learning could begin. Additionally, the students spoke more than a dozen different dialects, making the shared development of a common language one of the school's first goals. But, as the writer describes, "those were famine conditions. Yet the children in this school, just learning to speak to each other, had their School Council for self-government which received a gift of chocolate I sent them, duly electing a representative to come and get it and furnishing her with proper papers of authorization. They divided the chocolate fairly."[85]

A more skeptical writer, William Chamberlin, a journalist with the *Christian Science Monitor* who passed on information to US intelligence, described a school in which students in the higher grades "receive tasks in each subject, requiring from a week to a month for completion. They are then left free to carry out these tasks as they see fit."[86] He continued:

Visiting a school where this system was in operation I found the pupils at work in various classrooms, studying and writing out their problems in composition, algebra, and elemental chemistry. Sometimes the teacher was in the room, sometimes not, but the students were left almost entirely to their own resources. The teacher seemed to function largely in an advisory capacity, giving help only when asked. If the students preferred talk or games to study, the teacher usually overlooked it. Each student was free to choose the subject or subjects on which he would work on any particular day.

This absence of external restriction is a very marked characteristic of the Soviet school. The maintenance of discipline is in the hands of organizations elected by the students themselves, and while one seldom witnesses actual rowdyism in the classroom, one is also unlikely to find the strict order that usually prevails in the schools of other countries.[87]

Chamberlin questioned Lunacharsky, the commissar for education, about whether such a model provided sufficient education in basic skills such as grammar and spelling. Lunacharsky replied: "Frankly, we don't attach so much importance to the formal school discipline of reading and writing and spelling as to the development of the child's mind and personality. Once a pupil begins to think for himself he will master such tools of formal knowledge as he may need. And if he doesn't learn to think for himself no amount of correctly added sums or correctly spelled words will do him much good."[88] But, Chamberlin explained, it was hard to provide hard data on the success of the program, as "marks are proverbially an unreliable gauge of students' ability; and Russia has no grading system."[89] Examinations were also largely abolished, including those that had previously been necessary to gain entrance into institutions of higher education. Why? Because "it was believed that no one would willingly listen to lectures that were of no use to him."[90]

The revolution inspired a wide range of innovative thinkers in education and psychology. Lev Vygotsky, known as the "Mozart of psychology,"[91] created a legacy of influential work in child and adolescent psychology and cognition, despite being stymied and all but silenced under Stalinism. He began with a Marxist method and analyzed the way in which social relations are at the heart of children's learning process. He wrote that he intended to develop a new scientific psychology not by quoting Marxist texts but rather "having learned the whole of Marx's method" and applying it to the study of consciousness and culture, using psychology as his tool of investigation.[92]

Vygotsky used this method to investigate the creation of "higher mental processes," as opposed to more "natural" mental functions, which are biologically endowed. These higher mental processes are mediated by human-made psychological tools (for example, language), and include voluntary attention, active perception, and intentional memory.[93] He also traced the dialectical development and interaction of thought and language, which results in the internalization of language, verbalized thought, and conceptual thinking.[94] He argued that mental development is a sociohistorical process both for the human species and for individuals as they develop, becoming "humanized" from birth. Personality begins forming at birth in a dialectical manner, with the child an active agent in appropriating elements from her environment (not always consciously) in line with her internal psychological structure and unique individual social activity. For Vygotsky, education plays a decisive role in "not only the development of the individual's potential, but in the expression and growth of the human culture from which man springs,"[95] and which is transmitted to succeeding generations.

Through applied research in interdisciplinary educational psychology, Vygotsky developed concepts such as the zone of proximal development, in which joint social activity and instruction "marches ahead of development and leads it; it must be aimed not so much at the ripe as the ripening functions."[96] This view clashed with Piaget's insistence on the necessity of passively waiting for a level of biological and developmental maturity prior to instruction. Vygotsky devoted himself to the education of mentally and physically handicapped children; he founded and directed the Institute for the Study of Handicapped Children, which focused on the social development of higher mental processes among children with disabilities. He also discovered characteristics of "preconceptual" forms of thinking associated with schizophrenia and other psychopathologies.[97]

Vygotsky saw as the historical task of his time the creation of an integrated scientific psychology on a dialectical, material, historical foundation that would help the practical transformation of society. As he argued, "it is practice which poses the tasks and is the supreme judge of theory."[98] Although this task was incomplete upon his death, and both his work and the revolution itself were derailed by Stalinism (his work was banned under Stalin for twenty years after his death),[99] he made great headway in this process, and laid a foundation for others who have been inspired to further elaborate upon and develop his ideas.[100]

The immense poverty and scarcity of material resources after the Russian Revolution and the subsequent Stalinist counterrevolution distorted the revolutionary promise of education reform in the early years. Nonetheless, the Russian Revolution provides important examples of the possibilities for the creativity and radical reform that could be unleashed by revolutionary transformation of society at large—even amid the worst conditions.

While the adult literacy campaign's accomplishments were thus limited, and much of the data is hotly contested as a result of Stalinist distortions, it had important successes. In its first year of existence, the campaign reached five million people, "about half of whom learned to read and write."[101] While literacy statistics are hard to find, it is worth noting that the number of rural mailboxes increased from 2,800 in 1913 to 64,000 in 1926 as newspaper subscriptions and the exchange of written communications substantially increased—a notable corollary of increased literacy. In unions, literacy programs were quite successful. To give one example, a campaign among railway workers led to a 99 percent literacy rate by 1924.[102] Similarly, in the Red Army, where literacy and education were deemed crucial to ensure that soldiers were politically engaged with its project, illiteracy rates decreased from 50 percent to only 14 percent three years later, and 8 percent one year after that. On its seventh anniversary, the army achieved a 100 percent literacy rate, an immense accomplishment, even if short-lived, as new conscripts made continual education necessary.[103]

Perhaps more important than any of the data, however, are the plethora of stories of innovation and radically restructured ideas of schooling, teaching, and learning as students at all levels took control of their own learning, imbued with a thirst for knowledge in a world which was theirs to create and run in their own interests.

Conclusion

The complete transformation of education and literacy during the Russian Revolution exposes the lies at the heart of American education—that competition drives innovation, that punishments and rewards are the only motivations for learning, and that schools are the great levelers that provide every child with an equal opportunity to succeed.

If we have anything to learn from the revolutionary literacy campaigns of Russia, and to a certain extent in Cuba, it is that genuine learning triumphs in revolutionary situations that provide people with real opportunities for collective and cooperative inquiry and research; that literacy is always political; and that radical pedagogy is most successful when it actively engages people in the transformation of their own worlds—not simply in the world of ideas, but by transforming the material conditions in which reading, writing, and learning take place. Compare that to rote memorization of disconnected bits of information, bubble tests, and scripted, skill-based curricula that suck the love of learning out of children in our schools.

Radical educators should draw on these lessons wherever possible to fight for an educational system that is liberatory rather than stultifying, sees students as thinkers and actors rather than empty containers to be filled, and recognizes that collaboration and collective action are far more useful for our students than individualism and meritocracy.

But for most teachers, the opportunities to implement the lessons of these struggles are extremely limited as curricula are standardized and stripped of any political meaning, testing triumphs over critical thinking, and our jobs are increasingly contingent on how much "value" we've added to a test score.

It is no coincidence that the best examples of radical pedagogy come from revolutionary periods of struggle, as newly radicalized students and teachers put forward new visions of education and reshape pedagogy. As teachers, we know that students can't just ignore the many inequalities they face outside of the school building and overcome these through acts of sheer will. Genuine literacy that emphasizes critical thinking, political consciousness, and self-emancipation cannot happen in a vacuum. The creation of a liberatory pedagogy and literacy goes hand in hand with the self-emancipation of working people through revolutionary transformations of society as a whole.

Under capitalism, education will always be a means of maintaining class divisions rather than eradicating them. To imagine an educational system that is truly liberatory, we need to talk about fighting for a different kind of society—a socialist society in which, as Marx described, "the free development of each is the precondition for the free development of all." It is only by transforming our society to eradicate poverty, prisons, oppression, and exploitation in all its forms that we can fully unleash human potential and creativity.

Imagine a society in which teachers and students democratically decided what learning should look like and where learning was freed from the confines of a classroom. Imagine what true lifelong learning could look like in a world in which we were free to develop our own courses of study and unlock the creative potential of humanity. If we can learn anything from the history of education and literacy, it is that such a revolutionary transformation of society is both possible and urgently needed.

Acknowledgments

This book has been a collaborative project, a "dialogic" endeavor in the spirit of Freirian education. We would like to thank all the contributing authors for examining, discussing, and debating the ideas presented in this book in the spirit of advancing a revolutionary understanding of education.

We would like to thank Anthony Arnove, Julie Fain, Ahmed Shawki, and Dao X. Tran at Haymarket Books for making this project possible. Thanks as well to Jean Anyon, Paul D'Amato, Sharon Smith, and Lee Sustar in particular for their guidance on several chapters of the book. Others who provided invaluable feedback include: Sam Anderson, Rafael Feliciano-Hernández, Peter Lamphere, Peter McLaren, Jeremy Sawyer, Jeanne Theoharis, David Whitehouse, and Chris Williams. A portion of chapter 3 appears in the journal *Critical Education*, vol. 2, no. 8; thanks to editor Wayne Ross and the reviewers for their critique. Thanks also to Alan Maass for his tireless work editing *Socialist Worker*, the newspaper that helped us become writers and socialists. And we'd like to express our appreciation for help and guidance to Jody Sokolower of *Rethinking Schools* and Mary Compton and Lois Weiner, authors of *The Global Assault on Teaching, Teachers, and Their Unions: Stories for Resistance*. We extend special thanks, as well, to Kristina Crandall and Sarah Grey for their diligent assistance with copyediting.

We would also like to acknowledge and give thanks to our comrades, coworkers, friends, teachers, and students with whom we've developed the ideas herein, as well as to those who inspired in us a love of learning and liberation.

From Sarah in Los Angeles:

To Grandma More and those who helped to inspire a love of "learning and liberation": I'd like to thank my parents and grandparents for my intellectual curiosity and Grandma More, Mom, Emily, Aunt Martha, and Carolyn for being great educators. Much gratitude also to those who provided the love, ideas, and logistical support that made this book possible: Bruce Cooley, Daniel Fluckey, Ryan Whitney, Shaun Harkin, Sean Petty, the McKenna-Raghians, Kris, the Douglasses, the Taylors. And to the creative young intellects Cesar, Sequoia, Angie, Diana, Diego, Charlie, Olivia, Jenna, and Thomas: stay as smart, curious, and fun as you are now.

Thanks to the family at Fremont, Youth Opportunities Unlimited, and Central Region High School 16, and the activists in UTLA, PEAC, CEJ, ACCE as well as those involved in Occupy LA. Thanks in particular to David Rapkin, Gillian Russom, Randy Childs, Rebecca Sun, Jess Kochik, Cesar Montufar, Joe Zeccola, Bill Neal, Cindy Kaffen, and Peter Kuhns. And to all the Y.O.U. kids, especially Leadership!

From Jeff in Michigan:

Special thanks to the many people I've been lucky to learn from and collaborate with—at Arizona State, to Terry Wiley, Terri McCarty, Gustavo Fischman, Larisa Warhol, Maggie Bartlett, and Bärbel Singer; at Tempe Union, to Megan Karns Garvy, Kim Saad, and Birgit Zimmermann; in DC, to Michele Bollinger, Dave Zirin, Jesse Hagopian, Salomé Calvo, Liz Davis, Edith Echevaria, Ana Hernández, Signe Nelson, Micki Suchenski, and Natasha Warsaw. Most of all, my thanks go to the students of Abraham Lincoln Multicultural Middle School, who never allowed for a dull day and challenged me to see school in a whole new way.

I am indebted to Mildred Trude, Maureen Barry, Ralph Heister, Nancy Rosenberger, Judith Shepherd, and above all, to Rhonda Brown Ritchie—amazing teachers who showed me how to think, doubt, question, and reason. They may not agree with all the ideas I've settled on, but they helped me learn to decide for myself. Also, every so often we encounter a reading or an event that, well, sort of changes everything. Reading Sharon Smith's "Mistaken Identity" in the basement of the "cheese grater" at DePaul in 1994 did just that. To her, my thanks. To my parents, grandmother, godparents, and family go thanks for all their support.

Notes

Preface

1. See Noelle M. Ellerson, *Surviving a Thousand Cuts: America's Public Schools and the Recession* (Arlington, VA: American Association of School Administrators, 2010).
2. Erika Frankenberg, Genevieve Siegel-Hawley, and Jia Wang, "Choice without Equity: Charter School Segregation and the Need for Civil Rights Standards," Civil Rights Project of UCLA, January 2010, 37.
3. Quoted in Lee Sustar, "Solidarity City," *SocialistWorker.org*, February 28, 2011.
4. Pedro Noguera, *City Schools and the American Dream: Reclaiming the Promise of Public Education* (New York: Teachers College Press, 2003), 6.
5. Anthony P. Carnevale, Nicole Smith, and Jeff Strohl, *Help Wanted: Projections of Jobs and Education Requirements through 2018* (Washington, DC: Georgetown University Center on Education and the Workforce, June 2010), 14, cited in John Marsh, *Class Dismissed: Why We Cannot Teach or Learn Our Way Out of Inequality* (New York: Monthly Review, 2011), 86.
6. US Bureau of Labor Statistics, "Overview of the 2008–2018 Projections," table 2, cited in Marsh, *Class Dismissed*, 87.
7. Ibid.
8. Neta C. Crawford and Catherine Lutz, *The Costs of War since 2011 in Iraq, Afghanistan, and Pakistan: Executive Summary* (Providence, RI: Watson Institute for International Studies, Brown University, 2010), http://costsofwar.org.

Chapter 1
Schools, Marxism, and Liberation

1. Samuel Bowles and Herbert Gintis, *Schooling in Capitalist America: Educational Reform and the Contradictions of Economic Life* (New York: Basic Books, 1976), 29.
2. David McNally, *Global Slump: The Economics and Politics of Crisis and Resistance* (Winnipeg: PM Press, 2011), 23.
3. Economic Policy Institute, "The Great Recession's Long Tail: Third Anniversary Underscores Severity of Labor Market Woes," Briefing Paper #294, February 2, 2011.

4. OECD, "A Family Affair: Intergenerational Social Mobility Across OECD Countries," 7, www.oecd.org/dataoecd/3/62/44582910.pdf, cited in Marsh, *Class Dismissed*, 53.

5. Marsh, *Class Dismissed*, 52.

6. Jean Anyon, *Radical Possibilities: Public Policy, Urban Education, and a New Social Movement* (New York: Routledge, 2005),15.

7. Carnevale, Smith, and Strohl, *Help Wanted: Projections of Jobs and Education Requirements*, 14, cited in Marsh, *Class Dismissed*, 86.

8. Ibid., 89.

9. US Bureau of Labor Statistics, "Overview of the 2008–2018 Projections," table 2, cited in Marsh, *Class Dismissed*, 87.

10. See, for just one example, Brian K. Bucks, Arthur B. Kennickell, Traci L. Mach, and Kevin B. Moore, "Changes in U.S. Family Finances from 2004 to 2007: Evidence from the Survey of Consumer Finances," *Federal Reserve Bulletin* February (2009): A11.

11. R. Haveman and B. Wolfe, "The Determinants of Children's Attainments: A Review of Methods and Findings," *Journal of Economic Literature* 33 (1995): 1829–1878.

12. Anyon, *Radical Possibilities*, 21.

13. Ibid., 24.

14. Karl Marx, "On General Education," in *Selected Works*, Karl Marx and Friedrich Engels (New York: International Publishers, 1960), 398.

15. Karl Marx, *Capital* (London: Penguin Books, 1990) 1:284.

16. Paulo Freire, *Pedagogy of the Oppressed* (New York: Continuum, 2000), 73.

17. Myles Horton and Paulo Freire, *We Make the Road by Walking: Conversations on Education and Social Change*, ed. Brenda Bell, John Gaventa, and John Peters (Philadelphia: Temple University Press, 1990), 108.

18. Friedrich Engels, *Socialism: Utopian and Scientific* (Moscow: Progress Publishers, 1970), 128.

19. Paul D'Amato, *The Meaning of Marxism* (Chicago: Haymarket Books, 2006), 23–24.

20. Engels, *Socialism*, 130.

21. Lev Vygotsky, *Thought and Language* (Boston: MIT Press, 1986), 4.

22. Lev Vygotsky, *The Concept of Activity in Soviet Psychology*, ed. M. Cole and J. V. Wertsch (New York: M. E. Sharpe, 1981), 164.

23. Wayne Au, "Vygotsky and Lenin on Learning: The Parallel Structures of Individual and Social Development," *Science and Society*, 71 (2007): 290.

24. Freire, *Pedagogy of the Oppressed*, 12.

25. Peter McLaren and Ramin Farahmandpur, *Teaching Against Capitalism and the New Imperialism* (New York: Rowman and Littlefield, 2005), 53.

26. Bowles and Gintis, *Schooling in Capitalist America* (see chap. 4).

27. Ibid., 169.

28. Ibid. (see chap. 5).

29. Jean Anyon, "Social Class and the Hidden Curriculum of Work," *Journal of*

Education 162 (1980).

30. See ibid.

31. Ibid., 67–92.

32. *A Half Century of Learning: Historical Census Statistics on Educational Attainment in the United States; 1940 to 2000, Detailed Tables* (Washington, DC: US Census Bureau, 2010), table 4, www.census.gov.

33. John Bellamy Foster, "Education and the Structural Crisis of Capital," *Monthly Review* 63 (2011).

34. Mike Cole, "Contradictions in the Educational Theories of Gintis and Bowles," in *Bowles and Gintis Revisited: Correspondence and Contradiction in Educational Theory*, ed. Mike Cole (London: Falmer Press, 1988), 33.

35. Ibid., 35.

36. Ibid., 36.

37 . Karl Marx, *Contribution to the Critique of Political Economy* (Moscow: Progress Publishers, 1977), 6.

38. For those interested in an in-depth exploration of this topic, see Chris Harman, *Marxism and History: Two Essays* (London: Bookmarks, 1998), 7–54.

39. Harman, *Marxism and History*, 157.

40. Herbert Gintis and Samuel Bowles, "Contradiction and Reproduction in Educational Theory," in *Bowles and Gintis Revisited*, ed. Cole, 21.

41. Friedrich Engels, "Engels to J. Bloch, September 21, 1890," in *On Historical Materialism: A Collection*, Karl Marx, Friedrich Engels, and Vladimir Il'ich Lenin (London: Progress Publishers, 1972), 294.

42. Gary Orfield, *Schools More Separate: Consequences of a Decade of Resegregation* (Cambridge, MA: Civil Rights Project, 2001).

43. Daniel J. Losen, "Discipline Policies, Successful Schools, and Racial Justice," National Education Policy Center, October 2011, http://nepc.colorado.edu/files/NEPC-SchoolDiscipline.pdf.

44. See chapter 7, "The Socialist, Communist, and Trotsykist Parties," in Ahmed Shawki, *Black Liberation and Socialism* (Chicago: Haymarket Books, 2006).

45. Rakesh Kochhar, Richard Fry, and Paul Taylor, "Wealth Gap Rises to Record Heights between Whites, Blacks, and Hispanics," Pew Research Center Publications, July 26, 2011.

46. Keeanga-Yamahtta Taylor, "Race, Class and Marxism," *SocialistWorker.org*, January 4, 2011.

47. Marx, *Capital*, 1:414.

48. Marx, *Contribution*, 7.

49. Bowles and Gintis, *Schooling in Capitalist America*, 206.

50. Freire, *Pedagogy of the Oppressed*, 54.

51. Horton and Freire, *We Make the Road*, 103.

52. Anyon, *Radical Possibilities*, 98.

53. Gary Orfield and Chungmei Lee, *Historic Reversals, Accelerating Resegregation, and the Need for New Integration Strategies* (Los Angeles: Civil Rights Project/Proyecto Derechos Civiles, 2007), 27.

54. Gerald Grant, *Hope and Despair in the American City: Why There Are No Bad Schools in Raleigh* (Cambridge, MA: Harvard University Press, 2009).

55. Patrick J. Finn, *Literacy with an Attitude: Educating Working-Class Children in Their Own Self-Interest* (Albany: State University of New York Press, 1999), 169.

56. Jean Anyon, "What 'Counts' as Educational Policy? Notes Toward a New Paradigm," *Harvard Educational Review* 75 (2005): 74–77.

57. Bowles and Gintis, *Schooling in Capitalist America*, 245.

58. Mary Compton and Lois Weiner, eds., *The Global Assault on Teaching, Teachers, and Their Unions* (New York: Palgrave, 2008), 254.

59. Bowles and Gintis, *Schooling in Capitalist America*, 8.

60. Marx, *Contribution*, 6.

Chapter 2
The Struggle for Black Education

1. Quoted in Meyer Weinberg, *A Chance to Learn: the History of Race and Education in the United States*, 2nd ed. (Long Beach: University Press, California State University, 1995), 80.

2. See Brian Jones, "Charter Schools and Civil Rights: What Kind of 'Movement' Is This?," *Huffington Post*, October 15, 2010, www.huffingtonpost.com.

3. Weinberg, *Chance to Learn*, 13.

4. Allan D. Austin, *African Muslims in Antebellum America: A Sourcebook* (New York: Garland, 1984).

5. W. E. B. Du Bois, *Black Reconstruction in America: 1860–1880* (New York: Atheneum, 1969), 645.

6. Weinberg, *Chance to Learn*, 14–15.

7. See "Examination Days: The New York Free African School Collection," New York Historical Society, https://www.nyhistory.org/web/afs/; and Carter G. Woodson, *The Education of the Negro Prior to 1861: A History of the Education of the Colored People of the United States from the Beginning of Slavery to the Civil War*, http://andromeda.rutgers.edu/~natalieb/The_Education_Of_The_Negro_P.pdf

8. James D. Anderson, *The Education of Blacks in the South: 1860–1935* (Chapel Hill: University of North Carolina Press, 1988), 14.

9. Quoted in Weinberg, *Chance to Learn*, 16.

10. Du Bois, *Black Reconstruction*, 644; and Anderson, *Education of Blacks*, 7.

11. Anderson, *Education of Blacks*, 17.

12. Weinberg, *Chance to Learn*, 18–20.

13. Ibid., 25.

14. Quoted in ibid., 26–27.

15. Quoted in ibid., 27.

16. Du Bois, *Black Reconstruction*, 638.

17. Weinberg, *Chance to Learn*, 57.

18. Booker T. Washington, *Up From Slavery: An Autobiography* (New York: Doubleday, Page & Co., 1907), 30.

19. Quoted in Weinberg, *Chance to Learn*, 38.
20. Ibid., 38.
21. Anderson, *Education of Blacks*, 6.
22. Quoted in ibid., 7.
23. Quoted in ibid., 7.
24. Ibid., 21.
25. Ibid., 22.
26. Ibid., 19.
27. Du Bois, *Black Reconstruction*, 654–55.
28. Quoted in ibid., 655.
29. Quoted in ibid., 643.
30. Jack M. Bloom, *Class, Race, and the Civil Rights Movement* (Bloomington: Indiana University Press, 1987), 33.
31. Ibid., 32.
32. Anderson, *Education of Blacks*, 22.
33. Ibid., 21.
34. Weinberg, *Chance to Learn*, 44–45.
35. Quoted in Bloom, *Class, Race, and Civil Rights*, 34.
36. W. E. B. Du Bois, *The Education of Black People: Ten Critiques, 1906–1960* (New York: Monthly Review Press, 1973), 12.
37. Du Bois, *Black Reconstruction*, 665.
38. Eric Anderson and Alfred A. Moss, Jr., *Dangerous Donations: Northern Philanthropy and Southern Black Education, 1902–1930* (Columbia: University of Missouri Press, 1999), 36.
39. Anderson, *Education of Blacks*, 154.
40. Quoted in ibid., 165.
41. Ibid., 12.
42. Anderson and Moss, *Dangerous Donations*, 16.
43. Anderson, *Education of Blacks*, 59.
44. Ibid., 89.
45. Ibid., 51.
46. W. E. B. Du Bois and Booker T. Washington, *The Negro in the South: His Economic Progress in Relation to His Moral and Religious Development* (Northbrook, IL: Metro Books, 1972), 16.
47. Quoted in Anderson, *Education of Blacks*, 45.
48. Du Bois, *Education of Black People*, 27.
49. Anderson, *Education of Blacks*, 114.
50. Quoted in ibid., 274.
51. Quoted in Weinberg, *Chance to Learn*, 51.
52. Manning Marable, *Race, Reform, and Rebellion: The Second Reconstruction and Beyond in Black America, 1945–2006*, 3rd ed. (Jackson: University Press of Mississippi, 2007), 37.
53. Bloom, *Class, Race, and Civil Rights*, 60.
54. Weinberg, *Chance to Learn*, 71.

55. Quoted in Adina Back, "Exposing the 'Whole Segregation Myth': The Harlem Nine and New York City's Desegregation Battles," in *Freedom North: Black Freedom Struggles Outside the South, 1940–1980*, ed. Jeanne F. Theoharis and Komozi Woodard (New York: Palgrave MacMillan, 2003), 71.

56. Malcolm X, *The Autobiography of Malcolm X* (New York: Ballantine Books, 1964), 36.

57. Weinberg, *Chance to Learn*, 72.

58. Ibid., 77.

59. Ibid., 183–84.

60. Quoted in Jeanne Theoharis, "Alabama on Avalon: Rethinking the Watts Uprising and the Character of Black Protest in Los Angeles," in *The Black Power Movement: Rethinking the Civil Rights–Black Power Era*, ed. Peniel E. Joseph (New York: Routledge, 2006), 34.

61. Thomas J. Sugrue, *Sweet Land of Liberty: The Forgotten Struggle for Civil Rights in the North* (New York: Random House, 2008), 171.

62. Quoted in Wayne Au, *Unequal by Design: High-Stakes Testing and the Standardization of Inequality* (New York: Routledge, 2009), 38.

63. Sugrue, *Sweet Land*, 169.

64. Weinberg, *Chance to Learn*, 74.

65. Mark Naison, *Communists in Harlem during the Depression* (New York: Grove Press, 1983), 214–15.

66. Ibid., 215.

67. Ibid.

68. Martha Biondi, *To Stand and Fight: The Struggle for Civil Rights in Postwar New York City* (Cambridge, MA: Harvard University Press, 2003), 244–45.

69. Bloom, *Class, Race, and Civil Rights*, 77.

70. Ahmed Shawki, *Black Liberation and Socialism* (Chicago: Haymarket Books, 2006), 153–54.

71. Jeanne Theoharis, "'W-A-L-K-O-U-T!': High School Students and the Development of Black Power in L.A.," in *Neighborhood Rebels: Black Power at the Local Level*, ed. Peniel E. Joseph (New York: Palgrave MacMillan, 2010), 108.

72. Brown v. Board of Education, 347 U.S. at 483 (1954).

73. Sugrue, *Sweet Land*, 450.

74. Weinberg, *Chance to Learn*, 87.

75. Ibid., 90.

76. Ibid., 91.

77. Ibid., 99.

78. Bloom, *Class, Race, and Civil Rights*, 113.

79. Sugrue, *Sweet Land*, 459.

80. Weinberg, *Chance to Learn*, 93.

81. Theoharis, "Alabama on Avalon," 36.

82. Weinberg, *Chance to Learn*, 102.

83. See Adina Back, "Exposing the 'Whole Segregation Myth'" in *Freedom North*, eds. Theoharis and Woodard (New York: Palgrave MacMillan, 2003).

84. Jeanne Theoharis, "'I'd Rather Go to School in the South': How Boston's School Desegregation Complicates the Civil Rights Paradigm," in *Freedom North*, eds. Theoharis and Woodard, 132–33.
85. Weinberg, *Chance to Learn*, 106.
86. Ibid., 106.
87. Ibid., 105.
88. Theoharis, "'W-A-L-K-O-U-T!'",121.
89. Weinberg, *Chance to Learn*, 137.
90. Ibid., 137.
91. Jean Anyon, *Ghetto Schooling: A Political Economy of Urban Educational Reform* (New York: Teachers College Press, 1997), 63.
92. Ibid., 80.
93. Sugrue, *Sweet Land*, 470.
94. Ibid., 465.
95. Quoted in ibid., 484.
96. Theoharis, "I'd Rather Go to School in the South," 143.
97. Sugrue, *Sweet Land*, 483.
98. Theoharis, "I'd Rather Go to School in the South," 142.
99. Quoted in Sugrue, *Sweet Land*, 464.
100. Quoted in ibid., 467.
101. Reverend Herb Oliver shared these memories at a discussion: "The Strike That Changed New York" (panel, Museum of the City of New York, New York City, August 19, 2010).
102. Diane Ravitch, *The Great School Wars: A History of the New York City Public Schools* (Baltimore, MD: The Johns Hopkins University Press, 1974), 261, 318.
103. Jerald E. Podair, *The Strike That Changed New York: Blacks, Whites, and the Ocean Hill-Brownsville Crisis* (New Haven, CT: Yale University Press, 2002), 19.
104. Ibid., 101.
105. Ibid., 102–103. The letter to the teachers allegedly used the word "termination" but also instructed them to report to the Department of Education office for reassignment. Some argue that the community control board clearly did not have the authority to make such transfers. Regardless, the actions of the union before, during, and after the strike demonstrate a consistent hostility to the project of community control.
106. See Stephen Zeluck, "The UFT Strike: Will It Destroy the AFT?" in *Phi Delta Kappan* 50 (1969), 250–54. See also New York Civil Liberties Union, "The Burden of Blame: A Report on the Ocean Hill-Brownsville School Controversy," *Urban Education* 4 (1969): 7–24.
107. Podair, *Strike*, 100.
108. Ibid., 124.
109. Ravitch, *Great School Wars*, 366.
110. Joel Geier, a former leading member of the ISC, confirmed this over the phone on April 25, 2011. See also Milton Fisk, "The Independent Socialist Clubs and the Sixties," chap. 5 in *Socialism From Below in the United States* (Cleveland:

Hera Press, 1977).

111. Zeluck, "UFT Strike," 251.

112. See Dionne Danns, "Chicago Teacher Reform Efforts and the Politics of Educational Change," in *Black Protest Thought and Education*, ed. William H. Watkins (New York: Peter Lang, 2005).

113. This and other aspects of Shanker's turn to the right are detailed in Vera Pavone and Norman Scott, "Albert Shanker: Ruthless Neocon," *New Politics* (Summer 2008).

114. Podair, *Strike That Changed New York*, 142.

115. Jerald Podair made this argument during the discussion: "The Strike That Changed New York."

116. Diane Ravitch, "Resegregation," review of *In Brown's Wake: Legacies of America's Educational Landmark*, by Martha Minow, *New Republic*, October 14, 2010: 40–41.

117. Jonathan Kozol, *The Shame of the Nation: The Restoration of Apartheid Schooling in America* (New York: Three Rivers Press, 2005), 24.

118. Gary Orfield and Chungmei Lee, *Historic Reversals, Accelerating Resegregation, and the Need for New Integration Strategies* (Los Angeles: Civil Rights Project/Proyecto Derechos Civiles, 2007), 8.

119. Sugrue, *Sweet Land*, 487.

120. Ibid., 491.

121. Kozol, *Shame of the Nation*, 245.

122. Ibid., 246–47.

123. See Orfield and Lee, *Historic Reversals*, 4–5. See also Brian Jones, "Dr. King and the Achievement Gap," *Huffington Post*, January 10, 2011, www.huffingtonpost.com.

124. Quoted in Julie Bosman, "Obama Calls for More Responsibility from Black Fathers," *New York Times*, June 16, 2008. Buying into this same idea, many charter schools require parents to sign elaborate contracts that obligate them to participate heavily in school activities.

125. Michael Eric Dyson, *Is Bill Cosby Right? Or Has the Black Middle Class Lost Its Mind?* (New York: Basic Civitas Books, 2005), 87.

126. Carter G. Woodson, *The Mis-Education of the Negro* (Trenton: Africa World Press, 1990), xii–xiii.

127. Quoted in Jay A. Fernandez, "How Did 'Superman' Fly with the D.C. Elite?" *Hollywood Reporter*, October 14, 2010, www.hollywoodreporter.com.

128. Quoted in Nancy Hass, "Scholarly Investments," *New York Times*, December 6, 2009.

129. For further discussion on this point, see James Forman Jr., "The Secret History of School Choice: How Progressives Got There First," *Georgetown Law Journal* 93 (2005). In my view, Forman goes too far in making a virtue of necessity and misses the historic importance of the fight for public schools to secure the right to education.

130. Special thanks to Peter Lamphere, Jeanne Theoharis, and Sam Anderson for critical feedback on many of the issues covered in this chapter.

Focus On: The Indian Boarding Schools

1. This discussion relies primarily on these sources: David Wallace Adams, *Education for Extinction: American Indians and the Boarding School Experience, 1875–1928* (Lawrence: University Press of Kansas, 1995); Ward Churchill, *Kill the Indian, Save the Man: The Genocidal Impact of American Indian Residential Schools* (San Francisco: City Lights, 2004); and Leonard Peltier, *Prison Writings: My Life Is My Sun Dance*, ed. Harvey Arden (New York: St. Martin's Griffin, 2000).

2. There are various traditions among radical and progressive Native activists in terms of naming themselves. As such, this discussion uses the terms Native American, American Indian, and Indian interchangeably.

3. Cited in Charla Bear, "American Indian Boarding Schools Haunt Many," NPR.org, May 12, 2008, www.npr.org/templates/story/story .php?storyId=16516865.

4. Cited in Adams, *Education for Extinction*, 27.

5. Ibid.

6. Ibid.

7. Ibid., 20.

8. Ibid., 18.

9. Churchill, *Kill the Indian*, 13.

10. Adams, *Education for Extinction*, 15.

11. Ibid., 148.

12. Ibid., 150–51.

13. Dan Cook, "Northwest Jesuits Reach $166 Million Sex Abuse Settlement," Reuters, March 25, 2011, http://www.reuters.com.

14. Adams, *Education for Extinction*, 216.

15. Bear, "American Indian Boarding Schools."

16. Donald K. Sharpes, "Federal Education for the American Indian." *Journal of American Indian Education* 19 (1979): 19–22.

Chapter 3
Linguistic Justice at School

1. Quoted in *The Invisible Minority: Report of the NEA-Tucson Survey on the Teaching of Spanish to the Spanish-Speaking* (Washington, DC: National Education Association, 1966), 8.

2. Such students are often labeled *English Language Learners* or *Limited English Proficient* students. These terms identify students by what they don't know— English. *Emergent bilingual* is more accurate because it recognizes 1) that students already know a language, and 2) that students can and should maintain their home language while learning English.

3. Joshua Fishman, "The Displaced Anxieties of Anglo-Americans," in *Language Loyalties: A Source Book on the Official English Controversy*, ed. James Crawford (Chicago: University of Chicago Press, 1992), 167.

4. For overviews of this research see Ofelia García, *Bilingual Education in the 21st Century: A Global Perspective* (Malden, MA: Wiley-Blackwell, 2008); Ofelia

García and Colin Baker, eds., *Bilingual Education: An Introductory Reader* (Clevedon, UK: Multilingual Matters, 2007).

5.   See Colin Baker, *Foundations of Bilingual Education and Bilingualism*, 4th ed. (Clevedon, UK: Multilingual Matters, 2006), 215–16, and García, *Bilingual Education*, 134, for similar tables with more detailed differentiation.

6.   Eric Hobsbawm, *Nations and Nationalism since 1780: Programme, Myth, Reality* (Cambridge: Cambridge University Press, 1990), 44.

7.   Sue Wright, *Language Policy and Language Planning: From Nationalism to Globalization* (New York: Palgrave Macmillan, 2004), 31.

8.   Hobsbawm, *Nations and Nationalism*, 21.

9.   Jan Blommaert, "Language Policy and National Identity," in *An Introduction to Language Policy: Theory and Method*, ed. Thomas Ricento (Malden, MA: Blackwell Publishers, 2006), 246–49.

10. James W. Tollefson, *Planning Language, Planning Inequality: Language Policy in the Community* (London: Longman Publishers, 1991), 188–98.

11. Rama K. Agnihotri, "Identity and Multilinguality: The Case of India," in *Language Policy, Culture, and Identity in Asian Contexts*, ed. Amy B. M. Tsui and James W. Tollefson (Mahwah, NJ: Lawrence Earlbaum Associates, 2007), 188–89.

12. Although these formulations are mine, I must acknowledge Joshua Fishman and his use of Xmen speaking Xish in the Graded Intergenerational Disruption Scale for understanding language loss and revitalization.

13. Karl Marx and Friedrich Engels, *Manifesto of the Communist Party* (New York: International Publishers, 1948), 12.

14. Sinfree Makoni and Alistair Pennycook, eds., *Disinventing and Reconstituting Languages* (Clevedon, UK: Multilingual Matters, 2006), 9–30.

15. For example, English in Zimbabwe or French in Senegal.

16. Makoni and Pennycook, *Disinventing*; Jeff Bale, "International Comparative Perspectives on Heritage Language Education Policy Research," *Annual Review of Applied Linguistics* 30 (2010): 42–65.

17. David Harvey, *The New Imperialism* (Oxford: Oxford University Press, 2005), 44.

18. The Chuvash are one of a number of Turkic ethnic groups and are native to what is now central Russia.

19. Isabelle Kreindler, "A Neglected Source of Lenin's Nationality Policy," *Slavic Review* 36 (1977): 87.

20. V. I. Lenin, "Is a Compulsory Language Needed?," in *Collected Works* (Moscow: Progress Publishers, 1972), 20:71–73.

21. V. I. Lenin, "The Nationalities of Pupils in Russian Schools," in *Collected Works* (Moscow: Progress Publishers, 1977), 19:532–33.

22. Cited in Jeremy Smith, *The Bolsheviks and the National Question, 1917–1923* (New York: Palgrave MacMillan, 1999), 145.

23. See Smith, *The Bolsheviks and the National Question*, 144–68.

24. Tony Johnson, *Historical Documents in American Education* (Boston: Allyn and Bacon, 2002).

25. Bernard J. Weiss, ed., *American Education and the European Immigrant: 1840–*

1940 (Urbana: University of Illinois Press, 1982).

26. R. A. Carlson, *The Americanization Syndrome: A Quest for Conformity* (London: Croom Helm, 1987), 60.

27. Joshua Fishman, *The Rise and Fall of the Ethnic Revival* (Berlin: Mouton Publishers, 1985); Calvin Veltman, *Language Shift in the United States* (Berlin: Mouton Publishers, 1983).

28. Saul Cohen, *Education in the United States: A Documentary History*, vols. 4–5 (New York: Random House, 1974), 2931.

29. Ibid., 2933.

30. Ibid., 2971.

31. Ibid., 2972.

32. Crawford, *Language Loyalties*, 48.

33. Cohen, *Education in the United States*, 3012.

34. Deborah M. Herman, "'Our Patriotic Duty'": Insights from Professional History, 1980–1920," in *The Future of Foreign Language Education in the United States*, ed. T. Osborn (Westport, CT: Greenwood Publishing Group, 1998), 1–29.

35. Terrence G. Wiley, "The Imposition of World War I Era English-Only Policies and the Fate of German in North America," in *Language Policies in the United States and Canada: Myths and Realities*, ed. Thomas Ricento and Barbara Burnaby (Philadelphia, PA: Lawrence Earlbaum Associates, 1998), 211–41.

36. Sidney Lens, *The Forging of the American Empire: From the Revolution to Vietnam; A History of U.S. Imperialism* (London and Chicago: Pluto Books and Haymarket Books, 2003, originally published by Thomas Y. Crowell Company, New York, 1971), 236.

37. John F. McClymer, *War and Welfare: Social Engineering in America, 1890–1925* (Westport, CT: Greenwood Press, 1980).

38. John L. Watzke, *Lasting Change in Foreign Language Education: A Historical Case for Change in National Policy* (Westport, CT: Praeger, 2003).

39. Sidney Lens, *Forging of the American Empire*, 151–52.

40. Chris Harman, *A People's History of the World* (London: Bookmarks, 1999), 345–54.

41. Lens, *Forging of the American Empire*, 236–74.

42. Wiley, "Imposition of World War I," 216.

43. Ibid., 216ff.

44. Ignacio M. García, *Chicanismo: The Forging of a Militant Ethos among Mexican Americans* (Tucson: University of Arizona Press, 1997), 8–13; Guadalupe San Miguel Jr., *Brown, Not White: School Integration and the Chicano Movement in Houston* (College Station: Texas A&M University Press, 2001), 46–47.

45. San Miguel, *Brown, Not White*, 28; Justin Akers, "Fighting for Justice in the 'Factories of the Fields.'" *International Socialist Review* 34 (March–April 2004): 41–55.

46. I. García, *Chicanismo*, 10

47. Mario Barrera, "The Politics of Educational Change: Introduction," in *Mexican Americans and Educational Change*, ed. Alfredo Castañeda et al. (New York:

Arno Press, 1974), 76; I. García, *Chicanismo*, 7; Guadalupe San Miguel Jr., *Contested Policy: The Rise and Fall of Federal Bilingual Education in the United States 1960–2001* (Denton: University of North Texas Press, 2004), 6.

48. I. García, *Chicanismo*, 26.

49. O. García, *Bilingual Education*, 169.

50. I. García, *Chicanismo*, 27.

51. O. García, *Bilingual Education*, 168.

52. Dial Torgerson, "Start of a Revolution? 'Brown Power' Unity Seen Behind School Disorders," *Los Angeles Times*, March 17, 1968, quoted in Carlos Muñoz Jr., "The Politics of Educational Change in East Los Angeles," in *Mexican Americans and Educational Change*, ed. Castañeda et al., 85.

53. Meyer Weinberg, *A Chance to Learn: The History of Race and Education in the United States* (Cambridge: Cambridge University Press, 1977), 171.

54. Muñoz, "Politics of Educational Change," 86–96.

55. See Armando Navarro, *Mexican American Youth Organization: Avant-Garde of the Chicano Movement in Texas* (Austin: University of Texas Press, 1995), especially chapter 4; and Armando L. Trujillo, *Chicano Empowerment and Bilingual Education: Movimiento Politics in Crystal City, Texas* (New York: Garland Publishing, 1998), especially chapter 3.

56. See San Miguel, *Brown, Not White*, chapters 4–6.

57. See Navarro, *Mexican American Youth Organization*, chapter 4; San Miguel, *Brown, Not White*; Trujillo, *Chicano Empowerment*, chapter 3.

58. Trujillo, *Chicano Empowerment*, 124.

59. San Miguel, *Brown, Not White*, 168.

60. Robert A. Reveles, "Biculturalism and the United States Congress: The Dynamics of Political Change," in *Mexican Americans and Educational Change*, ed. Castañeda, et al., 205–15.

61. Ibid.

62. Sharon Smith, *Subterranean Fire: A History of Working-Class Radicalism in the United States* (Chicago: Haymarket Books, 2006), 217.

63. Rodolfo Acuña, *Occupied America: A History of Chicanos* (New York: Harper and Row, 1981), 367.

64. Joe Allen, *Vietnam: The (Last) War the U.S. Lost* (Chicago: Haymarket Books, 2005), 169–71.

65. Ibid., 205.

66. Smith, *Subterranean Fire*, 218–23.

67. Chris Harman, "Analysing Imperialism," *International Socialism Journal* 99 (2003), http://pubs.socialistreviewindex.org.uk/isj99/harman.htm.

68. For a comprehensive history of *Lau v. Nichols* and the Lau Remedies, see R. C. Salamone, *True American: Language, Identity, and the Education of Immigrant Children* (Cambridge, MA: Harvard University Press, 2010), 119–38.

69. Ibid., 120–22.

70. See Smith, *Subterranean Fire*, chapter 7.

71. O. García, *Bilingual Education*, 182.

72. Lance Selfa and Helen Scott, *No Scapegoats! Immigrants Are Not to Blame* (Chicago: Bookmarks, 1995), 15.
73. Ibid., 18.
74. Ibid., 2.
75. Quoted in ibid., 2.
76. For a fuller discussion of SB107, see Justin Akers Chacón, "The Preventable Rise of SB1070," *International Socialist Review* 73 (September–October 2010): 6–16.
77. For discussion of how SEI has been implemented in Arizona, see Karen E. Lillie, et al., "Policy in Practice: The Implementation of Structured English Immersion in Arizona," *Arizona Educational Equity Project*, July 8, 2010. For both this paper and a complete assessment of restrictive language policy in Arizona, see the homepage of the Arizona Education Equity Project at http://civilrightsproject.ucla.edu.
78. *Diné* is the indigenous term for the Navajo language.
79. This is illegal at the K–12 level, as the *Plyler v. Doe* Supreme Court case established in 1982. All children in the United States have the right to attend their neighborhood public school irrespective of immigration status.
80. Margot Veranes and Adriana Navarro, "Racist Fervor Becomes Law in Arizona: Calls for State Boycott Gain Momentum," *International Relations Center Americas Program*, June 5, 2005, http://americas.irc-online.org/articles/2005/0506prop200.html.
81. These last two points are based on my experience living in Arizona at the time. I was a doctoral student at Arizona State and also oversaw a local school district's English Language Learner program. I learned of the "chill" effect of Prop 200 from my own students and their stories of adult relatives who stopped attending free English classes, as well as from my coworkers who worked in those programs.
82. Nicole Santa Cruz, "Arizona Bill Targeting Ethnic Studies Signed into Law," *Los Angeles Times*, May 12, 2010, http://articles.latimes.com/2010/may/12/nation/la-na-ethnic-studies-20100512.
83. Crawford, *Advocating for English Learners*, 38–9.
84. Quoted in O. García, *Bilingual Education*, 183.
85. Crawford, *Advocating for English Learners*, 124.
86. Ibid., 185.
87. For example, New York state still offers the Regents high school exit exams in five additional languages besides English, and Texas still officially uses transitional bilingual education models.
88. Kate Menken, *English Learners Left Behind: Standardized Testing as Language Policy* (Clevedon, UK: Multilingual Matters, 2008).
89. Nancy Murray, "Profiled: Arabs, Muslims, and the Post-9/11 Hunt for the 'Enemy Within,'" in *Civil Rights in Peril: The Targeting of Arabs and Muslims*, ed. Elaine C. Hagopian (Chicago: Haymarket Books and Ann Arbor, MI: Pluto Press, 2004), 27–70.

90. David Folkenflick, "NPR Ends Williams' Contract after Muslim Remarks," National Public Radio, October 10, 2010, www.npr.org. For a tremendous and funny response to Williams's bigotry, see "Pictures of Muslims Wearing Things: Muslims Dressed in Their Garb" at http://muslimswearingthings.tumblr.com.
91. Deepa Kumar, "The Rise of Anti-Muslim Hate," *International Socialist Review* 74 (November–December 2010): 13–19.
92. Alicia Colon, "Madrassa Plan Monstrosity," *New York Sun*, May 1, 2007.
93. Daniel Pipes, "A Madrassa Grows in Brooklyn," *New York Sun*, April 24, 2007.
94. See Andrea Elliott, "Her Dream, Branded as a Threat," *New York Times*, April 28, 2008.
95. M. Wilmot, W. Weber, and M. Fenchel, *Dearborn Public Schools High School Operation Review Team: Final Report* (Ossineke, MI: Michigan Leadership Institute, 2009), 21, http://fordsonhigh.info/MLI_Dbn_High_Schools_Rpt.pdf.

Chapter 4
Obama's Neoliberal Agenda for Public Education

1. Leigh Dingerson et al., eds., *Keeping the Promise? The Debate over Charter Schools* (Milwaukee, WI: Rethinking Schools, 2008), xii.
2. Tamar Lewin and Sam Dillon, "Districts Warn of Deeper Teacher Cuts," *New York Times*, April 21, 2010.
3. Rehema Ellis, Victor Limjoco, and Alex Johnson, "Teacher Layoffs Raise Class-Size Tensions," MSNBC.com, March 1, 2011, www.msnbc.msn.com.
4. Ken Thomas, "Report: Low Graduation Rates in Many City School Districts," Associated Press, April 1, 2008.
5. Diane Ravitch, *The Death and Life of the Great American School System: How Testing and Choice Are Undermining Education* (New York: Basic Books, 2010), 210–11.
6. Nancy Krause, "Obama Weighs in on CF Teacher Firings," "Eyewitness News," WPRI online, March 10, 2010, www.wpri.com/dpp/news/president-obama-supports-central-falls-teacher-firings.
7. Brian Chidester, "Getting the Ax at Central Falls," *SocialistWorker.org*, March 8, 2010.
8. Naomi Klein, *The Shock Doctrine: The Rise of Disaster Capitalism* (New York: Henry Holt, 2008).
9. Samuel Bowles and Herbert Gintis, *Schooling in Capitalist America: Educational Reform and the Contradictions of Economic Life* (New York: Basic Books, 1976), 199, 238.
10. Jeff Bale, "The Stakes Are High in Michigan," *SocialistWorker.org*, March 28, 2011; Ed Brayton, "K-12 Funding Compromise Apparently Reached," *Michigan Messenger* online, May 19, 2011; Sam Inglot, "Early Budget Deal Announcement from Gov. Snyder Expected," *Michigan Messenger* online, May 19, 2011.
11. Howard Ryan, "Mass Teacher Layoffs and School Closures," *Labor Notes* 386 (May 2011).
12. "President Obama's Remarks to the Hispanic Chamber of Commerce," tran-

script, *New York Times* online, *The Caucus* blog, March 10, 2009, www.ny-times.com/2009/03/10/us/politics/10text-obama.html.

13. Jean Anyon, *Marx and Education* (New York: Routledge, 2011), 15.
14. See Maisha T. Winn and Nadia Behizadeh, "The Right to Be Literate: Literacy, Education, and the School-to-Prison Pipeline," *Review of Research in Education* 35 (2011).
15. Bowles and Gintis, *Schooling in Capitalist America*, 11.
16. James Crawford, "A Diminished Vision of Civil Rights: No Child Left Behind and the Growing Divide in How Educational Equity Is Understood," *Education Week*, June 6, 2007, www.edweek.org.
17. See "Charter Petition for the Alain Leroy Locke Charter High School," in *The Locke Transformation Project*, Green Dot Public Schools, www.scribd.com/doc/24665283/Green-Dot-Public-sic-Schools-original-Alain-Leroy-Locke-Charter-High-School-petition?autodown=pdf.
18. See Winnie Hu and Robert Gebeloff, "Growth in Education Spending Slowed in 2009," *New York Times*, May 26, 2011.
19. Cited in Anyon, *Marx and Education*, 85.
20. Sarah Knopp, "Charter Schools and the Attack on Public Education," *International Socialist Review* 62 (November–December 2008): 42–44.
21. Cited in Joanne Barkan, "Got Dough? How Billionaires Rule Our Schools," *Dissent* online (Winter 2011), www.dissentmagazine.org.
22. Jitu Brown, Eric (Rico) Gutstein, and Pauline Lipman, "Arne Duncan and the Chicago Success Story: Myth or Reality?," *Rethinking Schools*, Spring 2009, www.rethinkingschools.org.
23. Zein El-Amine and Lee Glazer, "'Evolution' or Destruction? A Look at Washington, D.C.," in *Keeping the Promise?*, ed. Dingerson et al.
24. A more probable hypothesis for why test scores dropped was that many more students were taking the SATs, the new additions being from lower-income and more disadvantaged backgrounds. See David C. Berliner and Bruce J. Biddle, *The Manufactured Crisis: Myths, Fraud and the Attack on America's Public Schools* (Cambridge, MA: Perseus Books, 1995).
25. Jean Anyon, *Radical Possibilities* (New York: Routledge, 2005), 21.
26. Ravitch, *Death and Life*, 8.
27. Ibid., 9–10.
28. Ibid., 125.
29. Mary Bruce, "Duncan: Katrina Was the 'Best Thing' for New Orleans School System," ABC News online, *Political Punch* blog, January 29, 2010, http://abc-news.go.com/blogs/politics/2010/01/duncan-katrina-was-the-best-thing-for-new-orleans-schools/.
30. Klein, *Shock Doctrine*, 6, and Leigh Dingerson, "Unlovely: How the Market Is Failing the Children of New Orleans," in *Keeping the Promise?*, ed. Dingerson et al., 17–34.
31. Seema Mehta, "The U.S. Education Secretary Says California Students in Peril," *Los Angeles Times*, May 23, 2009.

32. Barack Obama, "State of the Union Address," transcripts, White House, January 25, 2011, www.whitehouse.gov.
33. U.S. Department of Education, *Race to the Top Program: Executive Summary* (Washington, DC: US Department of Education, 2009), www2.ed.gov/programs/racetothetop/executive-summary.pdf.
34. "Race to the Top Program: Guidance and Frequently Asked Questions," US Department of Education, 2010, www2.ed.gov/programs/racetothetop/faq.pdf.
35. This information was on then-senator Gloria Romero's website, which is no longer available.
36. Dan Walters, "Obama's School Grants Are Side Issue in California," *Sacramento Bee*, December 8, 2009.
37. Amy Hanauer, "Profits and Privatization: The Ohio Experience," in *Keeping the Promise?*, ed. Dingerson et al.
38. Walter Alarkon, "Obey's Axe Hovers over Obama's $1.3B Education Program," *The Hill*, July 19, 2010.
39. Maria Glod, "The Schoolhouse Flunks; Education Dept. Takes Symbolic Step to Reconstitute No Child Left Behind," *Washington Post*, June 23, 2009.
40. *A Blueprint for Reform: The Reauthorization of the Elementary and Secondary Education Act* (Washington, DC: US Department of Education, 2010),www2.ed.gov/policy/elsec/leg/blueprint/blueprint.pdf.
41. Ibid.
42. Cited in Ravitch, *Death and Life*, 105.
43. Developing Government Accountability to the People, "Renaissance 2010," http://www.chicagodgap.org/et1.
44. "Teen's Beating Death Puts Pressure on Officials," NBC News, September 28, 2009, www.msnbc.msn.com/id/33057768/ns/us_news-crime_and_courts/t/teens-beating-death-puts-pressure-officials/.
45. Quoted in Melissa Tussing, "Pressure on CPS Board to Scuttle Renaissance 2010," *Medill Reports Chicago*, October 28, 2009, news.medill.northwestern.edu/chicago/news.aspx?id=143733&print=1; and "Report: School Closings Had Little Effect on Student Performance," *Medill Reports Chicago*, November 5, 2009, ccsr.uchicago.edu/news_docs/6882report.
46. Brown, Gutstein, and Lipman, "Arne Duncan and Chicago."
47. Andrew Spitser, "School Reconstitution under No Child Left Behind: Why School Officials Should Think Twice," *UCLA Law Review* 54 (2007).
48. Monty Neill, "Congress Needs a Different ESEA Blueprint," National Center for Fair and Open Testing, March 23, 2010, www.fairtest.org/congress-needs-different-esea-blueprint.
49. Ravitch, *Death and Life*, 179ff.
50. Ibid., 179.
51. Sam Dillon, "Formula to Grade Teachers' Skill Gains Acceptance, and Critics," *New York Times*, August 31 2010.
52. Sarah Knopp, "A Teacher Pushed to the Edge," *SocialistWorker.org*, October 1, 2010.

53. Eva L. Baker et al., *Problems with the Use of Student Test Scores to Evaluate Teachers* (Washington, DC: Economic Policy Institute, 2010), 2, http://www.epi.org/publications/entry/bp278.

54. Michael Stryer, e-mail communication, August 30, 2010, based on data from http://projects.latimes.com/value-added/rank/school/5/.

55. Diane Ravitch in a speech to seven hundred UTLA members, September 24, 2010.

56. Quoted in Libby Quaid, "Obama Backs Merit Pay, Charter Schools," Associate Press, March 11, 2009.

57. Barbara Miner, "The Debate Over Differentiated Pay: The Devil Is in the Details," *Rethinking Schools* 24, no. 1 (2009).

58. See Jesse Hagopian, "Teachers for CEO Merit Pay! Because Sabotaging the Global Economy Shouldn't Earn You a Bonus," *CommonDreams.org*, March 20, 2009, www.commondreams.org/view/2009/03/20-2.

59. Peter Lamphere and Meghan Behrent, "New York Teachers' Union Concedes on Merit Pay," *Socialist Worker*, October 26, 2007, 14.

60. The National Center for Fair and Open Testing, "Paying Teachers for Student Test Scores Damages Schools and Undermines Learning," November 19, 2009, www.fairtest.org/paying-for-student-test-scores-damages-schools.

61. David Berliner, *Poverty and Potential: Out-of-School Factors and School Success* (Boulder, CO and Tempe, AZ: Education and the Public Interest Center & Education Policy Research Unit, 2009), http://epicpolicy.org/publication/poverty-and-potential.

62. Peter Z. Schochet and Hanley S. Chiang, *Error Rates in Measuring Teacher and School Performance Based on Student Test Score Gains* (NCEE 2010–4004) (Washington, DC: US Department of Education, 2010), 35.

63. "Newt Discusses Education with Arne Duncan and Al Sharpton on Meet the Press," transcript, Newt Gingrich 2012, http://newt.org/tabid/102/article-Type/ArticleView/articleId/4657/Default.aspx.

64. Ravitch, *Death and Life*, 132.

65. Cited in Lee Sustar, "The War on Public Sector Unions," *SocialistWorker.org*, November 6, 2009.

66. Erica Frankenberg and Genevieve Siegel-Hawley, *Equity Overlooked: Charter Schools and Civil Rights Policy* (Los Angeles: UCLA Civil Rights Project, 2009), 6–7, www.civilrightsproject.ucla.edu.

67. "Pilot Study of Charter Schools' Compliance with the Modified Consent Decree and the LAUSD Special Education Policies and Procedures," Office of the Independent Monitor for the Modified Consent Decree, June 5, 2009. In Oakland, only 4.6 percent of charter school students were classified as special education, compared to 10.45 percent in district schools (see Ravitch, *Death and Life*, 215).

68. Ravitch, *Death and Life*, 141–42.

69. Frankenberg and Siegel-Hawley, *Equity Overlooked*.

70. Chad d'Entremont and Charisse Gulosino, *Circles of Influence: How Neighbor-*

hood Demographics and Charter School Locations Influence Student Enrollments (NCSPE Research Publication #160) (New York: National Center for the Study of Privatization in Education, 2008); and Robert Bifulco, Helen Ladd, and Stephen Ross, *Public School Choice and Integration: Evidence from Durham, North Carolina* (NCSPE Research Publication #172) (New York: National Center for the Study of Privatization in Education, 2009). See www.ncspe.org for both reports.

71. Frankenberg and Siegel-Hawley, *Equity Overlooked.*

72. National Assessment of Educational Progress, *America's Charter Schools: Results from the NAEP 2003 Pilot Study* (Washington, DC: National Center for Education Statistics, 2003).

73. *Multiple Choice: Charter School Performance in Sixteen States* (Stanford, CA: Center for Research on Education Outcomes, 2009), www.credo.stanford.edu. For a comprehensive review of the research on charter school performance compared with public schools, see Ravitch, *Death and Life*, 138–44.

74. Hanauer, "Profits and Privatization."

75. Joseph Mismas, "Ohio's For-Profit Charter Schools Make Great Businesses, Crappy Educators," *Plunderbund*, April 3, 2011, www.plunderbund.com.

76. David A. Stuit and Thomas M. Smith, *Teacher Turnover in Charter Schools* (NCPSE Research Publication # 183) (New York: National Center for the Study of Privatization in Education, 2009), www.ncspe.org.

77. Ravitch, *Death and Life*, 145.

78. Brown, Gutstein, and Lipman, "Arne Duncan and Chicago."

79. Ibid.

80. Robert D. Skeels, "CON: Why School Choice Plan Is a Bad Idea for the District," *Daily News of Los Angeles*, August 22, 2009.

81. Howard Blume, "Green Dot to Close Justice Charter High School," *Los Angeles Times*, March 22, 2010.

82. Robert D. Skeels, "Taking on a Charter School Closing," *SocialistWorker.org*, March 26, 2010.

83. Nancy Hass, "Scholarly Investments," *New York Times*, December 6, 2009.

84. Developing Government Accountability to the People, "School Closings," DGAP, www.chicagodgap.org/et4.

85. Bowles and Gintis, *Schooling in Capitalist America*, 265.

Focus On: Students, Parents, and Teachers Protest Gutting of Public Education

1. *Truthout* is a critical online source of news and commentary that describes its project as an effort "to broaden and diversify the political discussion by introducing independent voices and focusing on under-covered issues and unconventional thinking." We reprint this article with some minor revisions under a Creative Commons license from *Truthout* and with permission from its author, Rose Aguilar.

2. Louis Freedberg, "Districts Consider Even Shorter School Year," California

Watch, April 26, 2011, http://californiawatch.org/dailyreport/districts
-consider-even-shorter-school-year-10023.

Chapter 5
Teachers' Unions and Social Justice

1. Matthew DiCarlo, "Performance-Enhancing Union Contracts?" *Shanker Blog: The Voice of the Albert Shanker Institute*, October 1, 2010, http://shankerblog.org/?p=895.
2. Andy Becker, "Government Workers of the World Unite!," *Economist*, January 6, 2011.
3. Gus Lubin and Leah Goldman, "16 U.S. Cities Facing Bankruptcy If They Don't Make Deep Cuts in 2011," *Business Insider*, December 26, 2010, www.businessinsider.com.
4. Elizabeth McNichol, Phil Oliff, and Nicholas Johnson, *States Continue to Feel Recession's Impact* (Washington, DC: Center for Budget and Policy Priorities, 2011), www.cbpp.org.
5. Henry A. Giroux, "When Generosity Hurts: Bill Gates, Public School Teachers and the Politics of Humiliation," *Truthout.org*, October 5, 2010.
6. Finland, for instance, is ranked number one in education by the Program for International Student Assessment (PISA) and more than 95 percent of Finnish teachers are unionized. For a discussion of global education rankings and unionization, see Tim Walker, "In High-Performing Countries, Education Reform Is a Two-Way Street," *NEA Today*, March 31, 2011, www.neatodayact.org.
7. Alex Molnar, et al., *School Reform Proposals: The Research Evidence* (Boulder, CO: National Education Policy Center, 2002), http://nepc.colorado.edu.
8. See Gillian Russom, "The Case Against Charter Schools," *International Socialist Review* 71 (May–June 2010): 21–24. Chapter 4 looks at these and other problems with charter schools in more depth.
9. Bureau of Labor Statistics, "Economic News Release: Union Members Summary," press release, January 21, 2011, www.bls.gov/news.release/union2.nr0.htm.
10. Lee Sustar, "Public Sector Workers Under the Gun," *International Socialist Review* 69 (January–February 2010): 4.
11. *Education Week's Teacher Beat* blog; "Weingarten Weighs In on Obama Speech," post by Stephen Sawchuk, July 30, 2010, http://blogs.edweek.org/edweek/teacherbeat/2010/07/weingarten_weighs_in_on_obama.html?qs=Randi+Weingarten+race_to_the_top.
12. Stephen Sawchuk, "Unions' Tactics Diverge in Engaging Obama Agenda," *Education Week* 30, no. 1 (August 25, 2010).
13. Peter Lamphere, "Will NYC Teachers Fight?," *SocialistWorker.org*, December 17, 2010.
14. Elizabeth Green, "UFT Charter School Leader Will Leave after Clash with Teacher," *New York Sun*, April 22, 2008.
15. Ibid.

16. See National Education Association, "Race to the Top Proposed Changes Applauded," press release, February 12, 2011, www.nea.org/home/42442.htm.

17. Sean Cavanagh, "Teachers' Unions on Defensive as GOP Lawmakers Flex Their Muscles," *Education Week*, 30, no. 17 (January 19, 2011).

18. Bryan Kennedy, "Wisconsin: The Inside Story," *California Teacher* (April/May 2011): 4.

19. Sarah Knopp, "Needed: A National Teachers' Movement," *SocialistWorker.org*, March 16, 2011.

20. We will not discuss the "company union" model at length because we don't consider it to be a genuine part of the labor movement. A "company union" is one in which management has a hand in the organizing and running of a union. Usually this is done as a way of preventing genuine, independent unions from developing.

21. Lois Weiner, "Building the International Movement We Need," in *The Global Assault on Teaching, Teachers, and their Unions*, ed. Mary Compton and Lois Weiner (New York: Palgrave MacMillan, 2008), 254.

22. Compton and Weiner, *Global Assault on Teaching*, 178.

23. Marjorie Murphy, *Blackboard Unions: The AFT and the NEA, 1900–1980* (Ithaca, NY: Cornell University Press, 1992), 206.

24. Ibid., 27–28.

25. Ibid., 66.

26. Ibid., 83.

27. Ibid., 134–35.

28. Ibid., 131.

29. Ibid., 139.

30. Ibid., 142.

31. Ibid., 198.

32. Celia Zitron, *The New York City Teachers Union, 1916–1964: A Story of Educational and Social Commitment* (New York: Humanities Press, 1968), 17.

33. Clarence Taylor, *Reds at the Blackboard* (New York: Columbia University Press, 2011), 153.

34. Ibid., 45.

35. Ibid., 34.

36. See ibid., chap. 2, "Communist Front?"

37. Murphy, *Blackboard Unions*, 159.

38. Taylor, *Reds at the Blackboard*, 170.

39. Ibid., 241.

40. Celia Zitron's history of the Teachers Union, published just after its demise, reads more like a eulogy than a study meant to instruct future radicals. Zitron herself was affiliated with the Communist Party and was blacklisted from teaching in New York City. Thus, the history presented therein is told from the partisan point of view of an activist who was involved.

41. The American Federation of Labor (AFL) and the Congress of Industrial Organizations (CIO) did not merge to form the AFL-CIO until 1955.

42. In the United States the Communist Party put its particular interests ahead of the interests of the working class by purposely isolating the left-moving teachers from the more dynamic Congress of Industrial Organizations so that the CP would retain a base inside the AFL.

43. Taylor, *Reds at the Blackboard*, 127.

44. Ibid., 176.

45. Murphy, *Blackboard Unions*, 220.

46. Ibid., 223.

47. F. Glass, Eddie Irwan, and Marv Katz, "AFT Local 1021: Chartered 1949: United Teachers of Los Angeles," in *70 Years: A History of the California Federation of Teachers 1919–1989*, ed. F. Glass (Sacramento: California Federation of Teachers, 1989), 53.

48. United Teachers of Los Angeles, "UTLA History," UTLA website, www.utla.net/node/397.

49. Richard D. Kahlenberg, *Tough Liberal: Albert Shanker and the Battles over Schools, Unions, Race, and Democracy* (New York: Columbia University Press, 2007), 4.

50. Ibid., 4.

51. Ibid., 127–32.

52. Ibid., 69–91.

53. Ibid., 308.

54. Ibid., 318.

55. Philip Sheldon Foner, *US Labor and the Vietnam War* (New York: International Publishers, 1989), 133.

56. Taylor, *Reds at the Blackboard*, 83.

57. See compilation at "US Labor Against the War: Locals," US Labor Against the War website, www.uslaboragainstwar.org/section.php?id=52&offset=206.

58. Stephen Zunes, "Unions' Hawkish Foreign Policy Agenda Hampers Defense of Teachers," *Truthout.org*, May 22, 2011.

59. See Bureau of Labor Statistics, "Union Members—2010," press release, January 21, 2011, www.bls.gov/news.release/pdf/union2.pdf.

60. Michael Zweig, *The Working-Class Majority: America's Best Kept Secret* (Ithaca, NY: Cornell University Press 2000), 26.

61. Chris Harman, *Zombie Capitalism* (Chicago: Haymarket Books, 2010), 136.

62. For a thorough discussion of social class, see chapter 2 of Hal Draper, *Karl Marx's Theory of Revolution, Volume II: The Politics of Social Classes* (New York: Monthly Review Press, 1978). Even though Draper argues that government workers aren't part of the "proletariat" in the narrow sense that Marx tried to distinguish them from other workers, he also points out, contradictorily, that transit workers play an indirect role in production because they transport people to work where the latter will generate profits.

63. Friedrich Engels, *The Condition of the Working Class in England*, ed. David McLellan (Oxford: Oxford University Press, 2009).

64. A mid-nineteenth-century working-class political and social reform movement

in England and forerunner to an organized labor movement at the outset of British capitalism.

65. Karl Marx, *The Poverty of Philosophy* (Moscow: Progress Publishers, 1955), chapter 2, §5.

66. Engels, *Condition of the Working Class,* 232.

67. Written correspondence from Marx to Wilhelm Liebknecht dated February 11, 1878, in *Marx and Engels Correspondence,* Karl Marx (Moscow: International Publishers, 1968), www.marxists.org/archive/marx/works/1878/letters/78_02_11.htm.

68. For a further discussion of the trade union bureaucracy, see Tony Cliff and Donny Gluckstein, *Marxism and Trade Union Struggle: The General Strike of 1926* (London: Bookmarks, 1986).

69. See US Bureau of Labor Statistics figures at www.bls.gov/oco/ocos318.htm#earnings. The median salary data are from 2008 and the average starting salary from 2005–06.

70. Of course, most bureaucrats earn well less than $429,000, but they take their lead from the bureaucrats above them who set the tenor for the entire organization.

71. Lee Sustar, "The Lessons of Wisconsin's Labor Revolt," *International Socialist Review* 77 (May–June 2011): 1–4.

72. "Update: WEAC Urging Members to Come to Madison," statement by Mary Bell, NBC15.com, February 21, 2011, www.nbc15.com/news/headlines/ WEAC_Urging_Members_To_Come_To_Madison_116366454.html.

73. See "Social Justice Unionism," Educators for a Democratic Union website, https://sites.google.com/site/educatorssf/.

74. Jesse Sharkey, "Taking on the Board in Chicago," *Socialist Worker,* March 13, 2009.

75. Weiner, "Building the International Movement We Need," 257.

76. See Barbara Miner, "Networking for Union Reform: The Story of TURN," in *Transforming Teacher Unions: Fighting for Better Schools and Social Justice* (Milwaukee, MN: Rethinking Schools, 1999).

77. Sam Gindin and Michael Hurley, "The Public Sector: Searching for a Focus," *The Bullet—Socialist Project E-Bulletin,* May 15, 2010, www.socialistproject.ca/bullet/354.php.

78. Zaid Jilani, "Leader of Egyptian Unions to Wisconsin P'We Stand with You as You Stood with Us,'" *Truthout.org,* February 21, 2011.

79. Gillian Russom and Sarah Knopp, "Puerto Rico's Teacher Rebellion: An Interview with Rafael Feliciano Hernández," *Socliastworker.org,* May 26, 2008.

Focus On: The Madison Protests

1. Lee Sustar, "The Lessons of Wisconsin's Labor Revolt," *International Socialist Review* 77 (May-June 2011): 3.

2. Rick Pearson and Lisa Mascaro, "Wisconsin Recall Election a Test of Voter Sentiment," *Los Angeles Times,* August 11, 2011.

3. Sarah Knopp, "Needed: A National Teachers' Movement," *SocialistWorker.org,* March 16, 2011.

Focus On: Teachers' Struggle in Oaxaca, Mexico

1. Alejandra Favela, "Lasting Lessons from Oaxaca: Teachers as *Luchadores Sociales*: An Inside Account of the Historic Oaxacan Teachers' Movement and Why It Is Still Relevant Today," *Radical Teacher* 88 (Summer 2010).
2. Dan LaBotz, "Mexican Teachers Strike, Protest over Test-Driven Education," *Labor Notes* 387 (June 2011).
3. Ibid.
4. Javier Corrales, *The Politics of Education Reform: Bolstering Supply and Demand; Overcoming Institutional Blocks* (The Education Reform and Management Series, vol. 2, no. 1) (Washington, DC: World Bank, 1999), www.worldbank.org.
5. See ibid., 67.
6. John Gibler, "Teacher Rebellion in Oaxaca," *In These Times* 30, no. 9 (September 2006).
7. Cited in Favela, "Lasting Lessons," 69.
8. Lisa Kresge, *Indigenous Oaxacan Communities in California: An Overview* (Davis, CA: California Institute for Rural Studies, 2007), iii.
9. See the "Oaxacan Migration" page of the website for the Centro de Orientación del Migrante de Oaxaca, A.C. at http://comi.giving.officelive.com/migracion.aspx.

Chapter 6
Pedagogy and Revolution: Reading Freire in Context

1. In *A Brief History of Neoliberalism*, David Harvey notes the deleterious effect of the internalization of neoliberal principles of individualism and competition on the global justice movements of the late 1990s. Such an internalization would perhaps explain why Bill Gates's speech at the national American Federation of Teachers convention in 2010 did not lead to a general walkout or even a pie-ing.
2. Peter McLaren, *Che Guevara, Paulo Freire, and the Pedagogy of Revolution* (Lanham, MD: Rowman and Littlefield Press, 2000), 144.
3. Karl Marx and Frederick Engels, "The Annotated *Communist Manifesto*," in *The Communist Manifesto: A Road Map to History's Most Important Political Document*, ed. Phil Gasper (Chicago: Haymarket Books, 2005), 71.
4. Paulo Freire and Ira Shor, *A Pedagogy for Liberation* (Westport, CT: Bergin and Harvey Publishers, 1986).
5. Karl Marx and Frederick Engels, *The German Ideology* (New York: International Publishers, 1947), 60, www.marxists.org.
6. Freire and Schor, *A Pedagogy for Liberation*, 156.
7. Paulo Freire, *Politics and Education* (UCLA Latin American Studies, vol. 83) (Los Angeles: UCLA Latin American Center Publications, 1998), 9.
8. Karl Marx and Friedrich Engels, *Theses on Feuerbach* (Moscow: Progress Publishers, 1969), www.marxists.org.
9. Marx and Engels, in *Communist Manifesto: A Road Map*, ed. Gasper, 39.

10. Paulo Freire, *Pedagogy of the Oppressed* (New York: Continuum International Publishing Group, 2009), 81.

11. Ibid., 79.

12. Ibid., 128.

13. This critique extends equally to those on the left who look upon youth protesting at abortion clinics and at anti-immigrant rallies with a sense of pity about what has "happened" to "these children," rather than seeing them as individuals with ideas who need to be engaged and challenged.

14. Freire, *Oppressed*, 54 [emphasis in original].

15. Paulo Freire, *Pedagogy of the City* (New York: Continuum Publishing Company, 1993), 45.

16. Freire and Shor, *Pedagogy for Liberation*, 129.

17. Ibid., 109.

18. Ibid., 32, 125, 132–33.

19. Ibid., 39, 112, 129.

20. Freire, *Pedagogy of the Oppressed*, 194.

21. Freire and Shor, *Pedagogy for Liberation*, 92, 95.

22. Ibid., 107. For an excellent discussion of student resistance in very young children, see Aaron Neimark's "'Do You Want to See Something Goofy?' Peer Culture in the Preschool Yard," *National Association for the Education of Young Children: Voices of Practitioners* 9 (2008).

23. Freire, *Pedagogy of the Oppressed*, 163.

24. Freire and Shor, *Liberation*, 157.

25. Freire, *Pedagogy of the Oppressed*, 95.

26. Karl Marx, "Rules and Administrative Regulations of the International Workingmen's Association (1867)," in *Karl Marx and Friedrich Engels: Collected Works* (Moscow: Progress Publishers, 1975), 20:441.

27. Che Guevara, *Guerrilla Warfare*, 3rd ed. (Wilmington, DE: Scholarly Resources, 1997), 73.

28. The notion that his utopia is not an idealist conception of change appears throughout the majority of his later works. This phrase is from Paolo Freire, *Cultural Action for Freedom* (Cambridge, MA: Harvard Educational Review, Monograph Series no. 1, 1970, Penguin edition, 1972), 40.

29. For the sake of space, we will also have to omit discussion of the influence of radical Christianity, and liberation theology in particular, on Freire's concept of utopia.

30. Henry A. Giroux and Peter McLaren, "Paulo Freire, Postmodernism, and the Utopian Imagination: A Blochian Reading," in *Not Yet: Reconsidering Ernst Bloch*, ed. Jamie Owen Daniel and Tom Moylan (London: Verso, 1997), 150.

31. Freire, *Pedagogy of the City*, 115.

32. Many radicals had little knowledge or understanding of Stalin's counterrevolution in Russia and mistakenly looked to the Soviet Union as an alternative to capitalism. This was the primary contributor to the extreme disorientation of much of the global left in the face of the Soviet Union's collapse.

33. Among pre-K–12 teachers, the situation is even worse. The overwhelming drive toward data-driven, testing-based education has created an atmosphere of fear and trepidation about bringing anything "real-world" into the classroom without being able to somehow tie it to future test score increases.

34. Freire, *Politics and Education*, 24.

35. Ibid., 21.

36. For more on Freire's tenure in São Paulo, see Freire, *Pedagogy of the City*, and Bob Peterson, "Big City Superintendents: Dictatorship or Democracy? Lessons from Paulo Freire," *Rethinking Schools* 24, no. 1 (2009): 20–25.

37. Freire, *Politics and Education*, 46.

38. McLaren, *Che Guevara*, 193.

39. Freire, *Pedagogy of the Oppressed*, 89.

40. Peter Roberts, "Reason, Emotion and Politics in the Work of Paulo Freire," in *Social Justice Education for Teachers: Paulo Freire and the Possible Dream*, ed. Carlos Alberto Torres and Pedro Noguera (Rotterdam, The Netherlands: Sense Publishing, 2008), 109.

41. Freire, *Politics and Education*, 51; and Myles Horton and Paulo Freire, *We Make the Road by Walking: Conversations on Education and Social Change* (Philadelphia: Temple University Press, 1990), 60.

42. Pedro Noguera, "Bringing Freire to the Hood: The Relevance and Potential of Freire's Work and Ideas to Inner City Youth," in *Social Justice Education*, 37.

43. Ibid., 38.

44. Ibid., 47.

45. McLaren, *Che Guevara*, 57.

46. Stanley Aronowitz, *Against Schooling* (Paradigm Publishers, 2008), 159.

47. McLaren, *Che Guevara*, 194.

48. Freire, *Politics*, 27.

49. Victor Fernandez, "Massive ICE Raids in California," *SocialistWorker.org*, October 6, 2008.

Focus On: The Freedom Schools

1. Cited in Stokely Carmichael, with Michael Thelwell, *Ready for Revolution: The Life and Struggles of Stokely Carmichael (Kwame Ture)* (New York: Scribner, 2003), 387.

2. Cited in William Sturkey, "'I Want to Become a Part of History': Freedom Summer, Freedom Schools and the *Freedom News*," *Journal of African American History* 95, nos. 3–4 (Summer–Fall 2010): 348.

3. James R. Ralph, *Northern Protest: Martin Luther King, Jr., Chicago, and the Civil Rights Movement* (Cambridge, MA: Harvard University Press, 1993).

4. Cited in Daniel Perlstein, "Teaching Freedom: SNCC and the Creation of the Mississippi Freedom Schools," *History of Education Quarterly* 30 (1990): 311.

5. George W. Chilcoat and Jerry A. Ligon, "Developing Democratic Citizens: The Mississippi Freedom Schools as a Model for Social Studies Instruction," *Theory and Research in Social Education* 22 (1994): 147.

6. Robert Weisbrot, *Freedom Bound* (New York: Penguin Books, l991), 111.
7. See the Freedom School Curriculum Website at www.educationanddemoc-racy.org/ED_FSC.html for a historical overview, as well as exhaustive documentation of curricular materials used.
8. Cited in Paul Lauter and Dan Perlstein, "Introduction," *Radical Teacher* 40 (Fall 1991): 3.

Chapter 7
Literacy and Revolution

1. John Reed, *Ten Days That Shook the World* (New York: International Publishers, 1934), 14.
2. Jonathan Kozol, *Children of the Revolution: A Yankee Teacher in the Cuban Schools* (New York: Delacorte Press, 1978).
3. Cited in Alfie Kohn, *The Schools Our Children Deserve* (New York: Houghton Mifflin, 1999), 71.
4. Ibid., 38.
5. Ibid., 38.
6. Cited in ibid., 125.
7. Michael D. Shear, "Obama Speech Ties U.S. Need for More College Graduates to the Economic Recovery," *WashingtonPost.com, Higher Education* blog, August 9, 2010.
8. Harvey J. Graff, *The Literacy Myth: Cultural Integration and Social Structure in the Nineteenth Century* (New Brunswick, NJ: Transaction Publishers, 1991), xxxviii.
9. Ibid., 23.
10. Ibid., 48.
11. Cited in Kozol, *Children of the Revolution*, 83.
12. Robert F. Arnove and Harvey J. Graff, eds., *National Literacy Campaigns and Movements: Historical and Comparative Perspectives* (New Brunswick, NJ: Transaction Publishers, 2008), 5.
13. Ibid., 7.
14. Cited in Kozol, *Children of the Revolution*, 83.
15. Arnove and Graff, *National Literacy*, 9.
16. Kozol, *Children of the Revolution*, 49.
17. Marvin Leiner, "The 1961 National Cuban Literacy Campaign," in *National Literacy*, ed. Arnove and Graff, 173.
18. Ibid.
19. Ibid., 177.
20. Ibid., 176.
21. Ibid., 175.
22. Kozol, *Children of the Revolution*, 128.
23. Richard Fagen, cited in Leiner, "National Cuban Literacy Campaign," 173.
24. Kozol, *Children of the Revolution*, 51.
25. Cited in Leiner, "National Cuban Literacy Campaign," 178.

26. Ibid., 178. For a full description of the primer, See Kozol, *Children of the Revolution*, 12–18, and Leiner, "National Cuban Literacy Campaign," 178–80.
27. Leiner, "National Cuban Literacy Campaign," 178–79.
28. Cited in ibid., 179.
29. Ibid., 179.
30. Kozol, *Children of the Revolution*, 62.
31. Cited in Kozol, *Children of the Revolution*, 62.
32. Kozol, *Children of the Revolution*, 18.
33. Ibid., 14.
34. Cited in Leiner, "National Cuban Literacy Campaign," 183.
35. Kozol, *Children of the Revolution*, 19.
36. Cited in Paul D'Amato, "Tyrannies Ruling in the Name of Socialism," *Socialist Worker.org* August 29, 2008.
37. D'Amato, "Tyrannies Ruling in the Name of Socialism."
38. Samuel Farber, "Life after Fidel," *Foreign Policy in Focus*, May 7, 2008, www.fpif.org.
39. Kozol, *Children of the Revolution*, 196.
40. Quoted in Ivan Illich, *Deschooling Society* (New York: Marion Boyars Publishers Ltd., 1970), 18.
41. For more on the Citizenship Schools established by the Highlander School, see chapter 9, "Reading to Vote: The Citizenship Schools," in *The Long Haul: an Autobiography*, Myles Horton, with Judith Kohl and Herbert Kohl, (New York: Teachers College Press, 1998); Myles Horton and Paulo Freire, *We Make the Road by Walking: Conversations on Education and Social Change*, eds. Brenda Bell, John Gaventa, and John Peters (Philadelphia: Temple University Press, 1990), 67–195.
42. Horton and Freire, *We Make the Road*, 69–70.
43. Ibid., 72–73.
44. Ibid., 73.
45. Horton, *The Long Haul*, 107.
46. John L. Hammond, *Popular Education and Guerrilla War in El Salvador* (New Brunswick, NJ: Rutgers University Press, 1998), 5.
47. Ibid., 86.
48. Robert F. Arnove, "The 1980 Nicaraguan National Literacy Crusade," in *National Literacy*, 270.
49. Ibid., 282.
50. Horton and Freire, *We Make the Road*, 156.
51. See Matt Perry, "May 1968 across the Decades," *International Socialism Journal* 118 (Spring 2008).
52. Ibid.
53. "13 mai = Rentrée scholaire," The May Events Archive, Simon Fraser University (author translations), http://edocs.lib.sfu.ca/cgi-bin/Mai68?Display=188.
54. Ibid.
55. Cited in Perry, "May 1968."

56. Chanie Rosenberg, *Education and Society* (London: Rank and File Teachers), 28.

57. Perry, "May 1968."

58. Rosenberg, *Education and Society*, 34.

59. Ibid., 31.

60. Ibid., 33.

61. Cited in ibid., 36.

62. Ibid.

63. Alain Touraine, *The May Movement: Revolt and Reform*, trans. Leonard F. X. Mayhew (New York: Random House, 1971).

64. Rosenberg, *Education and Society*, 36–38.

65. Ibid., 39.

66. Kozol, *Children of the Revolution*, 84.

67. As Ben Eklof argues, there is a great deal of debate as to accurate measures of literacy at the time of the Russian Revolution. In 1897, according to Eklof, "only one in five subjects of the Russian Empire could sign his own name" and in rural areas "as late as 1910–1914 only fourteen to 41% of the population could read or write." Nonetheless, by other measures, the literacy rate is higher. Nicholas Timasheff argued that "by 1914, the literacy level in Russia had risen to forty-one percent." For more on this, see Ben Eklof, "Russian Literacy Campaigns 1861–1939" in Arnove and Graff, *National Literacy*, 128–29.

68. See chapter 10, "Communism and Education," in N. I. Bukharin and E. Preobrazhensky, *The ABC of Communism* (London: Penguin Books, 1969).

69. Lucy L. W. Wilson, *The New Schools of New Russia* (New York: Vanguard Press, 1928), 30–31.

70. Victor Serge, *Year One of the Russian Revolution* (New York: Holt, Rinehart and Winston, 1972), 362.

71. Cited in Eklof, "Russian Literacy Campaigns," 134.

72. Ibid.

73. Eklof, "Russian Literacy Campaigns," 133.

74. Ibid.

75. Serge, *Year One*, 362.

76. Lisa A. Kirschenbaum, *Small Comrades: Revolutionizing Childhood in Soviet Russia, 1917–1932* (New York: Routledge Falmer, 2001), 38.

77. Ibid., 73.

78. Ibid., 72.

79. See Dave Crouch, "The Seeds of National Liberation," *International Socialism Journal* 94 (Spring 2002). The discussion in the following two paragraphs is based on this article.

80. Ibid.

81. See chapter 23, "Education" in Arthur Ransome, *Russia in 1919* (Champaign, IL: Project Gutenberg, 1999), www.marxists.org.

82. See chapter 11, "Education in Soviet Russia," in Anna-Louise Strong, *The First Time in History* (New York: Boni & Liveright, 1922), www.marxists.org.

83. Wilson, *New Schools of New Russia*, 108.

84. Strong, "Education in Soviet Russia."

85. Ibid.

86. William Henry Chamberlin, "The Revolution in Education and Culture," in *Soviet Russia: A Living Record and a History* (Boston: Little, Brown, and Company [Atlantic Monthly Press Books], 1930), www.marxists.org.

87. Ibid.

88. Quoted in Chamberlin, "Revolution in Education and Culture."

89. Chamberlin, "Revolution in Education and Culture."

90. Ransome, *Russia in 1919*, 114.

91. See Stephen Toulmin, "The Mozart of Psychology," *New York Review of Books*, September 28, 1978.

92. L. S. Vygotsky cited in "Introduction," in *Mind in Society: The Development of Higher Psychological Processes*, ed. Michael Cole et al. (Cambridge, MA: Harvard University Press, 1978), 8.

93. Cole et al., *Mind in Society*.

94. L. S. Vygotsky, *Thought and Language*, ed. A. Kozulin (Cambridge, MA: MIT Press, 1986).

95. J. Bruner, "Prologue to the English Edition," in L. S. Vygotsky, *Collected Works*, eds. R. Rieber and A. Carton; trans. N. Minick, vol. 1 (New York: Plenum, 1987).

96. Vygotsky, *Thought and Language*, 186.

97. Alex Kozulin, "Vygotsky in Context," in *Thought and Language*, xlii.

98. L. S. Vygotsky, "The Historical Meaning of the Crisis in Psychology" in Vygotsky, *Collected Works*, 388–89.

99. J. V. Wertsch, *Vygotsky and the Social Formation of Mind* (Cambridge, MA: Harvard University Press, 1985), 14.

100. Thanks to Jeremy Sawyer for his research on Vygotsky and his valuable contributions on the subject in this chapter.

101. Wilson, *New Schools of New Russia*, 121.

102. Charles E. Clark, "Literacy and Labor: The Russian Literacy Campaign within the Trade Unions, 1923–27," *Europe-Asia Studies* 47 (1995): 1330.

103. Wilson, *New Schools of New Russia*, 131–32.

Index

About the Authors

Jeff Bale is assistant professor of second language education at Michigan State University. He teaches and writes about the history and politics of language education in US schools and about language policies targeting immigrant youth in Germany. His work has appeared in the *International Socialist Review*, the *Annual Review of Applied Linguistics,* and *Tertium Comparationis.* In addition, Bale taught English learners and German in urban public schools for a decade. In the District of Columbia Public Schools, he was a building representative for the Washington Teachers' Union. While teaching in Tempe, Arizona, Bale was active in school-based and community organizations challenging anti–bilingual education policies in that state. (photo: Jeremy Herliczek)

Sarah Knopp is a public high school teacher in Los Angeles. She has been teaching economics and government since 2000. A frequent contributor to the *International Socialist Review*, Knopp has also written for *Rethinking Schools, CounterPunch*, and *United Teacher*. She is an activist with United Teachers Los Angeles, a union co-chair at her school, and a dedicated participant in the movements for public education, immigrants' rights, and social equality. (photo: Misty Cervantes)

Rose Aguilar is the host of *Your Call*, a daily call-in radio show on KALW 91.7 FM in San Francisco. She is the author of *Red Highways: A Liberal's Journey Into the Heartland*. She is also a contributor to *Truthout*, a critical online source of news and commentary that describes its project as an effort "to broaden and diversify the political discussion by introducing independent voices and focusing on under-covered issues and unconventional thinking." (photo: Sue Blankman)

Megan Behrent is a high school English teacher in Brooklyn, where she has been teaching since 1999. She is also currently a graduate student pursuing a PhD in English literature at SUNY Stony Brook. She is a union activist and a UFT delegate from her school. As a longtime activist, she has been involved in campaigns for education reform, social justice, and for a more democratic and militant union. She is a frequent contributor to *SocialistWorker.org* on labor and education issues, and has also been published in *Labor Notes*, *New Politics*, and the *Harvard Educational Review*. (photo: M. B. Behrent)

Bill Bigelow is curriculum editor of *Rethinking Schools* magazine and author or co-editor of several *Rethinking Schools* books: *A People's History for the Classroom*, *The Line Between Us: Teaching About the Border and Mexican Immigration*, *Rethinking Columbus*, *Rethinking Globalization: Teaching for Justice in an Unjust World*, and *Rethinking Our Classrooms*, volumes 1 and 2. He lives in Portland, Oregon, and taught high school social studies for over thirty years. He is currently working on environmental justice curriculum. (photo: Susan Ruggles)

Michele Bollinger is a high school social studies teacher in Washington, DC, where she has been an activist for several years. She is a member of the Washington Teachers' Union, AFT Local 6. Currently, she is at work on *101 Changemakers: Rebels and Radicals Who Changed US History*, forthcoming from Haymarket Books. She is also the proud mama of Sasha, 7, and Jacob, 3. (photo: Dave Zirin)

John T. Green teaches history at Castro Valley High School. He lives in Hayward, California, with his wife and daughter. He is president of the Castro Valley Teachers Association and has represented the CVTA at the State Council of the California Teachers' Association. (photo: Izzy Goldberg)

Jesse Hagopian is a public high school teacher in Seattle and a founding member of Social Equality Educators (SEE), a rank-and-file organization of union teachers. Hagopian serves on the board of directors of the Haiti solidarity organization Maha-Lilo (Many Hands, Light Load). His writing has appeared in the *Seattle Times*, *TheProgessive.org*, *Black Agenda Report*, *Common Dreams*, *Truthout*, and *Counter-Punch*. (photo: Anna Ludwig)

Adrienne Johnstone has taught in San Francisco public schools since 2000. She ran for president of United Educators of San Francisco (NEA/AFT Local 61) in 2009 with a slate of candidates in the reform caucus Educators for a Democratic Union (EDU). She has written for the *International Socialist Review* and *SocialistWorker.org*. (photo: Adrienne Johnstone)

Brian Jones is a teacher, actor, and activist in New York City. Jones has taught elementary grades in Harlem and Brooklyn since 2003. His commentary and writings have appeared on MSNBC.com, the *Huffington Post*, *GRITtv*, and *SocialistWorker.org*. Jones is featured in the film *The Inconvenient Truth Behind Waiting for Superman* and has lent his voice to several audiobooks, including Howard Zinn's one-man play *Marx in Soho*. (photo: Kristin Lubbert)

Jessie Muldoon is a special education teacher in Oakland, California. She is a member of and activist in the Oakland Education Association and has written for the *International Socialist Review* and *SocialistWorker.org* on topics including labor and education reform. (photo: Isa Muldoon)

Gillian Russom is a high school history and geography teacher in Los Angeles. She is the East Area chair and a member of the Board of Directors for United Teachers Los Angeles. She has contributed several articles on education issues to the *International Socialist Review*. (photo: Jeannie Stahl)

Adam Sanchez is a social studies teacher in Portland, Oregon. His writing has been featured in *Rethinking Schools, Ecology of Education, SocialistWorker.org,* and the *International Socialist Review*. (photo: Lyra Butler-Denman)

Elizabeth Terzakis teaches developmental reading and writing and transfer-level literature and critical thinking courses at Cañada College in Redwood City, California. She holds master's degrees in English and creative writing from Brown University and Hollins University and a certificate in teaching adult reading from San Francisco State University. She is a regular contributor to the *International Socialist Review* and a member of the International Socialist Organization. (photo: Haymarket Books)

Keeanga-Yamahtta Taylor is a doctoral candidate in the department of African American Studies at Northwestern University. Her research looks at the rise and fall of the federal government's attempts at promoting single-family homeownership in African American urban communities in Chicago and Detroit in the aftermath of the riots in the 1960s and 1970s. For the 2011–12 academic year, Taylor was awarded the prestigious Ford Foundation Dissertation Fellowship and will also be a Northwestern University Presidential Fellow. She is active in local housing struggles in Chicago and is an organizer with the Chicago Anti-Eviction Campaign. Taylor has written for *CounterPunch*, the *Black Commentator*, *Black Agenda Report*, *Gapers Block*, and *New Politics*, among others. She is on the editorial board of the *International Socialist Review* and is a columnist for *SocialistWorker.org*. (photo: Eric Ruder)

About Haymarket Books

Haymarket Books is a nonprofit, progressive book distributor and publisher, a project of the Center for Economic Research and Social Change. We believe that activists need to take ideas, history, and politics into the many struggles for social justice today. Learning the lessons of past victories, as well as defeats, can arm a new generation of fighters for a better world. As Karl Marx said, "The philosophers have merely interpreted the world; the point, however, is to change it."

We take inspiration and courage from our namesakes, the Haymarket Martyrs, who gave their lives fighting for a better world. Their 1886 struggle for the eight-hour day reminds workers around the world that ordinary people can organize and struggle for their own liberation.

For more information and to shop our complete catalog of titles, visit us online at www.haymarketbooks.org.

Also from Haymarket Books

Schooling in Capitalist America: Educational Reform and the Contradictions of Economic Life
Samuel Bowles and Herbert Gintis

101 Changemakers: Rebels and Radicals Who Changed US History
Edited by Michele Bollinger and Dao X. Tran

IraqiGirl: Diary of a Teenage Girl in Iraq
IraqiGirl

Young Adult Fiction:

A Little Piece of Ground
Elizabeth Laird with Sonia Nimr

Oranges in No Man's Land
Elizabeth Laird

Red Sky in the Morning
Elizabeth Laird